Sydney in his twenties circa 1907. Photo courtesy of Gail Greenstreet.

The Life and Times of Sydney Greenstreet by Derek Sculthorpe
© 2018 Derek Sculthorpe. ALL RIGHTS RESERVED.
No part of this book may be reproduced in any form or by any means, electronic, mechanical, digital, photocopying, or recording, except for inclusion of a review, without permission in writing from the publisher or Author.

Published in the USA by:
BearManor Media
P O Box 71426
Albany, Georgia 31708
www.bearmanormedia.com

ISBN: 978-1-62933-308-3
BearManor Media, Albany, Georgia
Printed in the United States of America
Book design by Robbie Adkins, www.adkinsconsult.com
Front cover photo: *Publicity still of Greenstreet in character as Senor Ferrari in* Casablanca *(1942). Photo courtesy of Gail Greenstreet.*
Back cover photo: *Greenstreet (center) as Touchstone with Margaret Anglin (right) as Rosalind and Max Montesole as Corin in a scene from* As You Like It *during the St Louis festival to mark the Tercentenary of Shakespeare's death, June 1916. Photo courtesy of Gail Greenstreet.*

The Life and Times of
SYDNEY GREENSTREET

By Derek Sculthorpe

Acknowledgements

With grateful thanks to Gail Greenstreet for her kindness, patience and invaluable help. With thanks as always to my family for their encouragement and support.

"It's never too late to be what you might have been."
George Eliot

Contents

Introduction .... *vii*
1 *Man of Kent* *1*
2 *An Actor's Life* *8*
3 *American Adventure* *15*
4 *A Pastoral Idyll* *22*
5 *Happy Days in Pittsburgh* *30*
6 *Dissension in Harlem* *35*
7 *Enter, Colonel Savage* *40*
8 *Margaret Anglin* *46*
9 *A Farceur* *54*
10 *A King of Nowhere* *57*
11 *Sir Herbert* *62*
12 *The Rainbow Girl* *69*
13 *Lady Billy* *77*
14 *Comedian to Mitzi* *83*
15 *Mrs. Fiske's Dream Company* *91*
16 *The Theater Guild* *96*
17 *The Show Goes On* *105*
18 *Life with the Lunts* *112*
19 *There Will Be No Night* *120*
20 *The Black Bird* *126*
21 *The Blue Parrot* *135*
22 *Bogie and Sydney* *142*
23 *Background to Danger* *150*
24 *A Star of Tomorrow at Sixty-Four* *158*
25 *The Mask of Dimitrios* *164*
26 *Between Two Worlds* *173*
27 *Comedy at Last* *179*
28 *Still Learning* *188*
29 *The Laurel and Hardy of Crime* *197*
30 *Prelude to Night* *208*
31 *"Most unfortunate!"* *213*
32 *The Velvet Touch* *218*
33 *Flamingo Road* *225*
34 *Radio Swansong* *233*
35 *Finis* *237*
Epilogue *243*
Appendix: Film, Theater, Radio credits, List of Recordings .. *247*
Bibliography *267*
Notes *275*
Index *303*

Introduction

> *"He comes to the screen looking like a cross between Billy Bunter's father and a defrocked bishop ... The English intonation of his oily voice makes it sound like a benediction when he condemns one of his enemies to a sticky death. He watches them writhing with the complacent enjoyment of a connoisseur rinsing his tongue on a vintage port."*
>
> Leonard Mosley, "Oily-Voiced Sydney to Retire"
> *Singapore Free Press*, December 6, 1952, 2.

If Sydney Greenstreet had never succumbed to the lure of film, it is unlikely he would be remembered today outside theater circles, if at all. It was testament to his great acting skill that when he finally took the plunge at the age of sixty-one he immediately joined those other immortals of the silver screen and left an indelible memory in the collective consciousness. His debut as Kaspar Gutman in *The Maltese Falcon* was so strong that he seldom found such a satisfying role again. But despite the limitations imposed by his bulk, his age and the scripts he was offered, his long experience on the stages of the world meant that he always rose above his material. His marvelous speaking voice, wonderful intonation, perfect diction and the sheer ease of his acting ensured he was always in demand then, and warmly remembered today.

Greenstreet made only twenty-four films in an eight-year career, and as a result there have been few previous studies about him. An intended book by Homer Dickens never saw the light of day. There have been articles in magazines such as *Films in Review*, and chapters of books including *Close-Ups*. But the longest book about him so far was a joint biography/filmography with Peter Lorre. Ted Sennett's excellent *Masters of Menace: Greenstreet & Lorre* was published in 1979 and although long out of print is worth seeking out by all fans of their films and classic Hollywood in general. Although strong on his screen work there is little mention of Greenstreet's private life or his theater career; for instance, there is but a single reference to his wife. Fans of Lorre need look no further than Stephen Youngkin's *The Lost One*, surely one of the finest biographies ever written about a screen star.

This is the first ever book dedicated solely to Greenstreet and his art. It provides an in-depth study of his life and career spanning the first half of the twentieth century. I seek to redress the balance and show that he had a full life before he became famous. More than just a career record, this is a testament to those years and the many personalities he knew, from Sir Herbert Beerbohm Tree to Humphrey Bogart. Greenstreet's life spanned the decades and the continents, beginning in Victorian England and reads like a history of popular entertainment. He crossed over genres and eras, worked for leading impresarios such as Colonel Henry Wilson Savage and opposite such august stage personages as Margaret Anglin and Minnie Maddern Fiske. In theater, he played everything from Shakespeare to modern plays, veering off into farce, musical comedy and near Vaudeville along the way. In the 1930s, he was an integral part of the magical group of players organized by Alfred Lunt and Lynn Fontanne and as such was at the vanguard of some of the most compelling plays at a crucial time in history. Only after that did he enjoy a late-flowering screen career in the golden 1940s. Few had such a varied career as Greenstreet; but it was the same man who learnt his craft opposite Tree and Lou Tellegen, had fun with Peter Lorre and Humphrey Bogart, and encouraged young emerging players such as Zachary Scott and Montgomery Clift. There has been much attention on the Greenstreet-Lorre partnership, but Greenstreet worked just as effectively in different ways with Bogart and Scott in eight films.

Most of Greenstreet's films are readily available on DVD. Some are also available on Blu-ray, which provide excellent quality. His radio work has also been released on CD and is available on download from numerous organizations. The extensive Appendix has been carefully compiled and includes all his known work. The details of his theatrical and radio careers are the most substantial ever published. Also included are some collectable recordings. There are many evocative images of his life off-stage most of which have never been seen before, which appear by kind permission of his granddaughter Gail.

Greenstreet was a unique player who carved a niche as the most civilized of villains. It is not possible to confuse him with anyone else; his distinctive form and equally unmistakable voice bring him to mind long afterwards. I hope my story stands as a fitting tribute to a much-loved figure of our cinematic past who added immeasurably to the gaiety of nations.

The Life and Times of Sydney Greenstreet

1 Man of Kent

"Kent, sir - everybody knows Kent - apples, cherries, hops and women."

Mr. Jingle in *The Pickwick Papers* by Charles Dickens

"I am an Englishman by birth but I am really a citizen of the world."

Mr. Peters (Greenstreet) in *The Mask of Dimitrios*

Born in Sandwich, Kent, two days after Christmas 1879, Sydney Hughes Greenstreet was the fourth son of Tanner and leather manufacturer John Jarvis Greenstreet and Ann (nee Baker). Ann was a local girl and John hailed from Old Brompton in the north of Kent. Long since known as the garden of England, the county has a mild climate and lies in the south east of the country. Rather appropriately it was an Earl of Sandwich who invented the lunchtime snack for which the name of the town is now famous.

Sandwich lies to the east of the river Medway and so Greenstreet was a "Man of Kent" rather than a Kentish man. In medieval times, the distinction had some significance because the Men of Kent were descended from the Jutes and won for themselves certain rights from William the Conqueror at the time of the Norman Conquest, whereas the Kentish men merely surrendered. Some two miles from the sea, Sandwich was one of the Cinque Ports and under the reign of Henry VII became "the chief naval and military port of England."[2] Afterwards its importance declined and the port silted up. The town retains a picturesque aspect to this day and a number of impressive churches out of all proportion to its size. Although it is now a quiet backwater it still boasts ten medieval pubs.

The county has many literary associations, beginning with Geoffrey Chaucer and his *Canterbury Tales*. Kent has a strong connection to Charles Dickens who spent his formative years at Chatham and lived for a while in Dover. He knew the old Cinque Ports well and immortalized places such as Broadstairs in his literature. He described the quaint old half-timbered houses of Sandwich "bulging out over the road, with low lattice windows bulging out still farther so that the whole house appears to be leaning forward, trying to see who is passing on the narrow pavement below."[3] The Greenstreets were long-established in Kent which can be rightfully claimed as "their" county. The name literally means "dweller by a green road."[4] Specifically, the family had ancestors who lived in the village of Green Street near Faversham, Kent.

John Greenstreet married Ann Baker in September 1874 at St. Mary's church in Sandwich. They had eight children, five boys and three girls; Harry (born in 1875) was the eldest, there followed in quick succession Frank, Arthur, Sydney, Olive, Guy, Hilda and Margery. Between the eldest and youngest there was only eleven years. At the time of Sydney's birth his father was running a prosperous leather business in Sandwich which employed some twenty-one workers. The family also employed two servants and a nurse. The Oak tannery was close to the family home and the children used to play on the Roman walls adjoining the property. By 1891 they had moved to the nearby town of Deal.[5] A windswept maritime town, Deal is bigger than Sandwich and has a long sea front with a pebble-strewn beach. The coast of France is only twenty-five miles away and can be seen on clear days.

John's father William Greenstreet worked on the famous docks at Chatham as a carpenter. Several generations of Greenstreets were carpenters and artisans. John's mother Eliza died young in 1855 and three years later William died aged thirty-eight. Having thus lost both parents by the age of nine, John was sent to live with his maternal grandparents William and Susannah Cooper in Milton, Kent. The Coopers were a long-established family of tanners. His sister Eliza was sent to his paternal grandparents William and Martha Greenstreet in Eastchurch. To compound the family tragedy John's brother William died in 1859 at the age of fifteen.[6]

By 1871 John was working as a day laborer while lodging at the White Hart Inn at Sittingbourne a few miles away.[7] John was a favorite nephew of his unmarried uncle Venn Cooper and shortly

Sydney holding two family portraits from the Victorian era. Photo courtesy of Gail Greenstreet.

after Venn's death in 1872 at the age of forty-three, John became the manager of the Oak tannery in Sandwich. He named his third son after him.[8]

Sydney's mother Ann was the daughter of Henry Baker, a bookseller and stationer in Sandwich. After Henry's death in 1867, his widow took over the business and eventually his son Charles continued in the same line for many years in the same premises on Market Street. Ann had many siblings, her brother Frank was the town's chemist.[9] Ann became a governess employed by Mrs. Hannah Pratt, a farmer's widow of Eastchurch, to teach her six children. Mrs. Pratt was a Greenstreet before marriage and her unmarried sister Sarah also lived with her. It was while working there that Ann first met their nephew John Greenstreet and before long the two were wed. John's grandfather William Greenstreet, a carpenter, had lived in Eastchurch for many years and had served as parish clerk of the town.[10]

Sydney was always fond of eating and was a frequent visitor to the village bakery as a young boy; hardly a day went by when he didn't visit and buy some cakes with his pennies. One day when he was about seven he bought some sweet buns there and was so keen to tuck into them that he ran out of the shop and was knocked over by a horse and cart, breaking his leg. Some thirty-seven years later on one of his numerous visits to England he returned to the shop and curiously enough the same woman who served him then was not only still working there but remembered him and the incident with the horse.[11] Instead of congratulating him on his success all she said was "I told you then you ate too much!" as a rather churlish parting shot.[12]

The brothers were educated at Dane Hill House Preparatory School on Northumberland Avenue in the Cliftonville area of Margate. This was a private academy which prepared boys for Cambridge and Oxford. Sydney attended the school between the age of seven and seventeen, from September 1887 to June 1897, overlapping with his brothers. All of them were competitive, but although Sydney was the middle child he was the one who excelled on the sports field and surpassed them all.[13] As a boy he did well at rugby, cricket, soccer, hockey, tennis, swimming, boxing and fencing. He was so adept at all games that he was voted by the best players as the captain of the cricket, hockey and soccer teams at school.[14] He maintained that his only success at school was on the sports field and that he was not academic. As a youngster, he joined the South London Harriers Club, a famous athletics club that was one of the first to adopt professionalism and has since provided many British Olympic athletes. He continued to be a member of the club even after he moved to America.[15] He was an expert tennis player and according to a number of reports he held several amateur titles in the game and was "a one-time runner up in the Davis Cup."[16] All the family loved sports and they had their own grass tennis court at home.[17] Arthur in particular was a keen golfer who later won

Sydney's mother Ann (center), and two of his sisters, Olive and Hilda, circa 1910. Photo courtesy of Gail Greenstreet.

many trophies in the game. The town of Sandwich was also famous for its proximity to the Royal St George's Golf Club, one of the finest links courses in the world which has often hosted The Open Championship. However, the glory of the athletic field was not to be Sydney's route to immortality.

The Greenstreet's tannery was almost adjacent to the house in which they lived. Anyone who has lived in the immediate vicinity of a tannery will be unable to forget the noise and above all the pungent smell that the tanning process creates. Close to the building the air feels stifling and heavily laden with an odd mixture of things that in themselves are hard to identify. It is acrid, nauseating and possibly harmful to the environment to say nothing of the effect on the people employed to work there. At the very least it is the kind of odor that lingers on clothing if one is exposed to it for any length of time.

Not wishing to enter the family business, it was a chance meeting that led to Sydney's first big adventure. A friend of the family, described as "an old Cambridge pal" of his father happened to visit the house one night; he was a tea planter by trade. The teenage Sydney was so taken with the exciting life the visitor described that he persuaded his father to back his notion to go to Ceylon and run a tea plantation. Being business-minded his father acquiesced and Sydney caught a steamer to the island in September 1897. Tea-growing in Ceylon had only started less than thirty years earlier and was first centered at the hill capital in Kandy. Sydney faced the prospect of five years there if things worked out well.[18]

Unfortunately, it was not the romantic life he had envisaged. He had few companions with whom he could converse – most of the natives did not speak English. There were few other Englishmen or women there his own age and no real social life, unlike in India. Tea plantations tend to be located at higher elevations and many locales are isolated and sparsely-populated. Most of Sydney's nights were spent alone. He was, after all, only eighteen. In addition, he found the whole process of tea planting rather tedious and the working day was long and arduous. He began to miss his home. In those days mail took up to forty days to reach the island and letters from home were a real highlight. The greatest relief he had from the monotony and loneliness was in a set of the works of Shakespeare which his mother had packed in the base of his steamer trunk. For long hours in the time away from his work he studied them avidly and became familiar with all the characters of the immortal Bard. He may have missed out on the Cambridge education which his father had intended, but like many before him his informal education more than compensated for the loss.

He learnt all the rudiments of tea planting as a creeper, the name given to apprentices in the trade. Tea was once the province of the well-to-do, but during the nineteenth century it became the most popular beverage in Britain and much of its Empire. The process was highly dependent on the seasons and the best tea was produced during the first quarter of each year when the weather was cooler. Different altitudes had an effect on taste; the higher the plantation the subtler the flavor. Soil, location, type of plant and above all rainfall influenced growth and flavor. All these factors made the process a tricky business to negotiate. It required someone with patience and dedication. Sydney tried to adapt to the life on the island and learned Singhalese during his time there.[19] He also found time to improve his tennis, as his granddaughter related;

> "While he worked on the tea plantation he learnt, from a local native, some trick shots for tennis. Those trick shots made him a lot of money betting; at times, more than he did on the stage. The big trick was putting a spin on the ball so that it bounced once on the opponent's side but would spin back towards his side. He also was a pretty good golfer. With both these sports he looked too big to be much of a challenge but he was fast and light on his feet and had killer hand eye coordination."[20]

In his second year in Ceylon a sustained drought meant that many plantations were forced to close and his employer also went out of business. Sydney was only too glad to catch the first boat home that he could.

On his return to England in 1899 he became an agent for the Watney, Coombe & Reid Brewery based at Harrow, Middlesex, joining his elder brother Arthur. This venture lasted about a year. Sydney was not especially fascinated by brewing; it was just a means to an end. Although he was supposed to be selling he later admitted that he drank more beer than he ever sold.[21] In time the brewery business began to face economic problems. Two thousand pubs were closed and many men were laid off, including Sydney. Arthur stayed working in the brewery trade and became a Hop Merchant.

Casting around for a career, Sydney latched onto the one thing he enjoyed and which he felt he was good at; acting. During his year in the brewery business he had begun to play in amateur dramatics in and around London. His earliest successes on stage encouraged him to believe it was possible for him to make a living in the precarious business with perseverance and luck. He would need to apply himself but the chance was there.

2 An Actor's Life

"There is the greatest unstarred star of the English Stage."
Said by Sir Herbert Beerbolm Tree about Greenstreet, circa 1911: "From Shakespeare to Musical Comedy" *The Brooklyn Standard-Union,* October 28, 1923, 5.

Sydney had much experience in amateur theatricals in and around London and at one time was appearing in several productions across town. He won such applause as Marc Antony in a presentation of *Julius Caesar* at Deal that he announced to his family that henceforward he wished to be an actor. It was said that he "amazed his family and friends by the length and force of his Shakespearean recitations."[1]

His interest in the stage was something which raised the ire of his father who still planned a Cambridge future for him, or failing that, a good solid business career. Greenstreet *pere* disdained his son's high-flown notions of grandeur – he called him a "swell-headed young pup," and remarked, "The idea of thinking anyone would pay to watch you!"[2] That seemed to spur him into action to prove his father wrong. Sydney was fond of telling a story of his youth. "When I was a boy in London, my father warned me never to attend a burlesque show, because, he said, 'They're wicked, and you'll see things you shouldn't.' I went and I most certainly saw something I shouldn't have seen – my father in a box seat!"[3]

His mother had been surrounded by books in her father's shop and valued the written word. She always encouraged him in literature and was sympathetic to the idea of an acting career. It was she who gave him the funds to join the Ben Greet School in Bedford Street, London.[4]

Ben Greet first started touring in 1883 with his Woodland Players, and in 1896 founded his own academy of acting. There had been just a few earlier academies, but Greet was a pioneer in this

Sydney's mother Ann Greenstreet always encouraged his theatrical ambitions in the face of strong opposition from his father. She gave him the funds to attend the Ben Greet Academy in London. Photo courtesy of Gail Greenstreet.

area. The school was based at the Bijou Theatre, 3 Bedford Street, London and soon gained a reputation as one of the best of its kind. Greet was no theorist. According to the actress Margaret Webster, daughter of Dame May Whitty, he couldn't abide "fancy theaters, far-fetched analogies, scholarly discussions or gimmickry."[5] Greet's training was of the practical kind which set many actors on the right road. His only acting instruction was to reach the audience. A Christian-Socialist, part of Greet's mission was to educate and to reach people who would not normally come across the work of Shakespeare, such as children and the poor.

Greenstreet gave an audition for Greet in which he recited several lines from Shakespeare. He was readily accepted. Only halfway through his one-year term at the academy he was given his chance by Greet when he was entered into several modern London productions. The renowned British theater historian J. C. Trewin described the man and his approach:

> "Ben Greet was the classical manager the provinces knew best. A bulky, competent actor with a floss of white hair, he was absolutely untiring whether in Britain or in the United States ... [He] was an unexampled pastoralist: his company would play practically anywhere. Barry Jackson wrote to me once of a Greet production he remembered from his youth: *A Midsummer Night's Dream* in rural Warwickshire ... 'A wet day, clearing at sundown with a slight mist and a full moon. Being young I had sported a new pair of chamois gloves, and, applauding spiritedly, vanished in a cloud of French chalk.' These were the days when small-part actors, paid twenty-five shillings a week and equipped with the necessary 'Shakespearian shoes,' tights and a variety of wigs – provided, among much else, by themselves – would dutifully learn the cut texts and prepare for anything."[6]

The students at Greet's school learned very much by doing and preparing for anything was the order of the day. His companies were made up of the best players available but he stressed that there were no stars among them and that everyone was of equal importance. Each had to pitch in and accept any role. He had no time for ego or lofty philosophy. His practical no-nonsense approach suited his choice of play and the manner in which they were performed. Besides it was essential, especially on a long tour, that everyone pulled together. He used little or no scenery and a woodland glade was his preferred locale. The natural scenery forced the audience to concentrate their attention on the actors. It was also immensely practical and saved time and money on elaborate stage settings.

Greenstreet made his professional debut at the Bijou in a walk-on part in a Shakespearean play. He had his first speaking role as a murderer in *Sherlock Holmes* while the play was on a provincial tour in Ramsgate, Kent, in 1902. John Sayre Crawley played the leading role as he had on a tour of South Africa two years earlier. Crawley was the son of a clergyman from Northampton and was already an established actor. He was a dozen years older than Greenstreet and became rather like an elder brother to him as he was to all the younger players, showing them the ropes so to speak. The two shared many experiences on the road and became good friends. Crawley's first wife Constance was also in the company.[7]

Greet's company toured around London giving their pastoral plays at such venues as the Royal Botanical Gardens, Regent's Park and Lowther Lodge, Kensington. After that they took their show on the

Greenstreet played the tragic figure of Bruno Rocco in The Eternal City *on a long road tour throughout Britain in 1903 and again in 1904. Photo courtesy of Gail Greenstreet.*

road, chiefly visiting Oxford, Cambridge and Warwickshire. Much of Greet's impetus was centered on education and he gravitated to the main seats of learning. His players appeared annually for twenty years at Worcester College, Oxford and Downing College, Cambridge. Often, his choice of venue reflected romantic historical and literary links to the Elizabethan era. Such places as Wilton Park near Salisbury in Wiltshire which was reputed to have been where Shakespeare wrote and first acted in *As You Like It*. Ashbridge, Hertfordshire was where Elizabeth lived before she became queen. Naturally, he was drawn to Warwickshire and the company often played Stratford-on-Avon and the picturesque Warwick Castle. It was reminiscent of the old days of strolling players offering a spectacle not dissimilar to the Bard's own experience. Greet had been born aboard a naval recruiting ship of which his father was the commander and the navy remained close to his heart. Hence, the company often played at fundraising events and gave their pastorals for the Royal Naval School at Eltham among other navy establishments.[8]

Greenstreet appeared in several Greet productions and during much of 1903 toured as Bruno Rocco in *The Eternal City*. Rocco was described as a self-sacrificing character whose child is tragically shot and who ends up in prison. The play was controversial in its day, depicting what some commenters have described as a socialist view of religion and a number of critics even considered it irreligious. Nonetheless it was popular. This extensive tour took in most of the English counties including Devon and Cornwall in the South West, the home counties, the east and northern cities such as Hull and ventured to Scotland, travelling as far as Inverness. The production was well-received in most places and at Dover Greenstreet was among those adjudged to have handled their roles "excellently."[9] He toured again in the same play the following year.

From his own recollections, the apprentice actor had few real personal successes on the stage in England. He related scant anecdotes about his earliest roles apart from the unlikely sounding story that he once played a negro jockey in a musical comedy called *Kentucky* circa 1905. He claimed he had pictures to prove he was ever small enough to have played a jockey.[10] He played a number of roles in the allegory *Everyman* and once appeared as Flute in a special production of *A*

Greenstreet as Sir Toby Belch in Twelfth Night *one of his favorite Shakespearean characters. Photo courtesy of Gail Greenstreet.*

Midsummer Night's Dream at the famous Crystal Palace.[11] He also played with the renowned Sir Johnston Forbes-Robertson and his company.[12] By far Greenstreet's most illustrious role was as Falstaff in a production of *The Merry Wives of Windsor* at the Lyric Theater in London in 1904, a performance that was said to have been "especially noteworthy."[13] Only in his early twenties, he would seem too young for the role, but there was already something larger-than-life about him both physically and metaphorically-speaking. While others of that age might have set their sights on playing romantic leads such as Romeo or Hamlet, Greenstreet relished the character and comedy roles. He later said that he found audiences in England difficult. His experience was that they were not given to spontaneity. Nor did it help if a player was young and unknown; they were more interested in the well-established actors and would not give a newcomer a chance, he maintained. It was not until he arrived in the United States that he eventually began to find his feet as an actor and in time discover not only an appreciative audience but a way to communicate with them.

3 American Adventure

"Go west, young man."

(Credited to Horace Greeley)

The twenty-four-year-old Greenstreet arrived in New York on the *Numidian* in September 1904.[1] It was his first American tour with a group of players many of whom were of a similar age. One such was Sybil Thorndike who was not yet twenty-two and her brother Russell only nineteen. It was to be a baptism of fire for all of them.

The tour of the United States and Canada followed a similar pattern to the previous ones Greet had made. The company played at university and college campuses, visiting the principal seats of learning in both countries. Later tours expanded the number of establishments they visited and extended the list to high schools, technical schools, Country Clubs and parks. They played on the regular theater circuit in New York and other cities in addition to making personal appearances for private citizens.

The fourteenth century miracle play *Everyman* and the plays of Shakespeare were the mainstays of Greet's repertoire in the early years. He wanted to reach as many people as possible. His avowed intent was to perform the plays as Shakespeare had written them, in other words in the Elizabethan manner. He eschewed the then current fashion for cutting the texts to make them palatable for a modern audience, thus omitting all those passages deemed too crude for early Twentieth century sensibilities. This approach brought him into conflict with the prevailing mood of the time. It limited his audience, as did his insistence on having no stars in his company. However, he was always popular on the college circuit and made strides in the appreciation of Shakespeare among those who would never otherwise have come across his work, such as children and the poor. In the long term, he accomplished more than he has perhaps been given credit for, as Don-John Dugas' ground-breaking study *Shakespeare*

Greenstreet played a number of roles in Greet's production of the medieval allegorical play Everyman. *Sydney is seen here as Riches, circa 1905. Photo courtesy of Gail Greenstreet.*

for *Everyman* proves. Greet was an evangelist for Shakespeare and succeeded in spreading the word even though it might not have seemed so at the time.

Everyman received good notices in Los Angeles and other cities in the state of California, after which the company travelled to Oregon in December 1904 where they were met with much appreciation. It was a major event for everyone concerned. The local press reported; "The entire cast carried the audience to higher realms and the play will pass down to be remembered as one of the finest attractions that has ever appeared before a Salem audience."[2] Greenstreet made his Broadway debut in the same play in the role of Good Fellowship. In Minneapolis, a local critic praised the "intelligent and skillful actors" and noted that Greenstreet "plays Fellowship with just bonhomie."[3] *Everyman* was of obscure, possibly Dutch origin, and had first come to wide public attention with Frederick Poel, from whom Greet had acquired the rights. It was a surprisingly popular allegory and was even filmed twice some years later.

In most of the cities they played there was much advance notice and the plays were eagerly anticipated events. The world is much smaller now and it is difficult to imagine the effect of such tours. This was long before the days of air travel when ocean liners were the order of the day. There were few telephones and for travelling internally throughout America the train was the best known and most popular form of transport. Roads were not always of the best quality in rural areas in particular and stage coaches still linked many towns. Cars were a luxury at the dawn of the century and were not built for long journeys. It was a real event when a group of entertainers travelled thousands of miles from one part of the world to the other. Well known comedians such as W. C. Fields traversed the globe during the years before the First World War, travelling extensively in the British Isles, Europe and parts of what was then the British Empire including South Africa. With the coming of the war this cross-fertilization ceased and was never recovered.

At each college and university students were encouraged to help out and often took part in the plays. The production of *Hamlet* at the University of California in Berkeley was typical and had a great deal of input from students who filled many of the subsidiary roles.[4]

For the actors, it was demanding work and could be demoralizing at times. The Elizabethan texts needed careful study, and for the players who were often tired through constant travelling and devoid of physical comfort it was hard for them to give of their best. The itinerary was such that they were required to perform eight plays a week outdoors and in for the best part of nine months. They were not often praised for their work and were sometimes

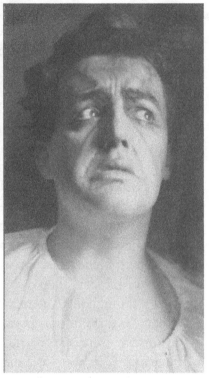

Sydney played a wide variety of Shakespearean roles especially during his years with the Greet company. He is seen here as "the melancholy Jacques" in As You Like It. *Jacques was one of the most philosophical of the great playwright's characters, famous for his "All the world's a stage" speech. Photo courtesy of Gail Greenstreet.*

Sydney as Casca in Julius Caesar. *Photos courtesy of Gail Greenstreet.*

dismissed by critics as mere amateurs. Nor were they well paid. It was a grueling schedule for them all. Any who were not used to roughing it soon fell by the wayside. The more robust ones stood up to it better. Lincolnshire clergyman's daughter Sybil Thorndike was accustomed to a spartan regime and was often called on to fill the breach when a leading lady was otherwise indisposed. As a result of her elevation she played almost a hundred roles during her American tours including many leads. However, even she was not immune from the illnesses doing the rounds. She looked back on her experience as something she would rather not recall; "The comfort, and even luxury, which we now associate with the States wasn't widespread then," she reflected in an interview in the 1970s, "There were several primitive places, and a lack of amenities which I'm sure I hope I've forgotten. With respect, but it was a joy when at last we returned to civilization."⁵ Being a touring player at that time was not for the feint-hearted; it required a strong constitution, total dedication and a real love of the art. Undoubtedly one of the most important things an actor learnt with the Greet company was the art of sheer survival which set them in good stead for their whole career.

Greet had not yet established his reputation in the United States on those early tours and a number of things went wrong. Apart from the lack of amenities in some of their chosen venues he also found himself in competition with other companies who presented the same plays. His dislike of using scenery made his plays less of a draw for those who preferred real spectacle and added to an overall impression of amateurism, even cheapness. The company had lost several experienced players and contained a number of novices who were feeling their way. Financial problems were seldom far from his thoughts and the biggest disaster of the 1904-05 tour was when his business manager absconded with all the company's money. The sum was estimated at between $2000 and $3000.⁶ Distraught, Greet managed to avert complete disaster by taking out short-term loans. Luckily, two Chicago businessmen came to the rescue and invited him to play at the Studebaker Theater in February 1905. Greet hastily organized a 'Shakespearean Festival' of seven plays in three weeks and arranged ticket sales in such a way as to encourage schoolchildren and undergraduates to attend. In addition, there were some attractive posters made, and he even engaged an Elizabethan musical expert to provide the music.⁷

Shakespeare was everything to Greet, almost like breathing. As a consequence, he had none of the preciousness that more cerebral actors might have displayed. Often it is an over-reverence for Shakespeare that kills the vitality of his work. Greet had a sure hand when it came to the comedies, especially *Much Ado About Nothing* and *As You Like It,* or the fantasies such as *A Midsummer Night's Dream.* His acting style was deemed far less successful in tragedy, but *Macbeth* and *Hamlet* were regularly given on the tours. In the first years of the twentieth century there was a thirst for culture. For instance, the three weeks the company spent in Chicago was viewed as "one of the chief society events of the year," and it was said that the "performances are attracting unusual attention."[8] After touring the state the tour finished with a farewell performance of the previously unseen miracle play *The Star of Bethlehem*. Afterwards Greet's company moved on to Canada where the players presented four plays at the McGill college campus in Montreal in June 1905 including *As You Like It* and *Two Gentlemen of Verona*. Greenstreet was one of those among the cast that was singled out as "deserving of special mention."[9]

At the end of his first tour in July 1905 Greenstreet travelled back to England via Glasgow with the Greet players. He toured with them in Britain during the summer, gaining more experience in the works of Shakespeare in such roles as Sir Toby Belch and Touchstone that he would come to know so well in the coming years. He also appeared in several roles in *Hamlet* including King Claudius, Fortinbras and Polonius. From the beginning of April, he had taken out an advertisement in the theater trade publication *The Era* to make potential employers aware of his pending return to Britain. He listed many of the roles he had essayed.[10]

At the end of the British season in October 1905, he returned to America with the Greet company on the *Philadelphia*.[11] The second tour was arguably more successful; it began in New York, took in the southern universities including Tennessee, and those in the Midwest before ending in the east. Again, there were numerous alfresco shows and appearances at many colleges and universities. The engagements at Princeton, Vassar, Harvard, Smith College et al became long-standing fixtures and followed a similar template to the appearance at Yale where *As You Like It* and *The Tempest* were given at the Lawn Club on a balmy afternoon and evening in June 1906.[12]

The most noteworthy innovation of the season was that the company played many shows for poor schoolchildren and adults. They played to several thousand children over the course of the tour.[13] This was exactly what Greet had set out to achieve and he built on his work with the young in the coming years.

The tours were hard work for the actors who endured long journeys by train crisscrossing the country. However, there was a real camaraderie among the players who interacted well. Greet encouraged married couples and siblings to join his company which not only made booking accommodation easier but helped to engender a convivial atmosphere. From all accounts, he was a strict disciplinarian but also a skillful teacher who took time out to help his players.[14] This work ethic stayed with Greenstreet throughout his career; the early lessons he learned in his acting apprenticeship were too engrained to be forgotten.

Sometimes the performances were not so well attended and the reviews negative. Nevertheless, in other locales their hard work paid off and in San Francisco the company were praised for the "quality of distinction in their work" and for the "sheer vocal beauty of the cast." In time, the shows came to be considered as "something not to be missed."[15] It was common practice in the company that none of the players were named. This anonymity emphasized the fact that the plays were ensemble works and ensured that there were no "stars" among the cast. However, there was a natural curiosity among the audience to want to know more about certain performers who stood out. Sometimes, for instance, Greenstreet and others were mentioned in dispatches. In *Twelfth Night*, "Sydney Greenstreet and J. Sayre Crawley were droll as to make-up and conception of the characters of Sir Toby Belch and Auguecheek" averred one commentator in Detroit.[16] The pair were noticed in Baltimore too, where one observer commented; "The scene where they watch Malvolio (Greet) throw bouquets at himself was altogether delicious."[17] The same critic remarked; "In comedy passages the Ben Greet players especially excel, throwing aside constraint and giving the humor the rein that Shakespeare evidently intended it should have."[18]

Besides Shakespeare and *Everyman*, the company sometimes gave plays by Ben Jonson, Tennyson and Moliere.[19] They presented the first ever performance of Christopher Marlowe's *Doctor Faustus* in America. Among other plays given at intervals were Sheridan's *The Rivals* and *School for Scandal* and Wilde's *The Importance of Being Ernest*. In *She Stoops to Conquer*, one critic noticed the excellent portrait of Hardcastle by Greenstreet in a production which captured "all the delightful spirit of Goldsmith"[20] Those patrons who were rich enough and had gardens of a suitable size could hire the Woodland Players for their own personal shows for birthdays, special occasions or maybe just to impress the neighbors.

4 A Pastoral Idyll

*"All the world's a stage,
And all the men and women merely players;
They have their exits and their entrances,
And one man in his time plays many parts ...."*

Jacques in *As You Like It*, Act II, Scene VII

By 1907 Greet's tours had become far better organized than some of the earlier ones. He concentrated his forces, employing smaller companies of only the best players. In addition, his repertoire was extended to include different plays. By then, Greenstreet was a mainstay of the company and was beginning to master his trade. The following year the Woodland players received the ultimate accolade when they played for President Theodore Roosevelt on the White House Lawn.

Greenstreet travelled extensively in the 1900s. Apart from the United States and Canada he visited parts of Europe including Italy and France with various companies. In addition, he went much further afield to Malta, North Africa, India, Australia and South America. He once claimed that he had performed in twenty-three countries, but actual details of these tours are scant.

On one of his return journeys to America he met Thomas Woodrow Wilson, then a principal of Princeton. The two struck up a friendship during the many long walks they took around the deck of the ocean liner. Wilson had a deep interest in the theater and was known to attend plays regularly. Despite his somewhat serious mien he obviously had a sense of humor and during his time in the White House it was said that he "used to slip out once a week for vaudeville shows."[1] Greenstreet was a frequent guest at his home near the campus.[2] In a few short years, Wilson became governor of New Jersey and by 1913 was president. Greenstreet appeared in plays given for him while he was chief executive. The two remained friends until Wilson's death in 1924. Greenstreet was also in the cast of other productions witnessed by President Warren G. Harding and Franklin D. Roosevelt, in addition to appearing for two Kings of England and the King of Spain.

Continuing his social mission to reach as many people as possible, Greet's company often gave benefit performances for a wide range of good causes, and such events proved popular. For instance, a production of *Everyman* was given at the Continental Memorial Hall in New York in aid of the Prisoner's Aid and City Missionary Society in April 1907. The play drew a capacity crowd and was judged a great success.[3] In many colleges and universities, the Players were welcomed back year after year. In Geneva, they often played between two large trees in the campus of William Smith College. The local newspaper reported; "Their work is so well known here that the mere announcement of their coming is sufficient to ensure them a large audience."[4] In addition, Greet was in demand to give lectures on the drama. He was popular among university audiences and he in turn was distinctly impressed by them; "The drama in America is becoming a vital thing, and most of the inspiration and encouragement of it is springing from these young college students," he wrote in a letter

Greenstreet on board ship. He estimated that he made forty trips back and forth across the Atlantic over the years. Photo courtesy of Gail Greenstreet.

Greenstreet excelled at make-up which was entirely his own creation. Here he is seen as Caliban in The Tempest. *Photo courtesy of Gail Greenstreet.*

from Augusta, Georgia to a friend in England. "There is hardly a university or college; from Harvard to Oregon, Virginia to Leland Stanford in California, where an English company has not been invited to give its representation."[5] Greet was so well thought of that The University of California even conferred upon him the then rare honor of a Professorship of Dramatic Literature.[6] He declined the offer because he did not want to be tied to one campus.

The 1907-08 season introduced Charles Reade's *Masks and Faces* and Nathaniel Hawthorne's *Tales of Wonder* alongside the Shakespearean favorites. These additions proved popular with all age groups.

Greenstreet was full of humorous anecdotes of his life on stage some of which became embroidered with each telling. One time at Boston in a production of *The Tempest* he was in almost full makeup as the monstrous Caliban when there was a knock at the door. It was a small boy with his laundry. The boy stood gaping at Greenstreet who was about to apply the fangs. "Say, mister," said the boy, "This is a pretty big show ain't it?" Greenstreet replied that it was rather elaborate. "Say, mister, any shootin' in it?" asked the boy. "No, my little fellow there is no shooting in the play" said Greenstreet." The boy looked him up and down; "Thought not; you take the place of the shootin' don't you? You're the big noise."[7]

Even when he was young Greenstreet was substantially built; he was about 5' 11" and weighed over two hundred pounds. Once in New York he was knocked down by a runaway horse and wagon. Surprisingly, Greenstreet was largely unhurt but the horse later died of its injuries which upset him a great deal; "Why the poor animal," he lamented, "He died because of me."[8]

Audiences were especially captivated by Greet's novel approach of open air performances, something which was soon taken up by other companies. These proved far more popular and profitable for him than those in regular theaters. A typical pastoral such as that near the Hotel Champlain at Plattsburgh, New Jersey in August 1908 made full use of the beautiful surroundings. The plays given were *Pandora – The Box of Mischief* and *Philemon & Baucis*. Greenstreet appeared as Zeus in the latter. A witness spoke of the charming setting of a "brightly lighted grove with ... tall evergreens." The following evening *Twelfth Night* was given in the same place. "It is rare," noted the local drama critic, "that the people of Plattsburgh have the chance of seeing at their own door a dramatic company of so high an order of merit."[9] Of course the only unpredictable element was the weather which often intervened to spoil the fun. It was then that the limitations of Greet's approach were exposed. For instance, a much-anticipated production of *The Tempest* at South Field in the grounds of Columbia University was driven inside by a real tempest. Torrential rain meant the company had to repair to the gymnasium where the play was given instead. However, the disappointment was more palpable than if the event had been abandoned altogether. In the big hall, the acoustics meant hardly anyone could hear the actors and a witness reported "the bare stage too robbed the fanciful idyll of the atmosphere of illusion, without which the whole performance seemed crude."[10] The audience felt cheated of seeing a magical play in the moonlight. But Greet was nothing if not a crowd pleaser and on the following day in the afternoon the company gave a rollicking version of *The Merry Wives of Windsor* in the Earl Hall where the acoustics were much better. "As each of the players appeared," wrote a local reviewer, "he or she was greeted with hearty applause. The audience seemed to regard the members of the company with affection and applauded the performance warmly."[11] In the evening the weather was good and *The Tempest* was given in the South Field and greeted with equal warmth.

There were other problems when the weather was too good. At one such alfresco event held in the height of midsummer, Greenstreet missed his cue when he took forty winks. It was a stiflingly hot and humid day and he knew he had about twenty minutes before he was needed on stage again. He found a pleasant spot on a shady knoll and dozed off. Suddenly he found himself being awoken by the stage manager and told it was his turn, but he was so drowsy he forgot what play he was in let alone what the next line was. He had to recite a song, but they had learned so many in the Shakespeare glee club that he went through almost the entire repertoire before he hit on the right one.[12] Perhaps his most memorable catastrophe was during a production of *As You Like It* at Bryn Mawr College in which he appeared as the banished duke. There was a large crowd and distinguished invited guests. A temporary stage platform had been set up near a clump of trees and during one scene there were three players involved; the others were both young but playing old men. In their doddering character personas one, Adam, reclined against a tree stump and another, Jacques was, in Greenstreet's words "lolling about." Suddenly the whole structure gave way and all three fell several feet. "Our Adam was really a young and energetic actor and he put up a hard fight first," explained Greenstreet, "With the agility of a twenty-year-old he leaped for the nearest tree, while some of the less compassionate spectators simply howled with glee at his metamorphosis. The branch gave way under the strain, and he followed Jacques and me into the pit. Fortunately, no one was hurt and we all scrambled out and ... continued the performance with all the *sangfroid* in the world." Greenstreet had the next line which drew much hilarity from the audience; "True it is that we have seen better days!"[13]

To Greet, the play was the thing and he would brook no cuts in the text. For instance, the version of *Hamlet* the company gave was in the seldom-performed 1603 version. In a production at Ann Arbor, in which Greenstreet appeared as Polonius with Sybil Thorndike as Ophelia, the play had to be given in two parts in the afternoon and evening which took a full five hours to perform.[14]

In October 1908, the company received the ultimate accolade when it was invited to perform for President Theodore Roosevelt and his family on the White House lawn. They were the first professional company ever invited. It was a spectacular affair and undoubtedly one of the highlights of the social season in Washington. Mrs. Roosevelt organized the event; she and her children had seen the Greet players give a performance on the wooded lawns near the President's house around Sagamore Hill the previous year, but her husband had not been able to attend at that time.[15]

The White House festivities began on the afternoon of October 16 when the plays were first given. Two of Nathaniel Hawthorne's *Tales of Wonder* were the ideal choice for the entertainment. The first was *Pandora and the Mysterious Box*, and the second *King Midas and the Golden Touch*. The cast was augmented by local children including cadets from the E and G High School dressed as elves and fairies. Young and old alike were completely enchanted by the whole thing. "To the north ... the White House ... to the south a fountain played; to the west were gaily bedecked crowds," noted *The Washington Times*, which went on to describe the event; "It seemed eminently fitting that the fairylike creatures of Hawthorne's imagination should be revived amid nature's surroundings in the sunlight, near flowing streams and upon historic ground."[16]

Anyone who was anyone was there and quite a few who thought they were someone. Several members of the government along with other dignitaries such as the Japanese and Chinese Imperial ambassadors were present. On the second day members of the public could buy a ticket and gain admittance in the hope of catching a glimpse of the president or the players. In total, there was an estimated audience of about three thousand on the grounds during the two-day event.

The marine band struck up "Hail to the Chief" then the President made a short speech welcoming the players and explaining that the proceeds would go towards a children's playground project. Turning to the actors he said "You're a pretty good-looking spectacle."[17] Around $2000 was raised for the cause. Observers noted that the president "laughed and applauded like any schoolboy," during the performance.[18]

Greenstreet was even invited by the president to use his bedroom as a dressing room. Roosevelt chatted with him while he changed his costume.[19] Soon the world moved on apace; within a few months Roosevelt left office and other changes came about; after two thousand years China no longer had an emperor.

A local correspondent described the atmosphere; "As the sun went down behind the hills back of the stage, a hazy fog came up from the river and softened the outline of trees and buildings, until the whole garden and its thousands of spectators became more a fairy grove than a real place."[20]

The reception for the plays was so warm that Greet talked of setting up a dramatic academy in Washington. He found the cultural atmosphere more receptive there, he said, than other parts of the country.[21] British players on tour always enjoyed staying in the city.

The success of the White House event was in contrast to some of the experiences the company had faced over recent months and years. The regular theater tours were hardly earning money anymore. In a forthright interview in *The Call*, Greet spoke about his disappointment. He said audiences in San Francisco and California in general were fickle and that once he had played to packed houses for three weeks and had such publicity as he had never known. Times had changed, to such an extent that now in the same places despite importing a high-class Russian symphony orchestra his company were not even able to pay their gas bill. "Perhaps it is the moving pictures or the cheap vaudeville houses that are doing the damage," he offered, "but legitimate theaters are suffering all over this country."[22] Despite his pessimism, the seal of approval from the White House enhanced his standing no end and he continued to go from strength to strength. His pastorals always made money and his companies became popular on the Chautauqua circuit which grew out of the adult education movement. Undoubtedly, he advanced the cause of drama considerably during his many tours of the United States, helping to popularize Shakespeare in the long term among many thousands who would otherwise never have been exposed to such culture.

In a sense, it couldn't get much better than performing for the president and it was shortly after that high note when Greenstreet left the Woodland Players and decided to make his own way in the land which he had already resolved to call his home.

5 Happy Days in Pittsburgh

> "With wonderful appreciation, splendid voice and ready sympathy, Mr. Greenstreet exacts from each part he plays the best and highest it has to offer."
>
> "Who the Players Are" *Pittsburgh Daily Post*, September 19, 1909, 4.

After leaving the Ben Greet Company in 1909 Greenstreet joined the E. H. Sothern and Julia Marlowe company for a touring play and then played in stock for several months at Pittsburgh. It was a happy time in a good company and he found the audiences there especially appreciative; the best, he declared, in the world.

Greenstreet decided to leave the Woodland Players at the beginning of 1909 after four and a half years and many tours of America, Canada and Britain. His association with Greet had started in 1901 and he had learned everything fundamental to his art in those eight years. Greet continued touring regularly in America until the outbreak of war in 1914. For four years, he ran the Old Vic Theatre in London and after that continued touring in the British Isles. He made later visits to the United States. He was knighted in 1929 for services to the Old Vic and to the cause of Shakespeare. Greenstreet kept in touch with the various Greet troupes that toured the States over the years and occasionally joined their ranks.

Greenstreet left the Woodland players because he felt he wanted to branch out into a far larger variety of work and accept some of the many offers that came his way. One such was an invitation to join Julia Marlowe on tour in the blank verse play *The Goddess of Reason*. Set during the French Revolution this premiered in January 1909 at the Majestic Theater in Boston, just eighteen months after it was written. It was the first and only play by Mary Johnston, an advocate of women's rights who was previously known for her novels including *To Have and To Hold* and *Audrey*. Julia Marlowe had a high regard for the work; "I am convinced," she declared, "that *The Goddess of Reason* is the greatest poetical drama yet written by an American."[1] True to her belief, she took the risk of starting the season with it. On the first night, the authoress joined the leading players at the curtain call.[2] Marlowe was one of the foremost stage actresses of the time who had made her theatrical debut as a child of ten in 1876 in a Midwest touring production of Gilbert & Sullivan's *H. M. S. Pinafore*.[3] She had a long and successful personal and professional partnership with manager E. H. Sothern who she later married. Their organization was one of the best; they had excellent resources and paid their players well. *The Goddess of Reason* was well-received during its tour and ran at Daly's Theater in New York until March 1909. Although the play was a tragedy, Greenstreet had a role as a judge that played more to his comedic strengths and offered some light relief.

In August 1909 Greenstreet joined up again with one of Ben Greet's companies for a week-long run at Columbia University. The company was run by Frank McEntee and included Eric Blind and Dudley Digges. The familiar repertoire comprised *A Midsummer Night's Dream*, *As You Like It*, *Hamlet* and *The Tempest* among others, and proved a decided hit with an audience of summer students and the general public alike. Only one day was lost to rain when *The Taming of the Shrew* was given in the gymnasium. Otherwise the weather stayed fine for the well-attended outdoor performances on the greensward of the campus for some magical performances beneath the bright stars.[4]

In September 1909 Greenstreet signed as the leading character actor with the Harry Davis stock company based at the Duquesne Theater in Pittsburgh, Pennsylvania. The son of a millwright, Davis had been born in London but came to the United States as a child with his parents. He started out as a carnival barker and soon became one of the leading impresarios of the era in Pittsburgh. He owned a dozen theaters and held numerous other interests including casinos. Four years earlier in 1905 he had established the first ever movie theater in the city. Davis was described as being "versatile and eclectic in his programming, moving between continuous vaudeville, popular melodramas, and … the headier repertoire of the art movement."[5] The Duquesne had been built in 1890 and along with the Alvin constructed the following year soon helped to establish Pittsburgh's reputation as a good theater town which attracted nationally-known stars. The Duquesne had a street level entrance with large ornate doors. The interiors were designed in the Moorish style and boasted a wide sweeping staircase. The stage was one of the widest in the city.[6] For several months in the summer of 1909 the theater had undergone renovation and redecoration. For its grand reopening in September a new stock company had been formed. Davis considered the company that he assembled that season to be the strongest in the history of the Pittsburgh theaters.[7]

The season began on September 27 with *The Road to Yesterday*, followed by *The Little Minister*. Greenstreet was soon cited as one of the most popular members of the cast both with co-players and audiences alike. In the farce *Are You a Mason*, in October, Greenstreet was said to be "contagiously humorous as the Grand Master."[8] In the western comedy *Rose of the Rancho* an observer praised him as "positively inspiring" as "Padre" Kincaid.[9] Other members of the company included Lillian Kemble, with whom Greenstreet often appeared on stage. She became better known as Lillian Kemble-Cooper and appeared with him again in *Lysistrata*. Many years later she made a handful of films including a small role as Bonny Blue's nurse in *Gone With the Wind* (1939).

Greenstreet was young and readily acknowledged that he was ambitious. He sought to widen his repertoire with a greater range of plays than he was accustomed to with the Greet Players. He proved to be a hit in the many different productions at the Duquesne that season. He did well in his natural métier of comedies such as *When Knighthood Was in Flower* and enjoyed himself in his familiar role in *As You Like It*. He showed his versatility. He caused great merriment as a pompous colonel in *Ranson's Folly*, a satire of army life; but he was equally impressive in a serious role in the anti-slave drama *The Dairy Farm*.[10] A local critic remarked; "The part of Squire Hurley the stiff-necked and self-willed owner of Dairy Farm was powerfully and winningly enacted by Sydney Greenstreet."[11] The material ranged from old standbys like *East Lynn* to popular musicals such as *Carmen*. *The Christian*, based on *The Sign of the Cross* was much admired at the time; an eyewitness remarked that it was "the best thing that the stock company ever presented," and that Greenstreet "did splendidly" in another serious role.[12] Audiences enjoyed his turn in the sprightly comedy *Mrs. Temple's Telegram*. A witness remarked; "As Wigson, the butler, Sydney Greenstreet caused much laughter and showed himself as a clever comedian."[13] This was echoed by another who said he was "side-splitting" in the farce *What Happened to Jones?*[14] In the satirical drama *A Temperance Town*, a witness said he "makes good in a quick change from a member of the 'Ramrods' (temperance zealots) to that of special pleader on behalf of a saloon keeper when on court trail."[15] It was said that he contributed "a finished bit of acting" as a general in the bittersweet comedy *When We Were Twenty-One*.[16]

Davis never missed an opportunity to create novelty and interest and on Mondays and matinees signed photographs of the company were made available. Each actor took it in turns.[17] When it was Greenstreet's turn it was announced in the press; "On Monday afternoon and evening, ladies attending the performance will be presented with souvenir autographed photographs of Sydney Greenstreet, one of the most popular actors ever seen on a Pittsburgh stage."[18] He achieved perhaps his best reviews while at Pittsburgh as Lancelot Gobbo in *The Merchant of Venice*. While the whole company was given "unstinted praise," it was said that Greenstreet gave "one of his comedy impersonations that is a real joy. The way he succeeds in getting at the real fun proved a treat."[19] He left the company at the end of April 1910 in order to return to New York. Davis took on two new players in May.

All in all, Greenstreet thoroughly enjoyed his time with the high-class company at the Duquesne and said he found the audiences in Pittsburgh to be the most appreciative he had so far encountered. He found audiences generally far more spontaneous in America than in England; if they liked you they let you know. In an interview at the time he contrasted the two countries and spoke of the attraction of his adopted land and its people; "They do not stop to inquire as to the actor's antecedents, where he is from or what he has done in the past," he reflected. "For this reason, and for many others, I like America, and I believe this is the country for a young actor to start his chosen profession."[20]

6 Dissension in Harlem

"This stock company undoubtedly has a brilliant future before it."

"At Other Playhouses - West End"
The New York Dramatic Mirror, May 10, 1911, 7.

After leaving Pittsburgh, Greenstreet played in stock and tried to get work in New York. The following year he joined Robert T. Haines' newly-formed stock company based in Harlem which initially had high hopes but soon ran into difficulties.

In September 1910 Greenstreet joined the tour of *My Cinderella Girl*, a musical comedy about baseball. The show had played to packed houses at the Whitney Opera House in Chicago for five months and the tour took in many small towns in Illinois and Indianapolis. It was equally well-received in those out-of-the-way one-night-stands, and at South Bend, Indiana, he was mentioned among the able support.[1] In November of that year he appeared in *The Nest Egg* in Plainfield, New Jersey. The star of the play was Zelda Sears who would later turn to writing herself; she was the author of several shows in musical comedy in which Greenstreet played prominent roles. The show transferred to New York but during rehearsals he was trying frantically to rush to his next scene and finding that the door to the set was locked he pushed against it too hard, bringing the whole flimsy edifice crashing down. "I never played the part," he explained, "they decided they couldn't take chances on the scenery. They re-wrote the part to fit an eight-year-old boy."[2] He had an even more disastrous experience in a production of *Hamlet*. Joseph Harworth was playing the titular role and Greenstreet had a minor walk-on part. He was advised by fellow player Edward J. Ratcliff in the wings "Never turn your back on Hamlet." However, Greenstreet's role required him to exit via a door at the back, so he had to walk backwards to the door. When he reached the door and with trembling hand he found it was stuck. He leaned his weight against it slightly and exited, but as he did so the scenery began to buckle. The audience started to laugh, while Hamlet in the foreground was in mid-soliloquy, unaware of what was going on. Suddenly the whole scenery began to move ominously and came crashing down into the orchestra pit while the musicians all ran for cover. Greenstreet made a hasty exit to the basement, unaware that he was the cause of the mayhem. Harworth was livid and came running at him with his large prop sword; "You ruined my play!" he shouted, "Now get out of this theater!" Then he lunged at him with his sword which eyewitnesses said he "brandished like a madman." Greenstreet left the theater hastily and roamed the streets still wearing his Elizabethan garb. A friend packed his trunk for him and it was reported that Greenstreet travelled to another engagement in Denver the next morning.[3]

In December 1910, he was invited by the American Dramatic Guild to take part in some pre-Elizabethan miracle plays in a similar vein to *Everyman*. In the seldom-seen morality play *Mankind*, he portrayed one of the abstract qualities; "Mr. Greenstreet made an amusing Nought," said one critic. In *The Second Shepherd's Play* it was said that he and the other shepherds "extracted a good deal of mirth from their parts in the rough Elizabethan manner."[4] Shortly afterwards he toured as a captain in the historical costume drama *The Duchess of Suds*.[5]

By March 1911 Greenstreet was back in a high-profile production when he was given a supporting role in *Thais*, a religious allegory based on the work by Anatole France. Tyrone Power, Snr. played a hermit in the Egyptian desert who believes he has a mission from God to save souls including the wayward Thais (Constance Collier) and the city of Alexandria which he considers beset by sin. The production at the Criterion Theater in New York received what is euphemistically known as a mixed reception. Essentially about the damaging effects of too much religion, it was dismissed by the drama critic of the *New York Press* as a "lame, insufferably dull" play of a "prolix, morbid and repulsive story." Even the music of Massanet was judged to be "inappropriate" to the period and the region in which it was set. The same critic noted that the first night brought "a large audience – for the most part composed, apparently, of friends of the management and actors." Apart from such sarcasm, he observed; "Among the subsidiary performers a word of commendation is due to Sydney Greenstreet, who as a cook to Thais endeavored to lighten the gloom by a little low comedy."[6] Despite lukewarm notices the play managed to last two months and closed in May 1911.

After the closure of *Thais*, Greenstreet joined the Robert T. Haines stock company for the spring and early summer season based at the West End Theater at 125th Street, New York. Haines had abandoned a career as a successful lawyer in order to tread the boards. After several years in vaudeville he became the managing director of his own stock company which was financed by real estate developer Ralph W. Davis. Haines promised elaborate productions in a varied program for the season. In addition to the evening performances they gave only two matinees weekly.[7] As his leading lady he had Beatrice Morgan, who was well-known to Harlem audiences. Despite the build-up, the company's opening production drew a generally poor reaction. According to the critic of *Variety* it was a real debacle. He criticized the choice of play, *Soldiers of Fortune*, as not favoring the leading lady, and the manner of its delivery. He brought attention to the fluffed lines, badly-dressed players, poorly-staged battle scenes, mumbling actors and the stilted nature of the acting of Haines himself. In addition, Morgan was said to be suffering from a badly ulcerated tooth. Among the supporting cast the same critic found Greenstreet and the others merely "tolerable."[8] However, *The New York Dramatic Mirror* flatly contradicted that assessment, noting that Greenstreet among others was "well cast and won the applause" and concluded that "This stock company undoubtedly has a brilliant future before it."[9] Yet another reviewer observed that Greenstreet made "a very humorous and corpulent MacWilliams."[10] Whichever version of events was closest to the truth, after the opening night Beatrice Morgan promptly handed in her notice. Thereafter she was keen to sever her connection with the company entirely. "I should prefer not to rush into print in this matter," she stated, while doing exactly that. "I regard both Mr. Haines and his wife as very charming people personally," she continued,

"But Mr. Haines does not understand the situation in Harlem … as Mr. Haines insisted on securing what I regard as inferior plays I could not afford to sacrifice what has taken me years to build up by playing second rate leads."[11] Two others left the company in her wake, an ingénue and a stage manager. Morgan received two weeks' pay even though she only played to the end of the first week. Haines tried to persuade her to stay but she was adamant. He later claimed that Morgan was "inclined toward 'dictatorship,' and this, of course would naturally be resented."[12]

Such an inauspicious start to the season made life difficult for Haines and the remaining company. Morgan was replaced by the inexperienced Marie Nordstrom and the engagement was completed. Most of the plays made a loss although there were some good individual performances. For instance, in *The Liars* Greenstreet was said to be good in support. The allegorical play *The Lion and the Mouse* left audiences baffled but it was reported that he and others "gave excellent work."[13] One of the highlights of the run was *Strongheart*, a play by William C. de Mille, a Columbia University graduate.[14] The first night audience was swelled by around 200 of de Mille's fellow students. Elder brother of Cecil B. De Mille, William followed his sibling to Hollywood and adapted a number of stage plays for the screen, including *Strongheart*, which became *Braveheart* (1925) when directed by Cecil. Such bright spots aside, by the end of the eight-week run at the West End, Haines had lost a considerable amount of money, although all bills were paid.[15]

Once the Harlem engagement ended, Greenstreet accepted the offer to stay with the company and transferred with them to the Savoy Theatre in Asbury Park, New Jersey. The entire run at the Savoy was due to last for five weeks in total. The first play they presented was *Secret Service* beginning on June 26, 1911. The production played to a packed house and received excellent notices. The local drama critic remarked; "Sydney Greenstreet imparted dignity and rotundity to the role of a confederate general."[16] The company then began rehearsals for the next production, *The City*. However, patronage fell away during the first week and so the play was about to be taken off. For two nights, the players consented to put on *Secret Service* under what was termed a commonwealth plan. It was then that the show's financial backer, Ralph W. Davis, withdrew his support and left the company high and dry. Having drawn out all his money from the bank he presented theater manager Walter Rosenberg with a dud check and blew town. By the time the check was returned to Rosenberg marked "No funds," there was no alternative but to disband the company. Leading lady Helen Holmes demanded her salary of $162.50 and filed suit against the owners of the company that comprised Haines, Mrs. Haines and Davis. It emerged that the company was not incorporated.[17] The other players – nineteen in all, including Greenstreet, had to accept their loss for the week. The audiences had dwindled significantly after the price of admission had been increased beyond a level that had been previously fixed, known as the Charles Champlain price.[18] Stung by the many problems he had encountered while running his own company, Haines abandoned the legitimate stage and returned to vaudeville. In time, he found some success on Broadway and even wrote his own plays. In addition, he made about a dozen films. He was a much-respected figure and once served as trustee of the Actor's Fund of America. He died from a cerebral hemorrhage at the age of seventy-five in his room at the Woodward Hotel in New York in May 1943.[19]

7 Enter, Colonel Savage

> *"Henry W. Savage had a genius for determining what Americans wanted in a musical show and for giving it to them in the most attractive form. If he had stayed in the realty field the world would have lost something of real importance to its joy of living."*
>
> "Henry W. Savage" *The Brooklyn Daily Eagle*, November 30, 1927, 8.

After his experience with the Haines company, Greenstreet toured in a repertory of plays, returning to the surety of Shakespeare. Soon he would encounter the colorful impresario Colonel Henry Wilson Savage and find a palpable hit in the long-running farce *Excuse Me*, which made the young actor known in the west and guaranteed him steady work for the next two years.

Greenstreet was back on sure ground in a repertory of Shakespeare plays in various companies, sometimes under the aegis of Ben Greet. Not all the performances went as planned; in the world of live theater there was always the unexpected. One scheduled performance on the roof of Public School 64 had to be changed because the extraneous noise from traffic and passing trams was so loud. Instead of the expected play, the rather frazzled manager appeared and announced that recitations would be given instead, in the vain hope of placating a restless and rowdy audience. According to one witness only those at the very front could hear a word that passed on stage. Naturally, a critic was on hand to describe the shambles; "When Mr. Greenstreet appeared to recite Kipling's "Gunga Din," one of [the audience] greeted him with "Oh, you Murphy!" I will not speak artistically of Mr. Greenstreet's delivery of the poem, but if you care to hear my opinion of the elevator train that jumped the track at that moment or the motor car that evidently blew up, I shall be pleased to tell you."[1] Another witness of the events described a slightly different viewpoint and declared that the performance was well-supported by an enthusiastic audience and achieved the seemingly impossible by keeping a thousand schoolchildren quiet.² The following night the company presented the intended play, *The Merchant of Venice*, in the school's auditorium in which Greenstreet appeared as Gratiano. The production was considered impressive and prompted one critic to remark; "No doubt everyone got at least ten cents' worth in watching Sydney Greenstreet, whose rotund but roguish Gratiano will bear comparison with any Gratiano that has visited New York in a number of years."³

Sydney circa 1910. Photo courtesy of Gail Greenstreet.

Greenstreet appeared in a variety of plays including contemporary works such as *Speed* by Lee Wilson Dodd which played at Collier's Comedy Theater from September 1911. The show was produced and directed by none other than Cecil B. de Mille. A pointed satire about motor enthusiasts it concerned a family who are obsessed with buying a faster car to such an extent that they re-mortgage their house and end up in debt and worse. Greenstreet featured as a "too-ardent admirer of Mrs. Jessup," a lady who is far more interested in cars than affairs of the heart.⁴ A reviewer commented; "Sydney Greenstreet as the unhappy broken-hearted man, proved excellent in the role of one who drowned his sorrows for four days in liquor. His actions as a drunk were perfectly natural and his figure added much to the fun which he invoked."⁵

In December 1911, Greenstreet was invited to join the cast of the farce *Excuse Me*. It was his first appearance for Colonel Henry Wilson Savage, beginning a lucrative association. The show was hugely popular and it was one of Greenstreet's first real American characterizations which made him known on the West Coast.

Savage was one of the most successful and influential impresarios of the American musical comedy stage of the period around 1890 until his death in 1927. Born in New Hampshire, he was a student at Harvard and began his career in the real estate business, at which endeavor he was most successful. He entered theatrical management by accident when the manager of a light opera company deserted his troupe and the stranded players appealed to him for help. From then on, he never looked back and it was said that almost all his shows were successful – an amazing record considering he made over fifty of them. He was an innovator too, and was the first to introduce grand opera sung in English. He succeeded by attracting and insisting on the best talent, paying them well and by making ticket prices affordable. It was a winning combination. He was what is usually referred to as a colorful character, which is often a backhanded compliment. He did not emerge well when recalled by P. G. Wodehouse and Guy Bolton in their cod-memoir *Bring on the Girls!* Wodehouse worked for Savage in the 1920s as a lyricist. Much of the book consists of entertaining but largely apocryphal anecdotes about the personalities of the period.

Excuse Me by Rupert Hughes was an immensely popular long-running farce set entirely on board a train travelling from Chicago to San Francisco. A special set was constructed which replicated a deluxe Pullman car with sleeping berths, a combination buffet, observation car and even wash rooms. Typical of Savage's thoroughness he sent his chief scenic artist to the Pullman workshops to make sure the set was accurate down to the last detail. The designer spent three months at the works and the finished result drew widespread admiration. The set designers cleverly achieved the impression that the train was travelling at speed.[6]

The play itself had little by way of plot but was full of familiar character types in farcical situations. The show ran for almost a year on Broadway before it toured extensively across America. It was always well-received wherever it played and tapped into the cultural significance of train travel in what were the glory years of rail transport. Greenstreet was not in the original New York production but soon became a firm favorite when he joined the tour. William P. Sweatnam was in the most prominent role as a porter. However, among the large cast Greenstreet was often singled out for his gem of a character study as the gentlemanly "Little" Jimmie Wellington "broken-hearted, blasé and full of wine," who is travelling to Reno to seek a divorce from his wife because she drinks too much. The joke was that his wife was also on the train and also seeking a divorce – because of his drinking problem. A reviewer commented on "his voluntary and repeated discourse on the virtues of his wife, whom, even under the stress of marital unhappiness he still declared to be a 'queen among women.'"[7] The show as a whole was harmless fun and kept audiences entertained from one season to the next across the country. Prior to his role in *Excuse Me*, Greenstreet was well known in the east but virtually unknown in the west. His appearance in the show remedied that. A Duluth newspaper commented that he was "one of New York's favorite comedians," and that "he has a personality that gets across the footlights and makes friends for him in the audience."[8] This observation proved especially true and audiences seemed to take to him. It helped that he was a distinctive and recognizable figure; a reviewer described him as "the fat man who makes you want to laugh when you look at him, because he is so good-natured and talkative."[9] Another remarked, "Mr. Greenstreet avoirdupois and indiscriminate goodwill to everybody and everything was an agreeable asset to an agreeable role."[10] At the time it did not seem an overstatement when a Chicago scribe said the show was "the best farce in twenty years," or when a San Francisco critic remarked; "*Excuse Me* is the cleverest and funniest farce yet given to the American public."[11] The first tour began in El Paso, Texas in December 1911 and over the following months visited the states of Illinois, Missouri, Utah, Nevada, California and Montana before ending in Winnipeg, Manitoba, Canada at the end of April 1912. The show spent three months in Chicago playing at the Studebaker. Savage's canny approach kept prices low; tickets ranged in price from 25c to $1.50.

Sydney enjoying a meal circa 1912. Photo courtesy of Gail Greenstreet.

In special matinees at some theaters the price was never more than $1 for the best seats.¹² *Excuse Me* proved a hit all round. It gave Greenstreet steady work and brought him to a far wider audience. He appeared in the show on and off over the next two years, visiting some cities twice over and receiving an even warmer welcome the second time around.

Greenstreet made a return visit to England in August and September 1912. The family was by then residing at 62 Nevern Square, Kensington, an exclusive fifteen-room boarding house run by his mother Ann.¹³ In September 1912, Sydney was best man at the wedding of his sister Margery to Frederick Daniel Davis, a civil engineer from Aberdeen, who had previously been one of the boarders at the house.¹⁴ The following year another sister Hilda married Arthur Dashwood Hayward, a surveyor, at the same church.¹⁵ Unfortunately, Sydney was not able to be present on that occasion. His other sister Olive never married. Of his brothers, Arthur worked as a commercial traveler in the brewing industry and eventually settled in Birmingham. Frank was a fine art dealer who lived in Chiswick. Guy was living in Fulham and working as an auctioneer's clerk. Eldest brother Harry had migrated to America in 1907 and was living in Nebraska. This trip marked the last time Sydney saw his father who passed away in March 1913 at the age of sixty-five.¹⁶

On his return to America, he next appeared for Savage in *What Ails You?* A wayward farce set in a health resort, the show employed a large cast and had over thirty speaking parts. In such a melee, it was hard for individuals to be noticed. However, one reviewer noted "Sydney Greenstreet falls out of bed with elephantine grace. It is funny and entertaining even when you hoped for more. The first night audience went home in high spirits."[17] A later critic remarked, "Two fat men, Greenstreet and Fisher, cause some fun by their work, the former getting the biggest laughs attempting to put on his shoes." However, that episode aside, the play as a whole was dismissed as "sunken-chested, weak-kneed, lame and nearly all-in" by *Variety*.[18] One witness took it for what it was and noted; "Among the freaks at this resort, Sydney Greenstreet stands first by sheer physical presence. With a physique like his he would have hard work not to be funny. Voice and facial expression help him in the good cause."[19] This time the Savage-Hughes combination failed to score and the hoped-for long run of the show never happened. Savage was practical and instead of the intended tour of *What Ails You?* opted to return to the crowd-pleaser *Excuse Me*, knowing it would be a sure-fire hit.

By Christmas Greenstreet was back on board for the tour of *Excuse Me* which played in Little Rock, Arkansas, Shreveport, Louisiana and Charlotte, North Carolina among many other places. The tour continued into January 1913 playing El Paso, Texas, and staying several weeks in San Francisco before moving onto Oregon and finishing in Kansas. Everywhere they played to packed houses and the show was still being hailed as "a farce that breaks all speed records" two years after making its debut.[20] The show was still recalled with great fondness thirty years later.

8 Margaret Anglin

"Comedy is, in fact, closer to my natural temperature of spirits."

Margaret Anglin, *Green Book*, 1911, quoted in Le Vay, John *Margaret Anglin: A Stage Life* (Toronto, Canada: Simon & Pierre, 1989), 13.

At intervals between his work for Savage, Greenstreet made returns to his beloved Shakespeare whenever possible. He stayed for some time with the Margaret Anglin company, appearing in several productions for her during a long tour and engagement at the Hudson Theater, New York. He also appeared with the Frank Lea Short players during the summer months in their pastorals given at country clubs and for causes such as the Suffragettes.

For the late spring and early summer of 1913 and again the following year, Greenstreet joined the Frank Lea Short Players. A high-class company, they took their cue from the approach of Ben Greet and gave their plays alfresco in college campus grounds, country clubs and parks. They once played at West Point where they presented *The Romancers* "under a bower of maple trees decorated with magic lanterns."[1] Greenstreet enjoyed himself in a swashbuckling role as Straforel, looking not unlike Captain Hook, in a production seen by 300 members and friends of the Marine and Field club. Proceeds were given to the Army Relief Society.[2] The play was a translation from a French original and the tour marked its debut in the United States. The prominent character of Straforel was a popular, larger-than-life figure, variously described as being somewhere between Falstaff, Don Quixote and Cyrano de Bergerac. At an open-air show in Richmond, Virginia, an observer said that Greenstreet "played Straforel with an air of bravado, an unctuous humor and an easy poise that marked the skilled actor and comedian."[3]

The company also gave a presentation of *Pomander Walk*, a quaint play about English life, on the lawn of the Bay Ridge Summer Home at the Crescent City Athletic Club on a warm June day in 1913. Many guests arrived by boat from Manhattan. "The play was given with a vigor and swing that was refreshing," wrote one witness. "Sydney Greenstreet provided much of the humor."[4] It sounded like a well-organized day in an idyllic setting towards the end of the leisurely pre-First World War era. "After the performance refreshments were served in the club house, and many of the younger people danced. A special boat left for the battery at eleven and many guests departed."[5] The following year the company gave the same play at Prospect Park for the Suffragettes in June 1914. It was a gala day for the Suffragists and their distinctive yellow sashes were in abundance, fluttering in the breeze. A stage was set up under a large tree "in the center of a broad green lawn owned by James McLaren just opposite the Lincoln Park entrance."[6] Among the players Greenstreet was welcomed as a "notable addition to the ranks" for the cause.[7] He played an effete gentleman and entered to the strains of "The Lass with the Delicate Air" sung by a concealed chorus. He gave yet another fine character study in a highly successful presentation; a witness said that he "acted with unction, poise and humor and the net result … was amusing in the last degree." The day was considered "one of the most successful in the history of the Suffrage cause" in Brooklyn.[8] The powers-that-be took exception to how well everything had gone and a week later arrested the head of the organizing committee, Mrs. Notman, demanding to know why she had not obtained a license for the performance. She replied that she did not think a license was necessary because it was for a charitable cause. The magistrate didn't accept that, maintaining that it was a purely political event and imposed fines.[9]

In 1913, Greenstreet was invited to join Margaret Anglin's prestigious company on tour and for a season at the Hudson Theater in New York. Anglin was one of the finest and most versatile actresses of her generation. Her productions were marked by their quality and intellectual freedom. Popular on the east and west coast and points

Greenstreet as Tuppy in the Anglin company's version of Lady Windermere's Fan *by Oscar Wilde, 1914. The play was one of several Wilde classics that Anglin presented and helped contribute to a revival of interest in the great playwright and wit. Photo courtesy of Gail Greenstreet.*

between she was often thought of as a great emotional actress but had a far wider range than that implies. She was once lauded by the critic of *The San Francisco Dramatic Review* as "an actress who has run the gamut ... from melodrama through farce and delicate, fanciful comedy to the deepest human tragedy."[10]

In the works of the immortal Bard, Greenstreet was in his true métier. Audiences and critics alike appreciated him. In *The Taming of the Shrew* both he and a fellow player were commended for the way they "managed to inject much comedy and individuality into their respective roles" as Biondello and Grumio.[11] These were normally only minor parts. He was widely praised for his "uproariously humorous interpretation of Sir Toby Belch" in *Twelfth Night* at the Hudson Theater, New York, in March 1914.[12] One reviewer commented that this was "altogether the most authoritative and richly amusing of the three somewhat similar parts he played. The ease and evenness of his work, the way in which he constantly contrived to give Sir Toby's smoky humor to our day – or to carry the spectator back into his own – was as rare as it was uproariously funny."[13]

He did well in a variety of works and was effective in an especially popular production of Oscar Wilde's comedy *Lady Windermere's Fan*. This adaptation was roundly lauded for the way in which it balanced the comedic and emotional aspects of Wilde's classic. Wilde was at that time enjoying something of a renaissance and Anglin was at the forefront of that. She also re-introduced *A Woman of No Importance* which, like *Lady Windermere's Fan* had not been staged in New York for over twenty years. The production drew widespread praise; one wrote that "nothing that has been staged in New York this season is entitled to higher commendation."[14] The rotund actor was cited for his fine character work; "As for Tuppy," observed one critic, "I defy you to find anywhere such an ideal actor for the role as Sydney Greenstreet." The same reviewer said the play was "profoundly touching, wonderfully real," It was shortly after this production that Anglin echoed Tree's famous sentiment about Greenstreet as "the greatest unstarred star of the English stage." Anglin said the same of him for the American stage.[15]

In 1914 Greenstreet toured Canada with the Anglin company in a repertoire of Shakespeare plays including *As You Like It* and *Antony and Cleopatra*. When they played His Majesty's Theater in Montreal in January the thermometer was close to 30F below freezing and unsurprisingly the house was not full, but those who turned up greatly appreciated the show.[16]

Greenstreet spent twenty-seven weeks on the road with the Anglin company in 1913/14. It was a fine season for connoisseurs of drama that was fully appreciated. In *As You Like It*, Anglin received many plaudits as Rosalind; so too did the entire company; "As Touchstone, Sydney Greenstreet was also very capable, and did his fooling in an intelligent manner," commented one review-

Watercolor and ink drawing of Sydney as Touchstone in As You Like It, *1913. Photo courtesy of Gail Greenstreet.*

er, "He had several scenes which were capital, and brought liberal applause."[17] Touchstone was the court jester who comments on the other characters and the play in general making it clearer to the audience what is going on. Anglin was an accomplished actress in serious drama and comedy. The works of Shakespeare were not treated as something precious and fragile, but something vibrant and living. *Twelfth Night* showed the strength of the company's approach. One observer noted "The rollicking comedy scenes were interpreted with a breadth of method and an unctuous humor created uproarious hilarity. Mr. Greenstreet gave us the best Sir Toby Belch we have seen in years."[18] Another perceptively observed that his portrait "has the depth and richness of tone of a seventeenth century Dutch painting."[19] Those productions at the Hudson drew widespread acclaim. Greenstreet was further praised for presenting Touchstone as "a very human being," and Anglin was lauded for the way she brought out the "human note and pathos" of Viola.[20] Anglin had been born in Canada and her company often played there, receiving a warm welcome every time. A Vancouver critic was especially taken with Greenstreet's rendition of Sir Toby in *Twelfth Night*, that "made one almost long to partake of the cup that cheers. His unctuous and all-pervading chuckle was hypnotic in its effect and the audience could not forbear joining in."[21] The role was one of Greenstreet's favorites; "In the part of Sir Toby," he once said, "one feels that the 'Great Dramatist' has written in his merriest and most understanding humor."[22]

He drew special praise for the variety of his work; the noted drama critic Walter Prichard Eaton singled out Greenstreet as the gem of the company. He wrote that Sydney was "a genuine "find," an accomplished artist" and called his "Shakespearean clowns and low comedy characters the most enjoyable in years." Eaton continued; "He is a young man too, not over thirty. His Sir Toby Belch is a rare treat, and, to show his versatility, he turns to Enobarbus in *Antony and Cleopatra* the next evening, and makes a vivid figure out of that bluff Roman soldier, which holds his audiences silent."[23] Enobarbus was based on a historical figure but was almost entirely Shakespeare's creation. Often cited as one of the most noble characters in the play he was given some of the most important speeches which encapsulated the author's positive views of Cleopatra.

At the end of a memorable season, one critic wrote "The company which Margaret Anglin has gathered together, is remarkable for its finish and perfection."[24] Anglin's companies were friendly and

In contrast to his usual comic performances, Greenstreet silenced audiences with his powerful portrayal of Enobarbus in Antony and Cleopatra, *1914. Photo courtesy of Gail Greenstreet.*

close-knit by all accounts and during the run of one of her plays in San Francisco two members of the troupe, Eric Blind and Frances Carson were married. Greenstreet had known Blind, a fellow Englishman, since the early days with Greet and was best man. Miss Anglin gave an informal wedding breakfast for the happy couple in her apartments.[25] Tragically, Blind died of pneumonia just over three years later in December 1916 while on tour in Philadelphia at the age of forty. His young widow Frances never married again. Many years later she made fleeting appearances in several Hitchcock films including *Shadow of a Doubt* (1943).[26]

9 A Farceur

"He sailed like a small blimp through bedroom farces."
Sennett, Ted *Masters of Menace: Greenstreet and Lorre*
(New York: E. P. Dutton, 1979), 11.

Greenstreet appeared in a variety of plays at this time which ranged from Shakespeare to farces. Some of the latter were unsuccessful but it was all grist to the mill and proved to be valuable experience. All the while he was honing his comic ability.

The farce *She's In Again* began life in France as *Ma Tante d'Honfleur*. It was adapted by two English writers and played in London as *My Aunt*. This in turn was re-written for the American stage by Tommy Gray, a Vaudeville sketch-writer. It was produced by Ned Wayburn who was previously known for his musicals. After a successful two-month trial in Philadelphia, the revamped play opened to mixed reviews at the Gaiety Theater, New York, in May 1915. Something was most definitely lost in translation. Much of the vulgarity of the French original was expunged to take account of American sensibilities, but in the process a large measure of the play's character and *raison d'etre* was lost. Critics felt that the humor of *She's In Again* was "of the cheap superficial Times Square type," and that Gray's conception of his characters placed them all in "Forty Second Street and points adjacent."[1] Comedienne Ada Lewis had the central role and was virtually on the stage for the whole of the third act, which was considered the closest to true farce by some. There was altogether too much shouting for many viewers, but some audiences appeared to appreciate it; one reviewer remarked that the play drew laughter "from the gallery and the orchestra alike."[2] However, the critics were unanimous that Greenstreet provided full value playing one of what would become a familiar gallery of butlers.

There followed *A World of Pleasure*, a sprawling revue which played at the Winter Garden Theater in New York from October 1915. Greenstreet essayed the role of a millionaire, but the critic of *Variety* felt that he was "rather sourly dressed for the role." The same observer found the whole performance tiresome and declared "On the whole one can think of little about *A World of Pleasure* to suggest anything but a night of monotony."[3] The music was by Sigmund Romberg, renowned for his operettas such as *The Desert Song*. He was immensely popular in the inter-war years. Although not as a singer, Greenstreet later

Sydney at the wheel circa 1914. Photo courtesy of Gail Greenstreet.

appeared in Romberg's *The Student Prince*. The Winter Garden was famous for its spectacular shows which mostly featured leggy chorus girls in fast-moving dances with vaudeville turns interspersed. *A World of Pleasure* was in a similar vein and involved twelve scenes and about a hundred performers. The ethos of the revue was encapsulated in the advertising byline "Music, Color & Girls" which summed up all that most among the largely male audience needed to hear.[4] The critic of the *Chicago Tribune* labelled it "the nakedest of the New York shows" which although intended as a criticism undoubtedly boosted business no end.[5] Even so it was only a modest success and ended its run after three months in January 1916.

In between engagements with Margaret Anglin and Herbert Tree, Greenstreet popped up in a number of other farces. At short notice, he was added to the cast of *A Pair of Queens* replacing the leading comedian. The show had run for several weeks at the Cort

Theater in Chicago and continued to be extremely popular despite numerous cast changes. When it finished at the end of July it was once more recast and Greenstreet left the show.[6] Later he joined a tryout for a livewire farce, *Here Comes the Bride*. Described by one viewer as "noisy horse-play from start to finish," the play was given in Buffalo and other outlying districts prior to an intended Broadway run. Not considered ready for the big time, the producers went back to the drawing board and it re-emerged some months later in a revamped format with several different cast members, including someone else in Greenstreet's role.[7]

In between such farces he sometimes joined up with one of the Ben Greet companies on the famous Chautauqua circuit. This was a highly popular tent show which was inspired by the adult education movement to take culture to rural towns and isolated communities across the United States. The week-long entertainment would consist of lectures, military bands and plays. In the summer of 1914 Greenstreet appeared as Sir Toby Belch in a production of *Twelfth Night* in one of the Greet companies run by William Keighley.[8] They played fifty-six dates over sixty-five days in western Pennsylvania and West Virginia.[9] In the summer of 1917 Greenstreet toured in the East and parts of Canada. That company was led by Grace Halsey Mills, who played Rosalind in a presentation of *As You Like It*. Greenstreet essayed his familiar role of Touchstone. The Chautauqua Festival week drew large audiences everywhere and the continuing popularity of the Greet players was proof of the enduring appeal of well-produced plays in capable hands. In Oswego, a critic remarked "Seldom has such an appreciation been given at a theatrical performance. The entire company is gifted and the reading of the Shakespearean lines was done with a perfection as rare as it was beautiful."[10]

10 A King of Nowhere

> "Sydney Greenstreet as the king won a distinct hit and shared honors with the star."
>
> "First Time Plays: Lou Tellegen's 'A King of Nowhere.' Albany, New York – Satire on Kings"
> The New York Dramatic Mirror, February 26, 1916, 15.

Greenstreet played King Henry VIII twice in the space of a year, firstly in *A King of Nowhere*. This was a far cry from the Henry of his pomp as presented by Shakespeare. It was a role to which the rotund actor was especially suited on account of appearance and personality and made a decided impression among theatergoers.

Romantic comedy *A King of Nowhere* first saw the light of day in Poughkeepsie in February 1916, before making its full Broadway premiere at Maxine Elliott's Theater the following month. After one week, it transferred to the Thirty-Ninth Street Theater. Despite the presence of romantic favorite Lou Tellegen in the leading role, the play as whole was deemed a miss. Nonetheless, Greenstreet as old King Henry VIII took the honors among the supporting cast. It was a role that appealed to him greatly and he spoke about his feeling for the part at length in an interview with *The New York Sun*. His was a different version of Henry, he said, just two years prior to his death, beset by fears and visited by the ghosts of his dead wives. Greenstreet revealed that he had studied the man closely and found him interesting "from a pathological viewpoint." He felt that the king's penchant for vulgar quips and slapstick affronts was a symptom of his feelings of guilt, and that his conscience would not let him rest; "I think the murder of his wives became too much for him," he commented. "He felt that he was losing his grip, even his mind, and like most people who won't admit a fault, he sought diversion. While it took the form of belaying gentlemen of his court and kindred sports, I believe his kingly instincts cropped out at

Greenstreet twice played the Tudor monarch King Henry VIII in the satire A King of Nowhere *(1916) and* Shakespeare's Henry VIII *(1917), It was a role he enjoyed and to which he was eminently suited. Photo courtesy of Gail Greenstreet.*

times. I have tried to show him this way – occasionally recalled by some subliminal better self, back shall we say, to etiquette."[2]

He won great praise for his inimitable performance as King Henry; one critic commenting that "his conception of the capricious and willful monarch is faithful and true"[3] Another opined; "He depicts royalty in some of its most humorous aspects: the characterization trenches close upon comic opera. But it is inspired by a wholesome Falstaffian humor and strikes a note that is a grateful relief from a

Greenstreet (left) as the unsuitable suitor of Martha (Oza Waldrup, right) in Friend Martha, *a comedy of Quaker life, 1917. Photo courtesy of Gail Greenstreet.*

volume of fustian and bombast."[4] The play as a whole was adjudged too meandering; "America has been more successful in providing Lou Tellegen with a wife than with a suitable play," commented one of the New York critics. Indeed, on the first night there was more interest in seeing Mr. and the new Mrs. Tellegen together (the actress Geraldine Farrar) than there was in what was going on in the play. Nonetheless, amid all the romanticism, Greenstreet was again noticed in a role that was ideally suited to his talents and appearance; "by far the most amazing person on the stage was Sydney Greenstreet," wrote one reviewer, "who played Henry with a fine sense of comedy."[5] An anonymous female watcher commented; "What a jolly soul was Henry. According to the way Mr. Greenstreet presented him, he would have cut a splendid figure in our best cafes that stay open at late hours. Everybody liked him and felt glad whenever he came on stage, for he knew how to make us laugh."[6] The make-up for the king's appearance was based on paintings by Hans Holbein. The play later toured successfully.

Greenstreet greatly admired leading man Tellegen, who had already made some films by that time. The darkly handsome Tellegen was indeed a romantic figure. Born in Holland of Greek-Spanish parents, in his youth he had studied sculpture with Rodin at the Conservatoire and even lived with the great man for two years. Switching to acting he rose to prominence as leading man to a succession of renowned European actresses. Firstly, he was with the German actress Agnes Sorma, with whom he acted in German; then Eleonora Duse for whom he learnt Italian; after which he spoke in French opposite Sarah Bernhardt. He first went to America with Bernhardt who suggested he learnt English, which he did in a short time.[7] An expert fencer, he had ample opportunity to display his skill in his heroic role in *A King of Nowhere*. Greenstreet said he learned more about acting from Tellegen than anyone else and praised him as the greatest living actor in terms of technique. He said he was a generous performer who did not mind sharing the limelight; on the contrary, he had the big-heartedness that accompanies greatness which wished to see everyone do well.

Greenstreet next appeared in Edward Peple's *Friend Martha*, a satirical play about a young Quaker girl who rebels against the tenets of her faith when her father pushes her into marriage with a rich but much older man rather than the boy she loves. Both Greenstreet and the play received mixed reviews, but most viewers were entertained. The *New York Dramatic Mirror* commented that he "gave a finished performance as the amorous elder."[8] Another wrote that "in the character of the distasteful elderly suitor [he] took full advantage of the well-turned phrases with which the author had provided him."[9] He followed that play with a good role as a medicine man in *Give and Take*, described at the time as a "raggedy comedy farce and operetta."[10]

In 1916 Greenstreet first applied for American citizenship by Naturalization. His final papers did not come through until almost ten years later. On his attestation papers, he cited several reasons for his decision. In his written statement, he said that he had no intention of ever returning to live England. "America is a land of greater opportunity for the actor and gives him wider scope for his art," he declared, echoing much of what he had said seven years earlier.[11]

11 Sir Herbert

"Such a charming fellow, and so clever: he models himself on me."

Oscar Wilde, speaking about Herbert Beerbohm Tree
(Quoted in *The New Yorker,* March 9, 1957, 136.)

Sir Herbert Beerbohm Tree was one of the leading actor-managers of the Edwardian era in England. In 1904, he set up an academy of acting at His Majesty's Theatre, the theatre he owned, in The Haymarket, London. This later became the illustrious Royal Academy of Dramatic Art (R. A. D. A.), through which some of the finest British actors have graduated over the years. In 1909, he was knighted for services to the theatre. He had three children and a complicated private life; he was the father of several illegitimate children including Carol Reed, the film director, and the grandfather of actor Oliver Reed.

Tree's association with America went back to 1895 when he first toured the country. He toured again in the following year. However, it was some time before he was able to make a return trip. In 1916, he returned to New York to take part in the Tercentenary commemorations of Shakespeare's death. After that he stayed until the spring of 1917 when he returned to England.

It was on this tour that Tree met Charles Chaplin for the first time, an encounter immortalized in Chaplin's autobiography. The two became friends. Tree was an early idol of Chaplin, who, as a boy of fourteen, used to imitate some of his character studies. "Sir Herbert was, I suppose, the dean of the English theatre, and the subtlest of actors, appealing to the mind as well as the emotions," wrote Chaplin, "Tree's conception of character was always brilliant. The ridiculous Svengali was an example; he made one believe in this absurd character and endowed him not only with humor but with poetry ... His acting was extremely modern."[1] At the New

Greenstreet (center) as Touchstone with Margaret Anglin (right) as Rosalind and Max Montesole as Corin in a scene from As You Like It *during the St Louis festival to mark the Tercentenary of Shakespeare's death, June 1916. Photo courtesy of Gail Greenstreet.*

Amsterdam Theater in New York, Greenstreet appeared as the host of the Garter Inn opposite Tree as Falstaff in *The Merry Wives of Windsor*. The production was a success and Tree received a score of curtain calls. It was only the third time he had essayed the role and in a short speech at the end of the performance said he hoped he was improving. One critic remarked that Greenstreet gave "a splendid character study" in his supporting role.[2] Another commented; "he makes just the right sort of round and rosy rascal and adds substantially to the general gaiety."[3] Part way through the run Margaret Anglin offered him a role in a special production of *As You Like It* in a Tercentenary pageant in St. Louis, Missouri, which he accepted. Cecil King replaced him in New York.[4]

Margaret Anglin's *As You Like It* was a spectacular open-air show that played during the week of June 5 to June 13, 1916 at Forest Park, St Louis, Missouri. The play was given on the banks of the River de Peres in "an open stage-space flanked by two 70ft oaks."[5] It was a huge operation that involved about a thousand players in total. Many of the citizens of St Louis were recruited for the

Sir Herbert Beerbohm Tree (left) as Cardinal Wolsey in Shakespeare's King Henry VIII.

Greenstreet (above) played the title role opposite Tree during the successful American and Canadian tour in 1917.

occasion. It was estimated that around 10,000 souls watched the colorful pageant over the course of the week. Among the main cast was Alfred Lunt, soon to become one of the most famous names in the theater and a big influence on Greenstreet's later career. In 1916 Lunt was just a jobbing actor.[6] *As You Like It* was one of Greenstreet's favorite plays in which he had appeared in nine different roles over the years.

Greenstreet recalled with fondness working with Tree and was full of stories of his whimsicality. A mercurial personality, Tree was not a great actor. It was said of him "The tall lanky figure with the carroty hair, restless pale eyes and soft purring voice, was only suited to fantastic roles. He remained to the last a gifted amateur ... But to an original intelligence rare among actors and an exuberant romantic imagination, he added a demonic energy that drove him irresistibly to the top of his profession."[7] If a play failed or bored him he would cut his losses and move on to the next project. He was the antithesis of the business-minded man and thought nothing of paying a good player hundreds of pounds for just a few lines if he believed that player was the best for a given role. It was his practice to replicate the *actualite* of each production. For instance, if a woodland scene in *A Midsummer Night's Dream* called for rabbits, he would use live rabbits. He was often derided by some of the more serious-minded critics for such apparent eccentricity. Greenstreet recalled a rehearsal of a production of *Joseph and His Brethren* in which Tree, in inimitable style, insisted on using a real flock of sheep. Tree was on stage waiting to deliver his lines. There was a long pause while the stage manager had to go to the stalls and wake up the actor concerned; "Forty-nine players and not one suited to his part," complained Tree, at which moment one of the sheep started bleating; "Except you," he said, addressing the sheep, "You're alright."[8]

Of all Shakespeare's plays, *Henry VIII* was among those that was least known. It was generally considered one of his lesser works and it was believed that his protégé Fletcher collaborated with him and indeed may have written a good deal of it. While not a great play it was a great spectacle and made a diverting historical entertainment. Tree first produced it at his own theater, His Majesty's, in London seven years earlier. There it enjoyed remarkable success, clocking up some 256 performances and as such was, surprisingly, one of the longest runs of any Shakespearean play in England. At the time of that production, Tree had expounded his philosophy:

> "I claim that not the least important mission of the modern theatre is to give to the public representations of history which shall be at once an education and a delight. To do this the manager shall avail himself of the best artistic and archaeological help his generation can afford him, while endeavoring to preserve what he believes to be the spirit and intention of the author."[9]

Tree was true to his word. Seldom produced, *Henry VIII* was, according to Greenstreet, little more than a colorful pageant. Nevertheless, it was an eagerly awaited event at the Lyceum Theater in New York in March 1917. A typically elaborate staging, it had five leading roles and involved some 150 players in all. It was such a major enterprise that a special train was hired to transport the whole company, costumes et al.[10] The lavish production was a hit and endorsed Tree's contention that if a play was worth doing it was worth doing well, regardless of expense. The combination of the elusive Tree and an equally elusive play proved an enticing prospect for theatergoers that spring. The production toured in Washington, Pittsburgh and around New York and was praised as "the most important and interesting theatrical event for many years."[11] Greenstreet had replaced Lyn Harding in the title role, and was in his element playing opposite Tree as Cardinal Wolsey. They both won many plaudits for their portrayals. One critic remarked that Greenstreet made Henry "human, likeable and entirely credible."[12] Another said of his performance "it was infused with such vigorous spirit and was so cleverly varied in mood that it stood out convincing and alive."[13] On tour in Montreal at the end of March, a witness wrote that he gave "an extremely artistic performance" as the King.[14] Those who bought tickets for some Thursday evening performances on tour were rewarded with copies of Tree's handsome book *Henry VIII and His Court* as a souvenir.[15]

At Rochester, Tree made something of a diplomatic *faux pas* when, at the curtain call he seemed to imply that the United States and Britain were allies in a common cause against Germany. "At that," a local reporter noted, "several persons left the auditorium." Although America entered the war barely a month later there was still considerable opposition to it, and politics were always best avoided, especially when the evening had gone so well. But Greenstreet was more in tune with egalitarian American sentiment. "Turning to Mr. Greenstreet, Mr. Tree invited him to say a few words. The actor ... said it was evident that Kings and Emperors were learning that the time had come when they must bow to the people."[16] On another occasion at the Star in Buffalo, Tree expressed his hopes of an end to war, a greater understanding between nations and what he termed a "new reformation of world peace."[17] Greenstreet took no part in the war, but like his elder brother Harry in Nebraska, registered for the draft in September 1918. Their brother Arthur was a captain in the Royal Army Service Corps for the duration of the conflict. Another brother Guy was a gunner in the Royal Garrison Artillery.[18]

Tree next played the title role in *Colonel Newcome* in New York in April 1917, which was a considered to be a great personal achievement. The play was based on *The Newcomes* by William Makepeace Thackeray, and the author's daughter, Lady Richie, was full of praise for the accuracy of Tree's performance. "It seemed a miracle!" she wrote, "Colonel Newcome alive and standing there before us!" By all accounts, Tree excelled himself, in what was adjudged a sometimes humorous and often moving portrayal of the old soldier who feels he is in the way of his family; "it can be recorded that tears, as well as laughter paid him tribute," noted a first-night critic. It proved to be his final performance on any stage. Among the supporting cast one reviewer noted that Greenstreet "pounds a lot of fun out of Fred Bayham."[19] Another commented that he was "ebulliently humorous" in the role.[20]

The energetic Tree had put a lot into his American tour, much of his time and energy and a great deal of himself. He was never a man to do things by halves. He had won many friends and plaudits in the process. The biographer of Tree's half-brother, the caricaturist Max Beerbohm, related what happened next on his return to London;

> "Herbert Tree, now sixty-four years old, had just returned from a ten-month whirlwind tour of the United States. Though his days were as hectic as ever and his love-life more than usually confused, Herbert was still radiant, bubbling over with projects and reminiscences and jokes. Max, meeting him one morning at Upper Berkeley Street, was amused at his quenchless vitality. A week or two later he fell downstairs and ruptured a tendon in his kneecap. He was operated on for this. Apparently with success: for a few days later he was sitting up in bed laughing, talking and peeling a peach. Suddenly he fell forward dead."[21]

Greenstreet felt Sir Herbert's death keenly; he admired Tree's vision, energy and generosity of spirit. Greenstreet had also been looking forward to many future collaborations with him. He spoke about him shortly afterwards. "He was a big man and a fine man, and understood actors perfectly," he recalled, "Once last winter I missed something obvious in my part. "Never mind, Greenstreet," he said consolingly, "nothing is more baffling to genius than the obvious."[22] He cited Tree as one of only four big stars he had ever known who had not a jot of jealousy or minded sharing the limelight.

12 The Rainbow Girl

"I am a comedian by inclination, avocation and experience."
"Sydney Greenstreet a Shakespearean Comedian"
South Coast Times & Woollongong Argus, March 7, 1950, 4.

By 1918 Greenstreet had established himself as one of the most popular and versatile of stage stars. He had a collection of over fifty photographs of himself in the makeup of some of the many different characters he had played in the course of his career which aptly displayed his versatility. The year was auspicious for him personally because he was married in May.

Most of his time was taken up by stage business, but not all. He would relax by playing sports, especially tennis, croquet and golf. Relax may not be the right word because he was fiercely competitive whatever game he played. He often spent his summers in Asbury, New Jersey, and played tennis at the auditorium courts there. At that time, he was considered "the best player in Asbury."[1] William A. Robinson, one of the leading players of the town, greatly enhanced his reputation when he once won a set off Greenstreet.[2] In this way, Sydney came to meet Dorothy Marie Ogden, who also spent her summers in the town. She often attended tennis parties and was a devotee of the stage. She was a prominent member of the elite social set whose father owned a summer home at 1603 Webb Street in Asbury.[3]

Dorothy was the daughter of James Crawford Ogden and his wife Jennie (nee Whitehead). Her father was well-known as the oldest undertaker in the state of New Jersey. He was also one of its most prominent citizens, listed as a freeholder and alderman of the town of Elizabeth. The family was descended from John Ogden, who fought in the Revolutionary War and was one of the founders of the settlement of Elizabeth.[4] Dorothy was a member of the Daughters of the American Revolution and traced her ancestors back to the Mayflower.⁵ She had a brother Harold (1884-1957) who was seven years her elder. Her father James had been married twice before he married Jennie Whitehead and had other sons to his first wife, the eldest of whom was Frank who was over twenty-five years older than Dorothy.

James had lost a child in infancy, a daughter to his second wife. He was around sixty at the time of Dorothy's birth. She had a closeted upbringing and understandably, he seemed to indulge his young daughter somewhat. For instance, he had several cars and gave one to her as a present for her eighteenth birthday. In 1909 that was a rare thing; few people even had cars, which cost an inordinate amount of money. He gave her a Hupmobile, and shortly afterwards she declared that so far, she had only had one accident with it. That accident must have been serious enough because her car was out of commission for some time.⁶ A couple of years later she was involved in a crash at Red Bank, New Jersey, when a Pope-Hartford auto collided with the Pullman touring car in which she was travelling with four friends. Dorothy was showered with shards of glass from the smashed windscreen which left her head badly cut.⁷ There being so few cars on the road driving lessons were not really considered necessary. In those days, one just had to get in and drive, but accidents were surprisingly common. Most cars cost between $500 and $1,000 then, but Ford undercut this price with his cheapest motor costing only two hundred and fifty dollars. The average wage was about $400 a year, but a mechanical engineer could make up to $5,000.⁸ Cars were increasingly popular in the decade but still mostly for the well-to-do.

In August 1910, Dorothy and her family enjoyed an open-air performance of *A Midsummer Night's Dream*, given at Asbury Park by none other than Ben Greet and his Woodland Players, which Greenstreet had left just the year before.⁹ It is quite possible that he was there too because he rejoined the company at intervals. The play was a precursor to the Queen Titania carnival and pageant in which the children of the town took part. The grand prize for the bonniest baby in the Baby Parade was a $1,200 Borden Buick car with extras offered by the editor of the *Asbury Park Journal*. Unsurprisingly this was eagerly sought after by every parent in town to

Dorothy and Sydney shortly after their marriage in May 1918. Photo courtesy of Gail Greenstreet.

the extent that the competition had never had so many entries. Queen Titania from the Ben Greet players was seen riding in the car during the first day of the parade.[10] Dorothy also organized a theatrical tea party for the Queen and the other maids in the company.[11] In the event the car was won by a twenty-months old girl whose parents had dressed her up as near as possible to look like a doll for the occasion.[12]

After a fairly long engagement, Dorothy and Sydney were married at her mother's house, 103 West Grand Street, Elizabeth, on May 12, 1918.[13] Sydney was thirty-eight at the time and Dorothy was twenty-six. Her father had died two years before at the age of eighty-five after a sixty-five-year career in undertaking. The couple sometimes returned to Asbury Park for the summers and the local press reported in July 1919 that Sydney was once again playing tennis between the rain showers at the auditorium courts and still found the locals "just as easy as ever to beat."[14]

The young couple set up home in a large apartment in New York located at 191st Street. In September 1920, their son John Ogden Greenstreet was born. There was initially some confusion about the name which led people to assume he was a girl, but Sydney put everyone in the picture; "In the case of my son, it is evident a mistake was made when my wife, in deference to me, had him originally christened Sydney. That is, certain newspaper persons reported the child to be a female. No, nothing, alas or fortunately, could be further from the truth."[15] His co-star Mitzi and other members of the cast of the show in which he was appearing were invited to the re-christening in December 1920. A visitor to the Greenstreet home shortly afterwards talked of Dorothy as being "blonde, beaming and friendly," and completely attentive to the needs of her young son who looked equally happy.[16]

Greenstreet's classical fans were surprised when he chose to do musical comedies. The decision, he said, was a purely financial one. With a wife and young son to support he felt that he needed the increase in revenue. When he first received a telephone call from the Klaw & Erlinger office he thought they had got him confused with someone else because, he said, he could neither sing nor dance. He was soon informed that he was not going to be called on to do either. He found it a major leap from the classical parts he was used to; "I have to bottle my pride about blank verses," he reflected, "and undertake the common or garden variety of character roles that give laughter to musical comedy,"[17]

He described the transition to popular revues as difficult. It was something of a comedown and he missed the chance to explore his art to the full. He was playing to a different crowd who were far less interested in what was happening on the stage. A great many had come to see the girls or hear a few songs. It presented him with a new challenge. He maintained that it required a skillful actor to actually attract and keep their attention in such shows; "They come in any time during the play and walk out any time," he explained, "a thing which another audience would never dream of doing. They aren't attentive and the subtle touches, almost infinitesimal, perhaps – an intonation of a word – which I may have practiced hours and hours in my room – are lost when some bony flapper comes out in tights to do a shimmy dance."[18]

Sydney with his wife and son John, circa 1922. Photo courtesy of Gail Greenstreet.

The Rainbow Girl was based on Jerome K. Jerome's story *Fanny and the Servant Problem*. Essentially an all-singing all dancing show it nonetheless stayed true to its source and presented an unusual story. Most shows of the type were singularly lacking in plot. It was essentially the tale of a musical comedy actress (played by Beth Lydy) who marries an English lord and the adventures she has in her new life. There was a lot of dancing *a la mode* and there was also much comedy mostly provided by Greenstreet as a haughty butler and Billy B. Van as an itinerant actor posing as a bishop. Van was a vaudeville comedian who started out with minstrel shows and worked in burlesque. He was popular in the post-World War One period and later had a near double act with the boxer James L Corbett after the latter ended his career in the ring. Van later quit the stage for health reasons and went to run a farm; he made some short films and was for some time a spokesman for soap. Some observers enjoyed the physical and philosophical contrast between the two players; the thin Van with his penchant for low comedy and the rotund Greenstreet with his assured high comedy sense. During the trial run in Philadelphia one critic felt Van was funny but that he was "out of key with the spirit of the book." He highlighted a number of problems with the production but recognized Greenstreet as the best of the lot; "If Mr. Greenstreet's fellow players could imbibe a little of his competence and if all of [lyricist Rennold] Wolf's stale jokes were eliminated, *The Rainbow Girl* might be converted into an enjoyable little play with musical interpolations – harmless and unimportant."[19] A Boston critic remarked that Greenstreet "seems out of place in entertainment of this sort."[20] However another said that he "gave the most artistic performance."[21] *The Washington Herald* observed that he "accepted with dignity some very enthusiastic applause for his share of the evening's work."[22] "He bears close watching," wrote another reviewer, "His comedy knack is authentic and distinctive. A funnier bit has not been seen in musical comedy in a month of Mondays."[23] In Chicago a critic commented on the plot which was more prevalent than usual in a musical of this kind, even though it was effectively a Cinderella story; "You will like the humor of Mr. Sydney Greenstreet ... far better I think, and will lament that his ample presence is less conspicuous than Mr. Van," he wrote.[24] The show was acclaimed as "one of the rare entertainments of the season," and Greenstreet caught the attention of most reviewers with his "variety of pomposities and range of chortles truly remarkable."[25]

Greenstreet enjoyed working with Van who he said was a generous performer. During the run of the play there was a special dinner given in Van's honor. The dinner took place at the Friars Club and Greenstreet was among those who provided the entertainment. Van

Greenstreet (left) with Billy B. Van, his co-comedian in The Rainbow Girl *circa 1919. Photo courtesy of Gail Greenstreet.*

was presented with an elaborate chest filled with silver tableware as a mark of the esteem of his compatriots. He made a short speech in which he vowed to continue the work he had started in assisting retired players and their families during their declining years.[26] Van and Greenstreet were among the leading personalities from the Broadway world who were invited to the Theatrical Day of the National Automobile Show at the Grand Central Palace in January 1918.[27]

In between his appearances in musical comedies, Greenstreet returned to his classical roots when the opportunity arose. For instance, he accepted an invitation from Viola Allen to join her company in a production of *Twelfth Night* at the Sleepy Hollow Country Club in Scarborough, New York in May 1919. He reprised his role as Sir Toby Belch in what sounded like a thoroughly charming night in idyllic surroundings. The grounds were open to the public and members of the club were encouraged to invite as many guests as they wanted. A train left Grand Central Station at 5.30 pm and brought a large number of guests. The play marked a brief return to the stage for Allen who had ended her long and highly-distinguished professional career the year before. All the actors gave their services for the benefit of Ossining Hospital. The alfresco performance was the first in the Garden Theater and drew great support from a large crowd. A club luncheon was given, then a dinner and after the evening show came supper and dancing. A special train was commissioned to take the guests back home at 1.30 am. Some $2000 was believed to have been raised.[28] The combination of Shakespeare played well beneath a starry sky in a semi-rural idyll worked its magic on those present. There was such a special "Fete de Mai" atmosphere that even the drama critic of *The Billboard* was sent into transports of delight; "Even the birds seemed to hush their song betimes and the shooting stars to have silenced their silvery jingle as they fell in clusters behind the distant hills," he wrote.[29]

13 Lady Billy

"Someone once asked me if I try to please my manager. I most certainly do not! I try to please myself first. I think an actor is his own harshest critic."

Myriam Sieve, "Sydney Greenstreet Jumps from Shakespeare to Musical Comedy - Tells Why Classical Productions Don't Pay" *The Billboard*, August 20, 1921, 22.

From 1919 to 1921 Greenstreet enjoyed a prominent role in the musical comedy *Lady Billy*. Another Henry W. Savage production, it was Sydney's first show opposite the diminutive song and dance sensation of the time, Mitzi Hajos, a real personality performer known to all and sundry as Mitzi.

In 1919 Greenstreet was considering an offer from the Sothern-Marlowe company to tour again in a repertoire of Shakespeare plays. But then he received a call from Henry W. Savage inviting him to take part in another musical comedy, *Lady Billy*. In the normal course of events he would have chosen the former offer. However, something about the character of Bateson the haughty butler caught his fancy and he decided to accept the Savage assignment instead. He later said that he felt that the character was one of his best. He explained the attraction; "[Bateson] typifies the true funny man, who is humorous though he has no sense of humor."[1]

He was roundly praised for his portrayal. A theatrical journal commented that Mitzi's "fat and faithful major domo, [was] acted with rare humorous poise by Sydney Greenstreet."[2] On tour in St Louis, Missouri, the drama critic lauded him as outstanding in support; "Not previously this season has an opening night audience stopped a performance in the middle of the second act to make known its joint appreciation for the star of a show and her chief assistant."[3]

Even in musical comedy he could not help but lapse into the classical drama where his heart lay. However, several critics appreciated his approach. One noted that "he played in a grand Shakespearean manner which is always funny in musical comedy when skillfully done."[4] But the show belonged to Mitzi who was then on the crest of her wave of popularity. The petite Hungarian-born performer Mitzi Hajos first made her name in such hit shows as *Sari*, *Pom Pom* (1916) and *Head Over Heels* (1918). On account of her size she often played boys in a hangover from the old pantomime tradition. An energetic personality of the kind that was popular in the frenetic 1920s, she became one of the most recognizable stars of the era, so much so that she was one of the few people to be known only by their first name. As one reviewer wrote; "Mitzi's personality, her singing and dancing continue to be the wonders of the modern musical stage."[5] Predictably, the uptown critics were not so enamored; the acerbic Dorothy Parker commented on one of her shows; "Mitzi ... is tireless in her efforts all evening. There are times, in fact, when, pleasant as she is, one wishes that she would just tire a little bit and go and lie down for a while."[6] But Greenstreet was always a welcome presence in the cast and the physical contrast of the two provided much of the show's appeal. One reporter remarked; "Sydney Greenstreet as a butler deserves mention, and his song "The Worm's Revenge" brought him forth for many encores on opening night."[7] The tour was equally as popular if not more so; "Whether the role of the old

Sydney's wife Dorothy with son John circa 1923. Photo courtesy of Gail Greenstreet.

Sydney has fun with his son John on the beach, circa 1923. Photo courtesy of Gail Greenstreet.

Sydney with his son John, circa 1923. Photo courtesy of Gail Greenstreet.

Sydney (right), with Dorothy (left) and son John (center), circa 1924. Photo courtesy of Gail Greenstreet.

secretary-chaperon was written particularly for him is unimportant," declared one observer; "Without him it would just be a minor role. With him it is a delight."[8]

In addition to acting Sydney also gave lectures and demonstrations at schools, colleges and universities. In 1923 for instance he gave *Fragments from Shakespeare* for the students of Boston University at the Colonial Theater. He gave excerpts from *Julius Caesar, Henry V* and *As You Like It*.[9] He delivered the same performance for the drama students of Mrs. Dow's School for Girls at Briarcliff.[10] He also presented a talk on "Shakespearian Clowns" at the Castle School for Girls at Tarrytown.[11] On that occasion he gave a recitation of "The Worm's Revenge" from *Lady Billy* in addition.[12] He gave similar addresses during a three-day session of a Drama Festival organized by the American Theater Association in May 1926. The festival took place at the Park Avenue Theater and included members of the Dallas Little Theatre in scenes from *Twelfth Night*.[13] At one school he was at first refused entry when the teacher failed to recognize him out of his makeup. In character, he had white hair and was made to look about 100 pounds heavier. He commented; "At last, having convinced them of my general honesty and purpose, two hundred pounds and thirty-four years, I adjourned to the lecture hall and talked. But was my

Sydney and his wife Dorothy enjoy a round of golf circa 1925. Photo courtesy of Gail Greenstreet.

audience attentive? How Shakespeare suffered! For so excited were these dear schoolgirls over their teacher's mistake and my youth and beauty – ahem! – that they giggled and tittered all afternoon. Miss Carroll McCormas as Lulu Bell is not alone in her efforts to disguise her handsome figure and tender years for art's sake," he joked, "Me too, Lulu."[14]

Greenstreet was often the life and soul of the party and immersed himself in the social life of the stage. He also took part in meetings of the Actor's Equity union and attended many special benefit entertainments for theater folk. For instance, he was the co-compere of the Boston Benefit for the Actor's Fund in the early 1920s which raised over $7,500. There was a packed house at the Colonial Theater in what was described as "one of the most noteworthy afternoons in the history of the Boston theater."[15]

Sydney relaxed away from work and often played golf with his wife Dorothy in the 1920s. He loved to play tennis and during a tour in Illinois for instance, it was reported that he was "vanquishing all opponents at the tennis courts of the Chicago Beach hotel."[16] He won a fair amount on bets on matches betting on himself, as his granddaughter related; "All I know about Sydney's tennis career is that he beat Don Budge (?) the same year Don won a Wimbledon title. The match I believe was in New York and my grandfather won enough on bets to live for a year."[17]

When the long run of *Lady Billy* at the Liberty Theater was coming to an end, Greenstreet was delighted to welcome a visit from his mother and sisters Olive and Hilda. They arrived on the Olympia in August 1921 and were keen to meet Dorothy and the new grandson. Sydney told Mitzi that his folks longed to see more of America than just New York "For my part the only reason I hated tours was because I got lonely for my folks," he explained, "Now I'm going to have them all along – six Greenstreets, count 'em. I've figured it out that we can see the country and live on my salary at the same time. If I went alone, I'd probably spend it all anyway. This way I'll make the whole family happy and have the time of my life myself!"[18] There were already other members of the Greenstreet clan in the United States and his mother's family, the Bakers. Sydney's eldest brother Harry had migrated to Nebraska in 1907. Harry first went to stay with his uncle Frederick Baker, his mother's brother, who had lived there since 1894.[19] Harry settled in Douglas, Omaha, Nebraska where he worked as a land examiner. He married a local girl, Lucille Curtis Race in March 1913. Sydney was best man at the wedding.[20] Harry and Lucille had a son (born 1917) who was christened Sydney in honor of his illustrious uncle.

Greenstreet's mother and sisters stayed with him for six months in total during which they toured around the country. They returned to England in February 1922.[21]

Sydney warms up on the tennis courts, circa 1926. A lifelong player, Tennis remained one of his favorite games. Photo courtesy of Gail Greenstreet.

14 Comedian for Mitzi

"[I remain with Mitzi] because she makes me happy, and so does my part."

"From Shakespeare to Musical Comedy"
The Evening Telegram - New York, November 14, 1923, 14.

After the closure of *Lady Billy*, Greenstreet appeared in a variety of productions, notably *The Magic Ring*. He played the odd serious role, then stayed several months with *The Student Prince* before returning for a final reunion with Mitzi.

He essayed the role of a villain for a change in Paul Wilstach's *Her Happiness*, the story of an innocent Italian girl and the unscrupulous entrepreneur who seeks to exploit her. The play opened at the Garrick in Washington, D. C., in October 1922 and was considered well-acted but not well-written. However, one reviewer remarked; "You are certain to enjoy Sydney Greenstreet, whose refusal to become a fiend and whose determination to remain human makes him one of the most charming villains of the autumn."[1] Nevertheless, despite his best efforts and those of popular leading actress Emma Dunn, nothing could "retrieve the play from the limbo of utter obliviousness and, at times, tiresome cant." Critic Harold Phillips observed that Greenstreet "is the embodiment of the impresario, a sort of push-cart personage who trades careers for unsullied souls, but in the last act he is the victim of the author's paradoxical whim, which makes him say and do things wholly destructive to the illusions he took so much pain and skill to previously create."[2] The play toured briefly, visiting Allentown, Pennsylvania and Wilmington, Delaware, but did not make the leap to Broadway. In complete contrast, he appeared shortly afterwards in a farce, *The Whole Town's Talking*. Anita Loos and husband John Emerson came across the original German play while on holiday in Europe. Together they adapted it for the American stage and it had a brief tryout tour around New

York in November 1922. The single-night debut at the Hempstead Theater, Long Island was especially well-attended and drew riotous laughter. The resident theater critic welcomed the arrival of the show, remarking that it made a refreshing change from stale vaudeville turns and too many movies.[3] A short tour moved on to Scranton and Wilkes-Barre, Pennsylvania where the show proved equally popular. Among the cast, Greenstreet "as the fellow who complicated matters by "fixing things" added to the fun," wrote one observer.[4] Despite the positive start the show did not transfer to New York as expected. According to Emerson "It was only on the road a short time, but everything happened to it. Members of the cast got sick and then [leading man] Jim Bradbury couldn't get the lines."[5] *The Whole Town's Talking* re-emerged the following year when it played on Broadway with a different cast, *sans* Greenstreet.

To Greenstreet, acting was an art and he was always working to improve his art in every way. Besides, he was interested in all the arts, especially painting and sculpting. Both he saw as an aid to acting. Sculpting was especially useful for thinking particularly about movement, he observed, and he often sculpted in his spare time.

His next big show was *The Magic Ring* which began with a tryout in Boston in April 1923, where it was originally entitled *Minnie & Me*. The show was something between a fantasy and a comedy with songs. The ubiquitous Mitzi played an organ grinder who discovers an old ring in an antique shop owned by Greenstreet. One rub of the ring transports her back three thousand years to the court of the Grand Vizier of Kashmir. The score was roundly praised; there were songs galore sung by the star with the help of a male operatic chorus and a female sextet of instrumentalists. Dynamo Mitzi danced as always and there were two other sets of dancing couples, Carlos & Inez, and Lyons & Wakefield.[6] Despite the busy stage Greenstreet drew much attention; one critic noted that his "character acting was superb."[7] Another remarked that he "delineates with wonderful cleverness the role of the bibulous antique dealer, who just loves liquor though he knows it is 'spoisonous.'"[8] Much of the comic relief devolved to him and he was ably supported by Janet Murdock who played his thrifty Scottish wife. Murdock would re-enter Greenstreet's life some years later when she became his housekeeper. The

Sydney (second from left) with some unnamed cast members of a musical comedy show, possibly The Magic Ring. *The lady second from right could be Janet Murdock. Photo courtesy of Gail Greenstreet.*

clever lyrics by Zelda Sears used words of more than two syllables and were praised as being "almost Gilbertian."[9] Among the cast was a young Jeannette MacDonald, described as a "slender blonde who possesses a light soprano."[10] Within a few short years MacDonald would team with Nelson Eddy and achieve outstanding success in screen musicals. However, *The Magic Ring* was Mitzi's show and most contemporary viewers saw her as "the magnet from which much of the charm radiates."[11] One even referred to her stint as a female Aladdin to be "the most brilliant success of her career."[12]

Greenstreet said he enjoyed his role in the show which he described as "the most charming drunk I've ever played. He is much more charming than a trio of Shakespearean drunks … although compared to a capacious Shakespeare role it is short rather than long."[13]

The Magic Ring marked the end of Greenstreet's twelve-year association with Henry W. Savage who died in November 1927. Shortly before his death Savage was reputedly one of the wealthiest showmen in the United States, worth an estimated $40 million and second only to John Ringling of the famous circus dynasty.[14]

Sydney and family, circa 1925. Photo courtesy of Gail Greenstreet.

Sydney on the golf course (with his wife watching in the background, circa 1925. Photo courtesy of Gail Greenstreet.

Continuing in musical vein, Greenstreet next appeared as Lutz the valet in *The Student Prince*. The show had been running for almost a year when he joined it in October 1925. A phenomenal success it ran for two years in total and an astonishing 608 performances at the Jolson Theater on 59th Street. It was by far composer Sigmund Romberg's most popular operetta. At the height of the Prohibition era it was an irony that was not lost on many that the show's most popular song was the rousing "Drink! Drink! Drink!" Despite his late entry into the show, Greenstreet contrived to bring his comedic talents to bear. Reviewing the show at Christmas 1925 one critic remarked; "A newcomer, the ponderously agile Sydney Greenstreet, gives rich comic tone to the farcical points of the evening."[15] The show continued until May 1926. During one incident back stage, he had an encounter with an indolent youth who was swinging on the knob of his dressing room door. "Mr. Greenstreet, according to eyewitnesses of the accident, dashed from the door in imminent need of a tailor and asked the boy how far he would have to go to find one. 'Roll over twice and you're there,'" answered the boy smartly.[16]

Sydney's golf dream: Sydney jokes with an unnamed friend about the number of trophies he has won. Photo courtesy of Gail Greenstreet.

Moving away from musical comedy for a spell, Greenstreet did well in a dramatic role in *The Humble*, an adaptation of Feodor Dostoievsky's stark and memorable novel *Crime and Punishment*. One reviewer described him as "conspicuously good" as the examining magistrate.[17] The run was all-too brief at Greenwich Village and many critics lamented the Americanization of the classic. However, they noted that Greenstreet and fellow Englishman Basil Sydney did the best work; the latter played Raskolnikoff.

Greenstreet followed that with a prominent role in *Junk*, by Edwin B. Self, described as "a simple play about a fat, modest hobo who loved a girl and gave her up to the boy she loved."[18] In fact the plot sounded anything but simple, and involved two friends, in love with the same girl, who rob a bank to provide the funds for a life-saving operation for the girl's grandmother only to discover it was all a ruse. As a result, one becomes a junk man and the other

Sydney had a leading role in Junk, *a short-lived comedy that ran at the Garrick Theater in January 1927. Photo courtesy of Gail Greenstreet.*

becomes governor of the state. Unsurprisingly it was deemed to be "crude ... mawkish and unbelievable." Nevertheless, the play had one redeeming feature, as critic Arthur Pollock noted, "Fortunately Sydney Greenstreet plays the junk seller. Mr. Greenstreet has a pleasant smile, an off-hand manner and shows what a good actor can do under ridiculous difficulties."[19]

By the time *The Madcap* opened in April 1927 it was said by many that Mitzi's star was on the wane. But if that was the case, her fans seemed to think otherwise. The packed houses during a seventeen-week run in Chicago were certainly testament to her sustained popularity. The story, derived from yet another French farce, concerned a daughter (Mitzi) who pretends to be younger for the sake of her mother who hopes to ensnare a rich lord (Greenstreet). Once again, Mitzi appeared much of the time in her child character. The show was pretty formulaic and although the songs were bouncy they were unmemorable. Observers noted that as usual she was surrounded by a cast of talent, including "a finished comedian" in the

Sydney and family circa 1927. Photo courtesy of Gail Greenstreet.

shape of Greenstreet, who was seen to best effect when teamed with fellow Britisher the tall and thin Arthur Treacher. One reviewer wrote that Greenstreet "brings down the house with his funny antics and amusing expressions."[20] Another noted that he enjoyed a "portly and portable part as a lord anxious to become a bridegroom."[21] Critic George L. David commented that Greenstreet was a conspicuous and "always welcome" presence. David wrote; "[He] played with his usual comic skill. Although he has excelled in comedy characters with a suggestion of the sinister or grotesque, his character had neither; but he made it amusing in his individual comedy style."[22] After a tryout around New York, the show arrived at the Lyceum in Brooklyn where it drew fair reviews but it was really during the spring and summer of 1927 that it took off in Chicago, after which it continued on to the Midwest until it finally re-emerged on Broadway to muted acclaim in January 1928. In total, it lasted a full year, clocking up some 429 performances. On its return to New York the production was "considerably cheered by a large audience at the Capitol last night," related one critic, who also commented on the songs Mitzi sang, one of which, "Step to Paris Blues" showed that her "voice was a bit thin for a real blues singer."[23] She continued performing well into the 1940s, by which time her glory days were long since behind her. She never made the transition to films and as a result is barely known today. Her true métier was the light musical comedy of the kind that flourished in the years after the First World War and once that fell out of favor she too vanished.[24]

15 Mrs. Fiske's Dream Company

"She was an inspired actress, a valiant soul...."
Harrison Grey Fiske tribute to his wife Minnie Maddern Fiske quoted by William A. Ettel, "Mrs. Fiske, Noted Actress, Walked Unrecognized Through Quiet Hollis Community" *Long Island Daily Press*, February 17, 1932, 2.

Greenstreet continued in his varied career, continually re-inventing himself. He had more than one string to his bow and moved swiftly from the waning world of musical comedy to the real theater once more. In November 1928, he accepted an offer from Mrs. Fiske to join her prestigious company on tour. It was a return to Shakespeare and he was much delighted at the prospect.

Minnie Maddern Fiske was considered to be one of the most important and influential American women of the stage of the first third of the twentieth century. She always maintained the highest possible dramatic standards, insisting on the integrity of artistic freedom. This brought her into conflict with the vested interests of the powerful Theatrical Syndicate which owned all the best theaters in the country and made every decision about who could be cast and which productions were deemed viable. As a result, Mrs. Fiske was isolated; she was forced into playing small venues such as churches, meeting halls and skating rinks. She suffered for twelve years in this way which meant that she ultimately died in poverty. An early advocate of animal welfare she was an influential figure because she was so well respected and widely admired far beyond theater circles. She campaigned against the barbarity of fur trapping and influenced the treatment of cattle on ranges. Her life was dedicated to the theater and she was practically "born in a trunk." She made her stage debut at the age of three and was touring as a child of six with her stage manager father and actress mother. She was an innovator in her profession who first introduced Ibsen

Mrs. Minnie Maddern Fiske (1865-1932), one of the foremost actresses of her time who ran one of the finest acting companies in America.

to American audiences, and gave some of the most well-beloved performances of the works of Shakespeare. Her aim was to introduce realism into acting which had hitherto often been beset by mannerisms and appeared stilted. Instead of giving several plays each season, her company concentrated on giving one play per year involving the best performers suited to the subject. Her tours began in the East and ended in the West, but because of the problems of venue she was based in Philadelphia. In New York, she played

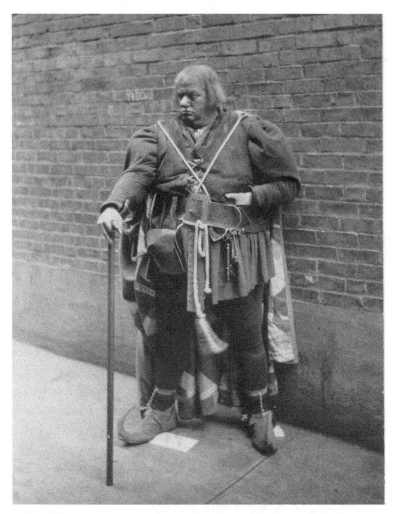

In Mrs. Fiske company's Much Ado About Nothing, *in 1928, Greenstreet provided comic relief as the pompous night-watchman Constable Dogberry, forerunner of the comedy policeman in popular entertainment. Photo courtesy of Gail Greenstreet.*

such little-known theaters as the Van Curler and the Wedgeway in Schenectady. Nevertheless, all her productions were so beautifully mounted that they tended to attract good and highly-appreciative audiences, at least during her glory years. It was not mere hyperbole that her company was billed as "America's foremost dramatic organization."[1]

Greenstreet was in his element with the company, savoring the chance to escape from being Mitzi's comic foil for a while. He spoke about his feelings at the time of joining up with them; "I never felt happier than when, upon reporting to rehearsal with the Mrs. Fiske Company I found myself associated with the most brilliant group of artists that could be gathered together in one cast. Mr. and Mrs. Fiske had made true the dream of my life – an acting company of such distinction that the word 'star' is superfluous."[2]

Her presentation of *Much Ado About Nothing* was a typically strong production with a musical setting. She maintained her standard of "only the best plays in the best manner possible."[3] When playing at the Broad Street Theater in Philadelphia a local critic remarked "nothing could be more convincingly humorous than the comedy of Sydney Greenstreet and Dallas Welford as Constable and Headbrough."[4]

He always loved the Shakespearean clowns best and excelled as Constable Dogberry. In Shakespeare's time policing was on a purely amateur basis and consisted mainly of night-watchmen. Dogberry was the epitome of the self-important petty official with delusions of grandeur who invariably used the wrong word and sowed confusion. As such he was the prototype of the bumbling policeman down the ages on stage and screen. Among others in the cast was Pedro de Cordoba, a distinctive actor of French-Cuban descent who was already well known as a film star. He went on to have a long screen career despite his assertion that he preferred the stage. Although Dogberry was a minor character, Greenstreet strongly believed that Shakespeare wrote no minor roles and that it was the mistake of some producers to cast the leading roles with stars and give no consideration about those in the smaller roles. He maintained that the Bard needed to be acted by experts who were able to do full justice to each role to successfully give life to the whole endeavor. He considered that an actor needed to study for five years in order to be able to speak blank verse intelligently.[5] When discussing the differences between modern and classical comedy, Greenstreet said that in Shakespeare's time the laugh needed to pointed; "A pause, a wink, a grimace, all will help to prepare your auditors for the laugh line which is to follow," he said, "the whole idea is in leading the audience to anticipate that something good is coming. But no matter what sort of comedy it is, the comedian has got to feel that the thing he is doing or saying is funny, otherwise it won't be."[6]

The tour began to great acclaim in Newark, New Jersey in November 1928 and did well in the theaters around New York, Baltimore and Hartford, Connecticut. The run at the Hollis Theater in Boston was said to be a tremendous hit. From there the company took the tour to Philadelphia. On the first night there, Christmas Day, 1928, there was a packed house, but during the week interest soon fell away. The city's newspaper reported; "Most of the time during her visit here Mrs. Fiske played to a bakers' dozen in the lower part of the house, and the sweetness of the production was wasted on the deserted rows of a gloomy floor."[7] It was dispiriting for all concerned and after such a cold response she closed the show in the first weeks of 1929 and the remaining dates in Pittsburgh were cancelled. Local drama devotees were left to ponder why such rarely-seen high art went unappreciated. There were many reasons why; lack of publicity, the choice of venue, the inclement weather, competition from other frivolous stage shows. Most assuredly the movies provided the greatest competition of all. No matter what it did, the stage could never hope to outdo the talkies which at that time had made their sensational entry in to the collective consciousness and captured the public imagination like nothing else.

Mrs. Fiske made two films but considered herself unsuited to the medium and never tried again. She was often sighted walking her dogs in the quiet suburb of Hollis where she had lived for many years; she was described by locals as a reserved lady with a regal bearing. She continued to plough her own furrow on stage and appeared to effect in comedies and many different types of plays always to a high standard and maintaining her artistic freedom. Unfortunately, her audiences kept declining to such an extent that by the time she died three years later her passing went largely unheralded.[8]

16 THE THEATER GUILD

"On the stage, we used to say 'tomorrow night.' Our best performance will always be 'tomorrow night'"

Virginia Macpherson, "Sydney Greenstreet is a Practical Joker at Home" *Schenectady Gazette*, August 1, 1945, 23.

There was a more somber mood ushered in after the heady days of the 1920s came to an end with the Wall Street Crash in October 1929. Somehow the urge to dance on tables or drink champagne from a lady's slipper seemed to have diminished. Before long the Depression years put a damper on everything, especially the theater. It was then that Greenstreet moved away from musical comedy and played a greater variety of roles. He made a series of acclaimed appearances for the respected Theater Guild, often in more serious-minded plays. In addition, he took part in a hit revival of a Greek comedy and even tackled some villainous parts.

By the end of the 1920s, Greenstreet was considered to be one of the "best known and highest paid entertainers of the English or American stage."[1] He was well paid by the standards of the time making over $4000 per annum.[2] This was far more than the average salary of $1,900. Wages were generally higher in the late-1920s than they would be at the end of the following decade, by which time his income was over $5000.[3] Before long the vast sums that could be made in Hollywood enticed a great many away from the theater to the film capital in what became an inexorable tide.

Greenstreet joined the Theater Guild at the end of 1929 and the first play he did with them was *Marco Millions*, Eugene O'Neill's satire inspired by the life of the thirteenth century traveller Marco Polo. Greenstreet played Kublai Khan, but did not go for the obvious approach. A critic remarked; "Instead of executing a caricature the Great Khan of Sydney Greenstreet is a mellow and sympathetic

Greenstreet as Kublai Khan in Marco Millions, *the first of several prominent roles he enjoyed during his time with the Theater Guild, 1929-32. Photo courtesy of Gail Greenstreet.*

figure that provides the necessary contrast between the philosophical oriental and the self-centered trade booster."[4]

Greenstreet was next elevated to the title role in the group's version of Ben Jonson's *Volpone*, succeeding Dudley Digges. A contemporary of Shakespeare, Jonson is not mentioned nearly so often,

Greenstreet (right) played the title role in the Theater Guild's acclaimed version of Ben Jonson's Volpone, *1930. With Earle Larimore (Left, standing on box) as Mosca, the Gadfly. Photo courtesy of Gail Greenstreet.*

although he contributed some of the great comedies of his age. The story revolved around three courtesans at the time of the Renaissance who each try to curry favor with Volpone in the hope of profiting in his will. Volpone – which literally means sly fox – plays them all off against each other. Greenstreet felt ill-at-ease with the part to begin with and struggled to capture the deviousness and hypocrisy of the character. He tried numerous things but nothing seemed to work. But once when he was rehearsing while staying at his summer house in the Berkshires as his young son was playing in a corner of the room, his son turned to him and suddenly exclaimed "Father, I don't like you!" It was then that Sydney realized that he had succeeded in capturing the essence of the role.[5] The critics were impressed; one remarked; "The shifting moods of Volpone, his utter levity and then his feigned illness are caught in the magic web of a fine artist of the theater when Sydney Greenstreet dons the flowing nocturnal robes."[6] He played to great effect opposite the agile Earle Larimore – the gadfly to Greenstreet's fox. Once again, the production was a tremendous success; "extraordinarily diverting stage entertainment" concluded the critics.[7]

Greenstreet next played the only human survivor in *R. U. R.*, a "brief and honorable" revival of Karel Capek's stark fantasy about robots.[8] *R. U. R.* (the initials stood for Rossum's Universal Robots) had first been performed in 1921 and was one of the most original plays of its time. It was the story of a company that develops robots to help mankind but the robots take over and kill the humans. The Theater Guild version was hailed as a highly effective and thought-provoking piece and all the actors were deemed "skillful."[9] The play's director was none other than Rouben Mamoulian who went on to a great career in Hollywood. His *Dr. Jekyll and Mr. Hyde* (1931) is an acknowledged horror classic. Among the cast was Henry Travers, who became a familiar face on screen. Albert Dekker, then known as Albert Van Dekker, played the leader of the strikers. Greenstreet was Beck the manager of the company. The highly effective production drew rare praise from the New York critics. Mamoulian recalled a key scene; "When the robots began to destroy people and objects, I had them walking in through doorways and windows, advancing towards the audience. As they stepped through the proscenium arch the lights went suddenly out."[10] It was a truly startling moment for the audience. Capek coined the term robot; his work was groundbreaking and prefigured Fritz Lang's *Metropolis* by several years. *R. U. R.* set the template for many a science fiction story for years to come and the theme of technology de-humanizing people is one that is likely to retain its relevance for some time. It seems curious that no one ever tried to make the play into a film considering how suited it was to the medium.

Greenstreet drew much laughter as the President of the Senate in Aristophanes' satire Lysistrata, *a surprising hit in 1931 which toured the following year. With unnamed cast members. Photo courtesy of Gail Greenstreet.*

When the English actor Herbert Druse died suddenly from pneumonia, Greenstreet was called in to replace him in the role of the Earl of Loam in a production of *The Admirable Crichton*.[11] J. M. Barrie's Edwardian satire concerned an upper-class family who are shipwrecked on a desert island and who are totally lost without their resourceful butler who ends up being in charge. But then once they are rescued everything returns to normal, or almost. Greenstreet gave a fine character study of the flustered and bumbling earl. In Rochester, it was said that he had long been "a favorite comedian of ours." The local dramatic critic noted that "he used his vocal tricks effectively again."[12] Another said he gave a "genial and delightful performance."[13] Along with Fay Bainter he was adjudged one of the most memorable in the cast. It was a well-mounted and popular production and the cast took six curtain calls.[14]

Greenstreet next popped up as the president of the Senate in a version of Aristophanes' *Lysistrata* starring Miriam Hopkins. It was for certain a remarkably old play but had only been seen in America for the first time in 1925 when a Russian company toured with it. The 1930 version struck a chord with audiences and critics alike. The story was set in Athens and the premise was a surprisingly timeless one. Tired of constant war with Sparta, a clear-thinking Lysistrata announces to both sides that their womenfolk will withhold all sexual favors until they end the fighting. At first the men laugh but when the women barricade themselves in the Acropolis the men soon come to their senses. One reviewer labeled it a "merry ribald frolic."[15] Hopkins and Fay Bainter shared the honors, but Greenstreet as the flummoxed president was noticed despite the relatively small size of his role. His part was a perfect satire of every self-seeking politician since time immemorial. It was such a popular show that when it toured later it stayed two or three weeks in places where it was only expected to last a week. By that time, Hopkins had left the show and was on her way to Hollywood; she was replaced in the cast by Jean Arthur, taking a sabbatical from movie-making.[16] The tour proved equally popular if not more so. Of Greenstreet an observer remarked; "Mr. Greenstreet has rocked audiences with laughter in this play, and, personally, if it were possible for all the patrons at the Majestic to meet him off stage, they would find that his flashing wit and keen sense of humor are just as natural and spontaneous as they are on the boards."[17]

In December 1931 Greenstreet appeared in a rare villainous role and made a distinct impression. The drama *Berlin* was set in the days just before the First World War and concerned spies, with Greenstreet as the head of the Secret Police. A critic remarked; "The

Greenstreet (left) enjoyed himself in a villainous role for a change as the head of the Secret Police in the spy drama Berlin 1931. *With left to right: Helena Rapport, Curtis Karpe and Helen Vinson. Photo courtesy of Gail Greenstreet.*

portly Sydney Greenstreet, who makes so genial a Shakespearean clown, plays the dark, relentless chief of police. He has moments when he trusts too much in the old-fashioned ways of being melodramatic, but most of the time he is an effective figure."[18] Another noted that he "makes a real character of Grundt, the most sinister character in melodrama since Professor Moriarty."[19] John Mason Brown felt he was too emphatic and wrote; "Not only does he scowl with the ugliest scowl that a Prussian could have ever produced, but he has donned a club foot for the occasion." Nonetheless, Brown praised Greenstreet's "rip-snorting and delightfully malign" performance as the most complete in a disappointing play, commenting, "Overact as he may, he is nonetheless a heart-stopping figure of terror."[20] Sydney later said it was one of his favorite roles.[21]

In March 1932, he had a supporting role as a colonel in the satirical comedy *Olivia Bows to Mrs. Grundy*, described by its author Roland Bottomley as a "free love argument in three acts."[22] Initially among the cast list was a young actor called Elisha Cook, Jr. However, Cook was switched to another play so the two did not act together at that time. The play started its tryout in Great Neck, Long Island before transferring to Washington from where it was expected to move to Broadway. Instead it underwent a further trial in Wilmington, Delaware where it was touted as "a comedy gem of undeniable genius" and reviews declared that the

Greenstreet (left) as the cunning uncle of Wang Lin with Jessie Ralph as his wife in The Good Earth, 1931. Photo courtesy of Gail Greenstreet.

"sparkling play keeps audiences in rare good humor." Greenstreet too was once again noticed; "the blimp furnished his part of the comedy," commented one reviewer.[23] Despite its apparent promise the show was taken off in Delaware after three days and moved to Hartford, Connecticut where it promptly disappeared from view. The cast all returned to New York without work.[24]

Later that year, Greenstreet appeared for the Theater Guild in *The Good Earth*. He played the role of the scheming uncle of Wan Lin, who was portrayed by fellow Englishman Claude Rains. It was deemed a variable adaptation of Pearl S. Buck's classic tale which employed some seventy cast members to good effect. Owen Davis and his son Donald were duly praised by some for the intelligent way they transferred the book, or at least part of it, to the stage. A particular talking point was the acting of Russian actress Alla Nazimova as the tragic O-Lan. One of the most flamboyant and recognizable personalities of the performing arts, Nazimova was always news. *Variety* commented that Greenstreet was "admirable as the rascally uncle."[25] It seems anomalous to modern audiences to employ Caucasian players in a play set in China, but such was common practice at the time and the film version of the same name followed suit.

In May 1932, there was a reunion of some of the Woodland Players for a special dinner given in Ben Greet's honor. Sir Philip Ben Greet had been knighted three years earlier and was by then one of the most respected and highly-distinguished figures in the theater with an international reputation. After numerous tours to America up until 1914 he returned to Britain and became instrumental in establishing the Old Vic as a leading light. Greenstreet and John Sayre Crawley along with many others attended the Shakespeare dinner at the Actor's Dinner Club and reminisced over old times. On May 9, a special production of *A Midsummer Night's Dream* was given by old and new players together at the American Women's Association Clubhouse.[26] Greet continued to tour but took a far less active role in proceedings as the years went by. He died four years later at the age of seventy-eight.

17 The Show Goes On

"Spun of all silks, our days and nights
Have sorrows woven with delights."

Francois de Malherbe *To Cardinal Richelieu*

Despite the uncertainty of steady stage work during the Depression, Greenstreet's theatrical career continued on its upward curve. In the early 1930s, he enjoyed another long-running success in the Jerome Kern musical *Roberta* which propelled Bob Hope to stardom. In contrast to Sydney's professional life he encountered personal sorrow with the sudden and prolonged illness of his wife Dorothy.

Greenstreet's private life had been hitherto settled but things began to go wrong in the early 1930s. At that time, his son John was a pupil at the exclusive Collegiate School in New York, one of the oldest and best-regarded Ivy League prep schools in the United States. The headmaster of that establishment, Cornelius B. Boocock, got to know the family quite well.

At the end of 1932, Sydney's wife Dorothy, then aged forty-one, began to show signs of becoming emotionally disturbed. It was not certain what exactly triggered her trouble, but it necessitated her complete removal to a sanatorium in January 1933. At first Sydney believed this would just be a temporary measure and that she would soon be back to being her old self. He told friends that she was away on a visit. However, when that visit extended to months and then a year, it was evident that she would not be better any time soon. He felt compelled to tell them the truth.[1]

Dorothy appeared to show no previous signs of any problems. Boocock, the headmaster of the Collegiate School that John attended described her as "a very calm, capable woman … who … seemed to have the interest of the boy very much at heart." Then something happened. Boocock had dinner with the family about two months before her trouble began. His impression at that time was that she

Sydney's wife Dorothy. Photo courtesy of Gail Greenstreet.

was "just a bit fed up with the brilliance of the spotlight which was focused by her husband on himself."[2]

Sydney's granddaughter recollected: "The family kept her fairly sheltered. It turned out she had mental health issues and by the time my dad hit ten she was in a mental health institution. The institute was located in the state of Milwaukee. And my father rarely saw her. She got so bad she didn't even know her own son."[3] It has not been possible to find more exact details about Dorothy's condition because the hospital said that it does not keep records going back that far.

Sydney with his wife and son circa 1930. Photo courtesy of Gail Greenstreet.

The Milwaukee Sanatorium for Nervous Diseases at Wauwatosa in Wisconsin was a privately-run home that had been established some fifty years earlier on a thirty-acre site along the Menomonee River. The founders of the place eschewed the then prevalent institutional approach and adopted the pioneering idea of a cottage system, providing a greater degree of comfort and engendered a feeling of being part of a community rather than in a hospital. At the same time, the administrators stressed the importance of the open air and the naturally soothing effects of a scenic location. It was considered to offer some of the best treatment possible in the country at that time and many non-Milwaukee residents were admitted, in fact they came from every state in the union.

At first Sydney and John visited Dorothy often. In one of his letters in August 1934 Sydney described an early visit to her and lamented "She is still a very sick girl." During that visit, they saw her every day for a week, twice a day for the first two days, but then she became agitated. The Doctor thought it was too much strain for her and they only went once a day after that. Sydney was upset and uncomprehending about her situation, but he was satisfied that she was receiving the best of care. He commented that the staff seemed well-trained and pleasant. Dorothy was often taken on drives by the head doctor's wife and occasionally on motor boat rides on the river. There were extensive grounds and the area was especially scenic and restful. The treatment of psychological problems was not so advanced but the doctor was of the opinion that her condition might improve when she reached the menopause.[4]

John moved to his next school in the Berkshires in the fall of 1934. Sydney became friendly with the headmaster, Dr. Seaver Buck. They often played golf together and during the summer months Sydney would sometimes stay as a house guest at the school. In many ways, Buck became a good friend and confidante to him, not only as someone to look out for his son, but someone to whom he could talk about his personal worries. Wherever he was in the country performing Sydney sent many letters to Buck during the time John was at the school. These letters chart not only his working life on the stage but his feelings about everything. They reveal Sydney as a concerned father, preoccupied with thoughts of his absent wife and show his worries about his health problems while constantly striving to do great work on the stage. An air of benevolence and great good humor irradiates the letters but beneath the veneer there is a palpable sense of anxiety and hints of deeper sorrow.

Most of his thoughts were about his son. For instance, Sydney knew that, like him, John was not particularly academic. He was disappointed at the grades he was getting and had a long talk with him about his school work. But although he urged him to apply himself to his studies, he was more concerned with the kind of person he was. He wrote to his friend that he realized John lacked concentration, and put this down to his rapid growth (he was 5' 7" at the age of thirteen). Sydney gave his own assessment of his son who, he said, despite his faults "has the big virtues honest, truthful, generous, loving; very sensitive."[5] He also knew how much John

Greenstreet in his element surrounded by a bevy of chorus girls in Roberta, a hit show despite critical derision. The nationwide tour lasted from 1933 until March 1935. Photo courtesy of Gail Greenstreet.

missed his mother and the effect of her situation on a sensitive boy should never be underestimated. Dorothy's illness was heartbreaking to them all and something they adjusted to over the years but never fully came to terms with.

Sydney's theatrical career continued unabated. He was a naturally ebullient soul who always seemed cheerful by all accounts, and friends had no inkling of his personal sorrow. Always the most professional of actors he lost himself in work and spent some sixteen months with a successful musical show which took up much of his time between 1933 and 1935.

The light musical comedy *Roberta* opened on Broadway in November 1933 to no great acclaim. It featured one Bob Hope in its cast, but neither his presence, nor that of Greenstreet could save the venture from the ire of the New York critics. Even so the show has come to be remembered for a variety of reasons, principally its music. Of Greenstreet, it was said he "had little to do." The show was generally derided by the critics; "If you miss it you haven't missed anything," hissed one reviewer, who pointed out that the only good thing about it was "Jerome Kern's sweet music."[6] The lyrics were by Otto Harbach. The outstanding song was "Smoke Gets in Your Eyes," which soon became a standard. Greenstreet even joined his co-stars Hope, Robert Middleton and Lyda Robert in singing "Let's Begin."[7] It was a show that two members of the cast had cause to recall. One was Fred MacMurray a young understudy described as "a bashful saxophone player." Fed up with not getting a chance to play a role, the story goes that one day he borrowed Bob Hope's hat and cane and took a screen test. He was successful and never looked back from there. Hope remembered it for more personal reasons; "I met my wife Dolores during the run of the show," he recalled, "And it was the turning point of my career. Thanks to *Roberta* I became a radio star and was bombarded with offers for movies."[8]

Despite what the critics said the show was hugely popular and continued at the New Amsterdam for eight months after which it did even better on the road. By that time, it had caught Hollywood's attention. A film version was hastily arranged which meant that the tour, which was due to continue in to June 1935, had to end early to make way for the movie premiere. It was a curious irony that was not lost on Greenstreet that the show was a victim of its own success and closed the tour that was still doing excellent business. He wondered aloud what the theater was coming to. The film starred Fred Astaire, Ginger Rogers and Irene Dunne, but some of the songs from the show were omitted and others added. The role that Greenstreet had played went to a little-known actor.

Seemingly content, Greenstreet was still preoccupied with thoughts of his wife and the calamity that had befallen them all. He became fatigued with overwork, constant travelling and the uncertainty of his wife's condition. He was run down and sometimes had mysterious "colds" that lasted for months. Once when the long tour of *Roberta* reached Boston his sense of depression overcame him for a while. He was with his son at the time. Sydney fell in the street and turned his ankle, but made no attempt to rise; "I just lay there and ruminated," he said, "Everything had seemed to be going wrong for several weeks. I was tired out. Here at last I was comfortably on my back. What matter if it was in the street? What matter if people were gathering in a circle and gaping at me?

I was resting, I was comfortable. For the first time in weeks nothing bothered me. I just didn't want to get up. I was completely content." However, he said that he made the conscious decision that he would get up and try again.[9]

18 Life with the Lunts

"They are going to be great."

Sydney's assessment of Alfred Lunt
and Lynn Fontanne in 1935.

In March 1935, while Greenstreet was lamenting the early closure of the *Roberta* tour, he was interviewed for a small role in a Shakespeare play. He didn't care much for the part offered and the salary was no improvement on what he was getting for the previous show. However, he decided reluctantly to accept the offer. The play was *The Taming of the Shrew* and the part was that of Baptista, the father of Kate. In this way began Greenstreet's association with husband and wife Alfred Lunt and Lynn Fontanne, one of the best and most influential teams in mid-century theater.

Greenstreet's initial ambivalence about the role soon melted away during rehearsals. He could see the way the Lunts worked; they were professional, dedicated and above all inventive. Greenstreet felt a huge sense of optimism and marveled at their wonderful conception of the play; he wrote to a friend they "are going to be great."[1] For his part, he tried various things to make more of his character than seemed possible and particularly wanted to make him amusing. In this he succeeded and the production was well-received by several hard-to-please New York critics. John Mason Brown felt the material was so familiar that little new could be achieved. He was moved to write that the play "has been turned into an inspired romp, because Sydney Greenstreet and Richard Whorf are admirable in the usually dead parts of Baptista and Christopher Sly, and finally because Lynn Fontanne and, even more especially, Alfred Lunt act Katherine and Petrucho with such invigorating gusto that they carry everything before them."[2] Another critic praised the experienced Greenstreet for his "delightfully hesitant" Baptista.[3] Some years later this production and the alleged backstage problems between the

Alfred Lunt (left) as Petrucho, Greenstreet (center) as Baptista and Lynn Fontanne as Kate in the critically-acclaimed production of The Taming of the Shrew *in 1935. It was Greenstreet's first appearance for the Lunts beginning an exciting six years in Sydney's career. Photo courtesy of Gail Greenstreet.*

Lunts inspired Cole Porter's musical *Kiss Me Kate,* with its memorable songs including "Brush Up Your Shakespeare."

The production was a great success and Lunt was keen to keep the ensemble together. He had long dreamed of having his own company and at last it had become a reality. He hailed the players he had assembled in the 1930s as the most versatile he had ever known. Among the others was Barry Thompson, a violinist, Richard Whorf, a painter, and S. Thomas Gomez, a linguist. Gomez sometimes understudied Greenstreet and after several years on Broadway he also went to Hollywood where he had some good roles such as the menacing Curly in *Key Largo* (1948). It was a wonderful group and Lunt realized that something magical was forming. "I've never been happier in the theater than I am at this time," he said, "It's unbelievable what energy these people have. Their initiative forever astonishes me. Moreover, we never quarrel. We are friends off stage, which is saying a lot."[4] Greenstreet always helped younger

Greenstreet (seated left) played German scientist Dr. Waldersee in Idiot's Delight, *the first of two Robert Sherwood plays which the Lunts presented. The production won the Pulitzer Prize in 1936. With Alfred Lunt (standing) and Edward Raquello (right). Photo courtesy of Gail Greenstreet.*

players. One such was Donald Buka, discovered by Lunt at the age of sixteen while a student at the Carnegie Technical School. He joined the company on tour and was given his chance in *The Taming of the Shrew* and *Idiot's Delight*. Greenstreet took time out to help tutor Buka in Shakespearean technique. Buka had a successful stage career and made several appearances in films including *Shock*

Treatment (1964). He later appeared regularly on television in some of the most popular shows of the day such as *Ironside*.[5]

Robert Sherwood was one of the leading American playwrights of the inter-war era. His hit *The Petrified Forest* was later made into a memorable film which first brought Humphrey Bogart to wide public acclaim. Sherwood's first stage success was with *The Road to Rome* in 1925 which took its cue from Hannibal's abortive attempt to capture the city. This introduced Sherwood's anti-war stance which informed much of his work. Similarly, *Idiot's Delight* was an anti-war piece concerned with a disparate group of strangers holed up in a hotel near the Swiss-Italian border. Lunt played a second-rate hoofer and Fontanne was a mysterious Russian who turns out to be from Detroit. Greenstreet played the role of a German scientist who is close to finding a cure for cancer. He even adopted an accent for the part. Although it was subsidiary role he felt it had great quality. His character becomes disillusioned with the impending war that all his work would count for nothing when mankind is intent on destroying itself.

Idiot's Delight was a comment on the political situation in Europe and was considered to be one of the best plays of 1936. It even won the prestigious Pulitzer Prize that year. However, many of the New York dramatic critics took great exception to this verdict. Among the play's supporters, John Mason Brown wrote; "Mr. Sherwood shows once again his uncommon ability to combine entertainment of a fleet and satisfying sort with an allegory which reaches for larger meaning."[6] It was, he said, "one of the Theater Guild's suavest productions" with "accomplished performances" by its cast.[7] Once the play began touring other critics were still more fulsome in their praise, concluding that *"Idiot's Delight* must be recorded as a play of a decade, not of a single season. Strange, stirring, humorous, tragic, brutal by turns, it won five-curtain-call applause for its players from one of the season's largest audiences."[8] Greenstreet was commended for his "thoughtful study" of the scientist.[9]

The Lunts next tackled a major work of the French dramatist Jean Giradoux. *Amphitryon 38* was pithily summarized by one commentator as "an essay on the disadvantages of being a god."[10] Alfred Lunt appeared as Jupiter. The play opened to great acclaim in New

York. Greenstreet was far less prominent than he had been in the previous play, even so he contrived to do his best; "Although cast in a comparatively small part," said one reviewer, "Sydney Greenstreet makes a little masterpiece out of the role of the trumpeter who takes his job too seriously. His thoughtfully realized interpretation adds considerably to the play."[11] Greenstreet accompanied them on their equally successful tour to Britain in 1938 which played to packed houses for most of the summer. The British critics were still more laudatory of the play, remarking that the translation was first rate. The drama reviewer in *The Times* of London declared; "You endow the historic with an air of impromptu that delights me."[12] Another was duly impressed by the "amusing, rippling dialogue" in "an evening of rare delight."[13] Greenstreet's friend, headmaster Seaver Buck caught one of his performances as the trumpeter and was so impressed he even referred to it in his commencement address to the school that year, which pleased Greenstreet no end.[14]

The Lunts sought to maintain a high standard and had a reputation as being hard taskmasters; their tours could be arduous and they demanded discipline. At times, according to those who knew him, Alfred Lunt could be miserly with impoverished cast members. However, when he first met Noel Coward, the playwright asked to borrow ten dollars. Coward said that not only would he pay him back quickly but that one day he would write a play for them. He was true to his word and not only returned the ten dollars along with a further ten dollars but wrote *Design for Living*, which was one of their earliest successes, in 1933. Greenstreet knew all about discipline and professionalism and he was one of the most valued members of the troupe. He refused all offers he received in order to continue working with them. Once, Sidney Howard offered him a role in a play but he reluctantly turned it down. The play was a revival of *They Knew What They Wanted*. Although flattered by the offer he was aware of the insecurity of the profession especially in the 1930s which also swayed his thinking.[15] Others in the company felt a similar sense of loyalty; Richard Whorf had spurned the offer of several film contracts for instance. On a personal level, it was said that "Alfred felt deep friendship" for Sydney.[16] He sometimes spent his summers with them at Ten Chimneys, their Swedish manor house at Genesee Depot, Wisconsin. Noel Coward was a frequent guest as were many other theatrical notables including Laurence Olivier and Vivien Leigh. The house was only about twenty-seven miles from the sanatorium in Wauwatosa where Dorothy was ensconced. Greenstreet maintained close ties with the Lunts long after he left the Company and entered films; he also stayed with them when he visited New York. He was one of the friends they "cared tremendously for" and recalled with the most fondness long after his death.[17]

Sydney and son John made a number of visits to England in the 1930s. Sydney (center) with John (left) possibly with Sydney's brother Arthur (right), 1938. Photo courtesy of Gail Greenstreet.

Greenstreet was extremely busy during the 1930s. Life with the Lunts was exciting, invigorating and challenging; it was also tiring. He was in his mid-fifties and not in the best of health. The Lunts' many tours wound around the country and encompassed most states, crisscrossing America east to west, north to south. One leg of their tour alone started in Chicago and passed through Missouri and Kansas before ending in Texas by which time the company had covered over 7,000 miles. They often ended the tours in Montreal, Canada. An old stager such as Sydney was used to the peripatetic life, having been travelling for the best part of forty years. Nonetheless, he admitted that it got to him. He confided to a friend that the constant round of train journeys, rehearsals, packing, unpacking, acting and travelling became wearying at times, and that his health often suffered. In addition, he worried continuously about the disparate strands of his little family.[18]

His son John was seemingly content at the exclusive $700 a term school in the Berkshirfes under the aegis of Sydney's redoubtable friend Dr. Seaver Buck. During some vacations John joined his father on the road at whichever hotel he happened to be staying in the course of his seemingly never-ending tours. Buck was a lifesaver at times to Sydney. In addition to all his duties as a headmaster and keeping a fatherly eye on John, Sydney relied on him to find out about train schedules, accommodate him at short notice and even put him in touch with a good dentist. Sydney had a lot of problems with his teeth. He often teased Buck mercilessly that he beat him at every game they played including golf, tennis, cribbage and chess. Buck obviously enjoyed the banter and had a good sense of humor; he called Greenstreet "a perfect peach."[19]

Life had not been easy for John as his daughter recalled;

> "My dad had a strange upbringing compared to current norms. He went to several boarding schools. With his mom away, he had to spend a number of holidays at the schools. Holidays being a time his father would be on a tour. His father who had beautiful handmade suits dressed his only child in knickers he bought in Harlem. No one had knickers let alone from Harlem. (His classmates were from families of some wealth.)"[20]

John was well-liked at the school. A friend remembered him as a "very pleasant guy, very amiable."[21] He made several visits to England during the 1930s with his father; in 1932, 1935 and 1938. According to Sydney, on the latter trip John made friends easily on board the ship with other college boys and girls his own age and thoroughly enjoyed his time in the country. In the summer of 1938, after staying for a while with Hilda and Fred in Wimbledon, father and son spent much of their spare time together and took a cottage in Sussex which was not far from a golf course. Golf was a game they both enjoyed. *Amphitryon 38* played to good houses during the entire tour and Sydney found the audiences delightful. On the boat home in September he said that the crossing was a little rough but that he took full part in all the activities going. He reported that he played deck tennis, ping pong and danced every night.[22]

Wherever they went on tour the Lunt company played to full houses and could have stayed for weeks in each place such was the warmth of their reception. The same was true with all their plays over the six years Sydney was with them. It was not a novelty for the troupe to receive a standing ovation every night. For instance, in Chicago, they played to almost 18,000 in two days.

For Greenstreet the public adulation contrasted with his private sadness. Since she had been admitted to the sanatorium in January 1933, Dorothy's condition was variable. At times when he visited she seemed to improve, but then the next time she would be worse. Sometimes she was fretful and unable to express herself clearly. In March 1935, he wrote "Saw Dorothy again on Sunday and it was indeed sad, vexed on me terribly, excited her, so my visit helped neither of us; I'm pretty discouraged."[23] His next visit she was different again. At the beginning, he harbored strong hopes of her return to him, but these hopes waned with the years. He marked each passing anniversary of the melancholy day she went away from him. When he was on tour it was not easy for him to reach Milwaukee and, depending where in the country the company were playing, it usually involved a long and circuitous journey. For instance, once when he was playing in Chicago he spent five and half hours coming and going in order to visit her. When he arrived at the sanatorium he found she was "decidedly better" and happy to see him, but the travelling tired him out.[24] His health did not seem robust and while in England he was forced to refuse a lucrative offer to recreate his role in the film version of *Idiot's Delight* because he was just not physically up to it. He wanted to do it but admitted that he was close to exhaustion; he expressed the fear that he might easily have collapsed entirely at any moment.[25]

19 There Shall Be No Night

> *"What I want, really, is any role which has color, philosophy, and the humane quality which makes a character warm and believable."*
>
> Charlotte Kaye, "Big Hit: Sydney Greenstreet"
> *Hollywood*, January 1943, 62.

Greenstreet continued his association with the Lunt company in their major late 1930s productions of Chekhov's *The Seagull* and Sherwood's *There Shall Be No Night*. Both enjoyed great critical acclaim and toured extensively. It was while on tour that Greenstreet was spotted by an aspiring film director who gave him the biggest break of his life.

The Seagull was Anton Chekhov's first attempt at a drama and made its debut in Moscow in 1896 where it was met with derision and Chekhov took refuge backstage. In the following years, it came to be hailed as one of the finest dramas of modern times and its author as one of the leading playwrights. There were several notable American productions but it had not been seen on the Manhattan stage for eight years when the Lunts revived it in 1938. It was an immediate hit and a London critic said it was "the most stimulating production of New York's theatrical March."[1] Greenstreet played the prominent role of Peter Sorin, a retired government official who has spent his life wanting to live but whose health is steadily breaking down. He lives in a sense vicariously through the main protagonist Treplev, in whom he recognizes himself when younger. The play was effectively a series of incisive character sketches and this production was deemed a fine ensemble piece. Even so, some singled out Greenstreet for special mention. The *Chicago Daily Tribune* said he was "outstanding."[2] New York critic Arthur Pollock wrote; "Somehow or other Mr. Greenstreet does not seem to project himself so sharply

Greenstreet was highly commended for his sensitive portrayal of Peter Sorin in Chekhov's The Seagull, *1938. The play was one of three with which the Lunt company toured extensively in 1938 and 1939. Photo courtesy of Gail Greenstreet.*

from the play as the others. He blends into it, is part of it, has a greater credibility than most of the rest. It is one of the finest things he has done."[3] The same critic later remarked "Sydney Greenstreet's is an excellent interpretation of the groping of an old man in search of the meaning of his unhappy lot."[4] "Another wrote that it was "an admirable portrait, excellently conceived and vividly drawn."[5] Even Robert Benchley opined "Sydney Greenstreet, from his chair, gives full value to some of the meatier lines in the play."⁶ Margaret Webster, who played Masha in that production, felt that most of the cast were uncomfortable in their characters but observed that only Greenstreet "seemed able continuously to be what he was."⁷ His acting appeared to be informed by his own personal sorrow and consequently reached a new depth of feeling.

A number of critics hailed Greenstreet's portrayal as a major highlight of the acting year. One commentator said his interpretation was "one of the most affecting performances of the season."⁸ Robert G. Tucker wrote; "the manner and the deftness with which Mr. Greenstreet etched this character was the very apex of superb acting. It was not the star part but it was of first rank in importance and significance."⁹

Among the company, the nineteen-year-old German-born actress Uta Hagen made a distinct impression as Nina. She later became a much-respected teacher of acting techniques and the author of several books on the subject. She enjoyed working with Greenstreet who she said she adored. She described working for the Lunts as "a twenty-four-hour-a-day affair; and I never forgot it – never!"¹⁰ The company took *The Seagull, Amphitryon 38* and *Idiot's Delight* on an exhaustive nationwide tour between 1938 and 1939, playing hundreds of one-night stands and some longer engagements. They alternated the plays to suit each town so that sometimes they might be doing the three different plays in the space of four days.

The company next revived *The Taming of the Shrew* in aid of the Finnish War Relief Fund. Once again Greenstreet played Baptista and the production was praised as being "full of color and japery."¹¹ Again they toured the same circuits. They started in Washington in October 1939 and traversed the country visiting the usual venues in Wisconsin, Minnesota, Iowa, Nebraska and California et al. The tour ended with a week-long run at the Alvin Theater in New York in February 1940. If anything, the 1939/40 version of the play was considered even livelier than the 1935 model, with a large cast that included midgets and acrobats. It went over well and most viewers agreed that the Lunts had given Shakespeare a much-needed shot in the arm.

In his fifth appearance for the Lunts, Greenstreet played the music-loving Uncle Waldemar in *There Shall Be No Night*. Author Robert Sherwood had written the play in only twenty-six days and the inspiration was a moving Christmas radio broadcast about the Russian invasion of Finland. Whatever the source, the critics were generous in their praise; "It is a memorable experience in the theater," wrote one, "and shows that American drama still has something to say for itself, and in almost Hellenic proportions."[12] The resemblance of Uncle Waldemar to the Finnish composer Sibelius was remarked upon. "Sibelius, you know, toured in this country," observed Greenstreet, when interviewed backstage; "Alfred Lunt had a picture of him and brought it to me. We asked Bob Sherwood about it." The composer was also famous for having no hair. This necessitated a Greenstreet visit to the barbers; "But before I did I made sure everybody concerned thought it was a good idea. I didn't want to make myself look a sight on the streets until I got an O. K."[13] He received some of his best notices; one commented that he gave "a distinguished performance."[14]

Among the cast was a twenty-year-old actor called Montgomery Clift who had shown promise early and had made his Broadway debut at the age of fifteen. Already well-known as an intense actor he had a real love of the stage and a thirst to learn and understand. According to his biographer "[Lynn Fontanne] and Monty spent hours talking about the theater and sat with Sydney Greenstreet reading Shaw and Shakespeare."[15] In his usual way with youngsters, Greenstreet encouraged Clift who often visited him.[16]

The Lunts were not especially political, but *There Shall Be No Night* was politically provocative at the time. The United States was not involved in the war nor did it wish to be. Witnesses said "the rehearsals were electric as Lunt infused the company with his own personal passion about Finland."[17] Lunt's stepfather was Finnish. The characters were quietly inspirational with an understated heroism born of the true patriotism that never waves a flag. This was embodied in Waldemar, symbolic of the nation who, with his niece, elects to stay to face the advancing Russians and almost certain death. "Inspired playing and inspired acting have rarely found

Lynn Fontanne (left) with Greenstreet in a scene from There Shall Be No Night, *1940. Greenstreet drew some of the finest notices of his career as Uncle Waldemar in Robert Sherwood's moving play about the Russian invasion of Finland. When the tour reached Los Angeles a certain John Huston was in the audience and offered him a role in a Hollywood film. Photo courtesy of Gail Greenstreet.*

such an ideal meeting ground" wrote one reviewer who declared that Greenstreet "plays his role to the life."[18]

The play ran on Broadway from April to December 1940 with breaks in between and then toured. It was a tremendous success and won the Pulitzer Prize in 1941. Even on tour and against the background of the escalating war in Europe it retained its power. *Variety* commented that it "still explodes in the theater with the immediacy and concussion of a bomb," and noted that all the cast "play with irresistible conviction."[19]

The later plays that the Lunts presented were successful but in many ways, *There Shall Be No Night* was not just their personal high watermark but showed the continued relevance of the theater in national life at a crucial time in history.

The Lunts continued to receive popular and critical acclaim during their forty-year stage career. When Alfred Lunt died in 1977 he was only the third person for whom the lights of Broadway were dimmed in tribute. The Globe Theater was later re-named the Lunt-Fontanne in their honor.

When the tour of *There Shall Be No Night* reached the Biltmore Theater in Los Angeles it so happened that a young screenwriter and aspiring director was in the audience. He had not yet directed a film of his own, but all that was soon to change. His name was John Huston.

20 The Black Bird

"I'll tell you right out I'm a man who likes talking to a man who likes to talk."

Kaspar Gutman to Sam Spade,
The Maltese Falcon

Greenstreet's film debut was one of the most memorable for a man of any age, but for a man of sixty-one who had never stepped before a camera before it was all the more impressive. Serendipity appeared to be at work, and not for the first time. However, if he had followed the advice of his agent, it would never have come about. For years he had received film offers but every time his agent had advised against them. For once he decided not to go with what his agent said, but to follow his own instincts and accept. His forty years on the stage had seemed to prepare him for the moment. Not only was it an excellent role it was with a peerless cast in one of the landmark films of the 1940s. On the surface, it appeared to be a mere whodunnit, but it was different in so many ways from all the detective thrillers that went before and set the template for most of those that followed.

After seeing him as Uncle Waldemar in *There Shall Be No Night*, Huston went backstage to meet Greenstreet. The two got on well from the start and became friends from that day. After years of saying no to movies, Sydney finally said yes. Huston succeeded where others had failed and soon Greenstreet was on his way to Hollywood. He was initially offered $1000 a week with a four-week guarantee.[1] Huston had caught him at exactly the right moment. Greenstreet was not getting any younger; he was feeling increasingly tired and the thought of being in one place greatly appealed to him after so many years on the road.

The genesis of the film is recounted best in the book *The Maltese Falcon, John Huston, director* (see bibliography). Hammett's classic

"Here's to plain speaking and clear understanding." Greenstreet made one of the most memorable of screen debuts as Kaspar Gutman in The Maltese Falcon. *Photo courtesy of Gail Greenstreet.*

was written in 1929 and brought to the screen within two years. In the 1931 version, sometimes known as *Dangerous Female,* the Irish actor Dudley Digges played the role of Gutman. In a curious shadowing of careers, the two had first acted together in their Ben Greet days, and Greenstreet had followed Digges in the title role of *Volpone* for the Theater Guild. Digges also played The Examiner in the 1930 model of *Outward Bound,* as he had in the original stage version. They were the same age but although Digges appeared in about forty films and made his screen debut a dozen years before Greenstreet, the former much preferred the theater and is not as well remembered today. That is unfortunate because Digges was a fine actor in his own right adept at curious character roles. He had good timing and encapsulated much of the erudition and decadence of Gutman in such simple things as the use of a monocle. The most notable difference was the sheer physical presence of Greenstreet in the later version used to great advantage by Huston. The script was similar, but with subtle differences; for instance, when Gutman says "Why, I feel toward Wilmer as if he was my own son," it is Sam Spade who adds the rejoinder "It's possible to get another son, but there's only one Maltese Falcon." It made more sense for Gutman to say that line and carried far greater resonance, especially when Greenstreet added, turning to Bogart "When you're young you simply don't understand these things." The underlying homosexuality of the gang of three was also more apparent in the earlier version, for instance, when Gutman strokes Wilmer's face affectionately several times. Director Roy del Ruth was working before the Hays Production Code was brought into effect. Huston was working at a time of greater restriction but wanted to make it equally apparent in other ways, as Elisha Cook, Jr. (who played Wilmer) recalled; "You know what Huston wanted to do? He wanted to put fake eyelashes on me. Wouldn't that have been great? But he said, 'No, I'd better not go that far.'"[2]

A second version of the film was altered substantially from Hammett's original and released under the title *Satan Met a Lady* (1936), but bore little resemblance to either films. Several characters were changed; Gutman, for instance, became Madame Barabbas, played by that excellent character actress Alison Skipworth.

Gutman was quite clearly a decadent character who is first introduced in his well-appointed hotel room. Even though it is about midday he is wearing a dressing gown and one recognizes at once that he is a man of considerable means with time on his hands to pursue rare *objet d'art* around the world. Urbane and something of a *dilettante*, he is thoroughly ruthless underneath. He has others to do his bidding and never actually gets his hands dirty; he does not

"The stuff that dreams are made of." Peter Lorre, Mary Astor and Greenstreet feast their eyes on the black bird. The famous statuette used in the film sold for $4 million at a Bonham's auction in 2013. Photo courtesy of Gail Greenstreet.

exert himself but is the hub around which the others revolve. As such he is one of the most important characters in the film.

Huston worked out everything to the last detail and this quality marked the film out not only from the previous versions of the story, but from all other murder mysteries. Cook spoke of the innovative way Huston worked, and how much everyone cared about the project;

> "He wanted to shoot one scene without a cut – the one where we're all in the room and I'm beggin' Greenstreet to let me kill Bogart … Now John wants this in one shot – never been done before. So, he said, 'We're going to close down and rehearse this for a day or two.' Jack Warner heard about it; he came down to the set. He said, 'No way you're going to close down in my studio for two days.' So, Huston and Bogart walked off the set. That shot runs 950 ft. without a cut – ten minutes of film."[3]

Huston and his cinematographer Arthur Edeson carefully worked out the complex sequence in detail beforehand. Everyone worked hard to bring it off and after shooting finished all the crew members "heartily applauded Bogart, Greenstreet and Edeson and his camera operators."[4]

There was a protective feeling among the cast who wanted to keep what they were doing under wraps until the last moment. They devised a number of ruses to keep visitors at bay. Huston spoke about the making of the film in an interview in the 1970s. He felt that the strength of the old studio system was one of the key factors in its success:

> "I considered the Hammett novel practically a screenplay, and we had a wonderful time making the movie, no sense of making a classic of course. Everybody just had a lot of fun doing what they were doing and liking themselves doing it. Imagine assembling that cast today – Bogie, Mary Astor, Greenstreet and Lorre, Gladys George, and the rest. That was something which only the old studio system could supply."[5]

Another key ingredient was the music of Adolph Deutsch, one of the foremost composers of the time. His beautifully-arranged score was apt for atmosphere, subject and above all, characters. For instance, the scene when Gutman suddenly realizes that Wilmer has fled was perfectly synced to the choreography of the fat man marching from room to room looking for him. Greenstreet had long passages of dialogue to learn and in his usual methodical way had memorized the script for weeks in advance, as he had for years on the stage. Lorre had a casual attitude towards learning scripts. He and Bogart would arrive at the studio at 8:55 am and Greenstreet would be there waiting. As Lorre recalled; "How did you like the script? Greenstreet asked me suspiciously, "I don't know," I said, "I haven't looked at it yet." Sydney blinked, fidgeted and went off." About twenty minutes later Sydney knocked on Lorre's door and asked him the same question. "I rolled my eyes and shrugged," related Lorre, "It's alright I guess. But on page five you could say something else. Well, in an hour we had changed fifteen pages. We did it as a team. Sydney was pleased and did it letter perfect."[6]

An emotional Wilmer Cook (Elisha Cook, Jr.) threatens Sam Spade (Humphrey Bogart, right) while Kasper Gutman (Greenstreet, sitting) and Miss O'Shaughnessy (Mary Astor) look on in a tense scene in The Maltese Falcon *(1941). "I've never had a better cast," observed Huston. Photo courtesy of Gail Greenstreet.*

Huston had a sure way of handling all the different actors. As David Shipman astutely observed; "Huston made it clear that he cherished [Greenstreet's] serpentine delivery and his love of being listened to."[7] The film made Huston's reputation and he later reflected on how much it meant to his career at that early stage; "Just think of a completely inexperienced director's bringing Sydney Greenstreet from New York," observed Huston, "They gave me the actors I wanted. Being in charge of my own casting has allowed me not to have to do as much directing over the years."[8] If he had not been able to persuade Greenstreet, Huston discussed alternatives. On a long list, there was the gargantuan Eugene Pallette with his frog-like voice; Edward Arnold, who was the embodiment of the patrician politico; the explosive Lee J. Cobb and even Billy Gilbert, remembered mostly for his appearances in the films of Laurel and Hardy.[9] Greenstreet's Englishness was crucial to the character and set him apart from all the others. He made the part so entirely his own and unwittingly set the template of the erudite villain for others to follow in his wake.

Despite his long years on stage, Greenstreet still needed reassurance before the camera, as Mary Astor recalled in her memoir;

> "Poor Sydney! He never did live down the Fat Man. I don't think he ever did a picture later in which that hiccupy laugh wasn't exploited. He was a very fine, very versatile actor, within his physical limitations. The *Falcon* was his first picture and he was nervous in that first scene – that same long-winded monologue – as though all his years in the theater counted for nothing. He said to me, "Mary dear, hold my hand, tell me I won't make an ass of meself!"[10]

He had no cause to worry. At the first showing a particularly hard-to-please tryout audience were asked to fill in report cards nominating the player who had given the best performance. Almost unanimously the answer came back the Fat Man. Before long Greenstreet was nominated for the Oscar as Best Supporting Actor, narrowly missing out to Donald Crisp in *How Green Was My Valley* (1941). *The Maltese Falcon*, which was shot in eight weeks and cost less than $300,000, was also nominated as Best Picture, as was Huston for his screenplay.[11]

Huston commented; "There's always talk about the difficulty of making the transition from stage to screen, but you wouldn't know it to watch Greenstreet; he was perfect from the word go, the Fat Man inside out. I had only to sit back and take delight in him and his performance."[12]

As a leading light of the stage, Greenstreet's performance was watched with interest by his friends, colleagues and fans alike. As *Variety* noted, it took a stage actor of his renown to do full justice to the role;

> "Critical and audience spotlight will be focused on Sydney Greenstreet, prominent member of the Lunt-Fontanne stage troupe, who scores heavily in his first screen appearance. Player displays consummate ability as an artist of high rank, and solidly holds attention through several extensive

dialogue passages that could easily fall apart in less competent hands."[13]

Many of his friends had been surprised when he took the plunge into films, and some warned him against it. He described his own reaction to seeing himself on screen for the first time; "I was both excited and horribly embarrassed when I first saw myself on the screen. Suddenly I was overwhelmingly conscious of a thousand little mannerisms I didn't know I had. It was a startling discovery."[14] He reckoned the camera added fifty pounds to him because he was shot from ground level "There's a standing gag at Warner Brothers that every cameraman who has to photograph Greenstreet gets a stiff neck," he joked.[15]

The film critic of *The Times* of London encapsulated Huston's achievement succinctly: "Mr. Dashiell Hammett has at last found a director, Mr. John Huston, who can translate into the appropriate cinematic terms the abrupt, nervous prose, the inhuman detachment, the shuddering abhorrence of the sentimental and the heroic which makes his novels something more than mere detective stories."[16]

Considered one of the earliest of the cycle of classic film noirs, *The Maltese Falcon* has been discussed at length since its debut. Cineastes have deconstructed it and it has been the subject of numerous books and articles. An interesting viewpoint was offered in one of those books on the hitherto overlooked significance of the fat man in noir. In *Screening Genders,* Jerry Mosher wrote perceptively of how Greenstreet's appearance as Gutman "would prove to be a performance as iconic as that of Bogart."[17] In his excellent chapter "Hard Boiled and Soft-Belied" Mosher made some cogent observations on the nature of the role of the fat heavy in noir and especially some of the actors who followed in Greenstreet's wake.

For all its modernity, the film was also in many ways theatrical. For instance, the use of interior sets sometimes for extended periods, the small cast of characters, the use of language and also the exits and entrances of the characters. Gutman is a suitably theatrical character with his love of words and expansive gestures. It is noticeable that none of the crooks die predictably in a hail of gunfire as was usually the case in most crime dramas of the era. On the contrary the nonchalant way in which Gutman and Cairo bid their adieus and make their leisurely exit gave the characters greater resonance. Although the audience hears about their fate, the abiding image is of them leaving together to continue merrily on their way in their search for the falcon and committing who knows what acts of diabolical villainy in the future.

After the phenomenal success of the film, Warner Bros. planned a sequel almost immediately. *Further Adventures of the Maltese Falcon* intended to use the same cast, but was never made.[18] As soon as Hammett asked for a $5,000 retainer to write the sequel, Jack Warner lost interest in the idea.[19] Considering that lightning rarely strikes twice, perhaps it was just as well.

21 The Blue Parrot

"Might as well be frank, Monsieur, it would take a miracle to get you out of Casablanca, and the Germans have outlawed miracles."

Senor Ferrari to Victor Laszlo in *Casablanca*

After he finished work on *The Maltese Falcon*, Greenstreet returned to the Lunt's company on the road. But no sooner had he arrived than he was asked if he would consider making one more film appearance, with the option of another. Warner Bros. realized they had something and tempted Sydney with the offer of a lucrative contract. That did the trick and he was persuaded to stay in Hollywood for just a while longer.

The rollicking adventure *They Died with Their Boots On* (1941) was one of Errol Flynn's best and most popular films in which he played George Armstrong Custer. This highly fictionalized account was done with all the gusto the studio was famous for, and employed a fine cast in an irresistible yarn. Greenstreet turned up in a small but pivotal role as Lt. General Wingfield Scott seen mostly during the Civil War sequences. He was seen later when Custer's wife (Olivia de Havilland) pleads for his help to find a military post for her disillusioned husband. Greenstreet had only a few scenes but left an indelible impression as always. Especially memorable was the scene when he is first introduced in the restaurant; "Just time for a quick snack today," he informs the waiter cheerily as he reels off four or five courses from the menu. Suddenly he bemoans the lack of creamed Bermuda onions, and a previously disconsolate but quick-thinking Custer offers him his. Impressed by such a generous act, the General soon gets Custer his longed-for entrée into the fighting once more, going over the head of Custer's arch enemy Major Taipe. The real Scott was also a substantial figure weighing

Greenstreet (left) as General Wingfield Scott shares a plate of creamed Bermuda onions with Major Custer (Errol Flynn) in Raoul Walsh's rousing adventure They Died with Their Boots On *(1941). Photo courtesy of Gail Greenstreet.*

well over 300 pounds, and was widely known for his gargantuan appetite. He became so corpulent that he was not able to mount his horse. He was apparently a far bigger eater than Greenstreet who was said to be "fastidious about his food and consumes only normal proportions."[1] It was unimportant that Scott had probably resigned by the time the events were supposed to have taken place, or that he was not half as jolly as presented by Greenstreet. This was not history, it was entertainment and Flynn was perfect for the leading role. No-one else had the same savoir faire or seemed so incredibly likeable. The brio he brought to the part was entirely in keeping with the approach of the film as a whole. Max Steiner's rousing score was unforgettable and the old marching song "Garry Owen" was never used to such effect.

The making of *Casablanca* has been the subject of several books and its cultural significance has inspired millions of words, numerous learned university theses and a poem. In 2005 there was even a musical version which debuted in China. It is a curious irony that one of the most popular movies of all time was based on an unproduced stage play, *Everybody Comes to Rick's*. Like many classic films, it owed much to chance and the serendipity of time, studio and place. It was born in confusion with several of the leading players disinterested and unwilling to take part. When filming started, the script was not even finished. It was so uncertain that when Ingrid Bergman asked the director who she was supposed to be in love with she was told to "play it between."[2] Perhaps this uncertainty made the film the hit it undoubtedly was and remains.

Screenwriter Hal Wallis had much input into the film and he chose Greenstreet for the small but important role of Senor Ferrari. He was one of the first to be cast. To entice him he was offered a special contract that gave him $3,750 a week. This was over $2,200 more than his usual salary.[3] Initially his scenes were scheduled to take two weeks to shoot, but he had some additional dialogue with Paul Henreid and Bergman so his assignment lasted a fortnight longer. In total, he was employed for almost four weeks and finished shooting his segments on July 25, 1942. This meant that, for his five minutes of screen time he was one of the highest paid actors in the film. For the notoriously miserly Jack Warner the extra budget requirement was deemed "a minor disaster by the studio's standard."[4] If Greenstreet had not been secured for the role, J. Edward Bomberg was lined up as a replacement, but luckily there was no difficulty persuading Sydney to accept. Despite the small size of his role, Greenstreet was fifth billed and his name featured prominently in all publicity in large letters. He was also depicted on several of the posters and much of the promotional material. Indeed, some posters featured only Bogart, Bergman and Greenstreet. An especially evocative one depicted them in a stylized café setting encircled by cigarette smoke as Rick and Ferrari play a game of chess. In the film Rick plays chess with himself but the allusion is apt for the psychological nature of all Bogart's films with Greenstreet. A French poster showed Bogart and Bergman in close-up with a background of mosques and minarets and the familiar white-suited figure of Senor Ferrari aka Sydney complete with cummerbund and fez shown mostly in shadow.

The sight of Greenstreet in his fez swatting flies is as much a part of the *Casablanca* experience as Bergman's luminous beauty, the constant talk of letters of transit or the eminently quotable lines; "Why did you come to Casablanca?" "I came here for the waters." "But Casablanca is a desert." "I was misinformed." The fly-swatting routine was not in the original script and was entirely Greenstreet's idea. Several writers have commented on the large number of European emigres in the film: Bergman, Conrad Veidt, Henreid, Lorre, Greenstreet and Rains among the principals, which helped give the film much of its feeling of depth. The cast alone speaks well for the strength of the studio system. A recent author noted that "The Englishmen, Rains and Greenstreet, are key to the film's success."[5] The music was a decisive factor; from the dramatic score by Max Steiner to the romantic singing and playing of Dooley Wilson, especially "As Time Goes By" which made the film seem timeless.

Greenstreet had such a presence that he made Ferrari one of the most memorable characterizations in the film. As "the leader of all black-market activity in Casablanca," Ferrari is a rival to Rick but again the two have a regard for each other. Although all out for himself, Ferrari sometimes shows his human side such as when he says to Laszlo "I'll make one suggestion. Why, I do not know. It cannot possibly profit me." It is interesting that whenever sequels were suggested, Greenstreet was always one of the first names on the cast list.

The film was premiered in New York in November 1942 and was an immediate hit. It made $4 million at the box office in the United States and $3 million in the rest of the world.[6] It has continued to make money ever since. The premiere coincided with the invasion of North Africa by Allied troops which followed on from the battles of El Alamein that had turned the tide of the war significantly in the Allies' favor. In Churchill's famous phrase it was "the end of the beginning" of the war. This mood seemed to chime in with the sentiment of the film and particularly the stirring scene when the "Marseillaise" is sung. Ironically, the Office of War Information prevented *Casablanca* from being shown to troops in the region in order not to offend Vichy supporters.[7]

In contrast to many films of the era, the reputation of *Casablanca* has grown with the years. Indeed, it seems more widely known

Senor Ferrari (Greenstreet, left) peruses an elusive letter of transit while Ilsa Lund (Ingrid Bergmann) looks anxious in a publicity still for Casablanca. *Photo courtesy of Gail Greenstreet.*

and loved than any film of the 1940s, even among those who are unfamiliar with classic films or purport not to like black and white movies. Tellingly, the colorization of the classic did not prove popular because it added nothing to it but rather detracted from the whole thing. Not only is the film still incredibly popular but it has been discussed at length by such luminaries as the Italian writer and philosopher Umberto Eco who called it, among other things, "a palimpsest for future students of twentieth century religiosity."[8] Despite such obscure semantics he also recognized that the film was much loved. Leonard Maltin considered it quite simply the "best Hollywood movie of all time."[9]

It matters little that there were in reality no such things as letters of transit or that there were no uniformed Germans stationed in Casablanca. The American conception of north Africa was always likely to be vague at best and a considerable way from the real thing

Iconic: Rick (Bogart, left) and Ferrari (Greenstreet, right) discuss the future in a scene on a lobby card from Casablanca. *With Oliver Drake serving the drinks.*

but that was part of the fun. As a critic observed at the time of the fiftieth anniversary of the film's release, "*Casablanca* creates a world both preposterous and irresistible, as dreamlike as the studio fog that fills the closing scene."[10]

The cast was so perfect together that the urge was to keep the momentum going and use them to great effect in other films. Several projects were mooted. One of the first ideas was *Brazzaville* in which Bogart and Greenstreet would recreate their *Casablanca* roles and the female lead would be played by Geraldine Fitzgerald.[11] It was widely reported that filming would begin in the spring (of 1943) after Fitzgerald had completed a Broadway assignment, but the movie was never made. As for Greenstreet, his elevation to the star ranks brought many more offers his way. He was lined up for the role of a priest in *Mission to Moscow* (1943), a curious pro-Soviet drama-documentary also directed by Michael Curtiz.[12] Pat O'Brien was later assigned the role but in the event neither actor appeared in the film. Greenstreet was also slated to co-star again with Bogart along with George Raft and Edward G. Robinson in *Heroes without Uniform*, a tale of the merchant marine in wartime based on a story in the *Saturday Evening Post*. However, the project ran into the sand.[13] Another possibility was the chance to play the Emperor Nero in a version of *Quo Vadis?* It would have been great fun to have seen him in such a role but the project was never realized and it was another eight years before the book was filmed.[14] Greenstreet was also penciled in as a late replacement for Charles Laughton in *The Dragon Seed*, but luckily perhaps proved to be unavailable at the time and the part went to Akim Tamiroff.[15]

22 Bogie and Sydney

"Bogie and Sydney could switch you from laughter to shock in a split second."

Peter Lorre "A Bogey Man Returns: Peter Lorre Trying to Both Scare, Amuse" *Buffalo Courier-Express*, November 4, 1962, 28A.

The films Greenstreet made with Peter Lorre have attracted a lot of attention over the years, but Sydney made five with Humphrey Bogart; two are considered *bone fide* classics and the others are fascinating in their own right. *Across the Pacific* and *Conflict* (1945) show two great actors at work in some ways just as *simpatico* as Greenstreet and Lorre but in a different way. Always adversaries they had a degree of admiration the one for the other which added an unexpected dimension to their work.

Seldom mentioned by cineastes, *Across the Pacific* (1943) was an unheralded gem which re-teamed four of the talents that made *The Maltese Falcon* so perfect – Bogart, Mary Astor, Greenstreet and director John Huston. Originally to be entitled *Aloha Means Goodbye* it was at one time announced that Dennis Morgan and Ann Sheridan would play the leading roles, but the studio was keen to retain the *Falcon* team.

Bogart played Rick Leland, an American agent posing as a discredited army major in order to discover who is helping the enemy to gain a foothold in the Panama Canal. He takes an ocean voyage to the zone with two others, Dr. Lorenz (Greenstreet), a university sociologist based in the Philippines and Mary (Astor) whose reasons for travelling seem vague.

Greenstreet was philosophical about playing another villain, "A good actor should be able to play Shakespeare or Noel Coward or Frank Capra," he remarked. "As for me, I don't worry about a role so long as it's a positive one and not a negative."[1] The screenplay was by Richard Macauley and there was some clever and witty dialogue. Greenstreet had problems with the scene where he tries to commit Hari Kiri before the small shrine. The cameraman Arthur Edeson seemed to be taking some time getting the shot and Sydney had to kneel down time and again; "My knees are getting creaky," he remarked, "Let's take this and get it over with." Bogart heckled from the sidelines; "What are you complaining about? You can thank the Japs that their Hari Kiri ritual includes a pillow to kneel on."[2] Greenstreet and the Chinese actor Sen Young were instructed in Japanese dialogue by a technical advisor. At the outbreak of the war the unfortunate man was sent to an internment camp in Los Angeles.[3]

For Bogart, it was an extension of his screen persona; tough, cynical, often one step ahead of everyone else. Some of the familiar hard-boiled *Falcon* dialogue came into play. It was as though Huston had an ability to draw out the unique inherent qualities in each of his actors. He embellished certain characteristics and turns of phrase which helped make each character believable and appealing. For instance, Greenstreet's oft-repeated refrain "Most unfortunate!" after someone has been murdered, a phrase he used regularly throughout his film career. Huston used Greenstreet's mastery of stagecraft and Shakespearean grandiloquence to great effect.

The three principals gelled so naturally, so much so that it did not feel as though they were acting. Their ease of playing together and the playfulness underlying their performances was particularly apparent. "The three players' work ... is well-nigh perfect," commented *The Film Daily*, "and Huston's direction again is incisive, clear-cut and forceful with a fine grasp of mood."[4] There were some fine Hustonian touches such as the scene in cinema. It helped that the cast was relatively small, and all the supporting players did good work. As Dr. H. F. G. Lorenz, Greenstreet gave an insightful portrayal of suave villainy. It was easy to imagine him as a university sociologist with a love of all things Japanese. His admiration for them and immersion in eastern culture makes him contemptuous of his own country and its alliances. Lorenz was a wonderful character whose ultimate failure was that he was unable to believe entirely in the cause to which he aligned himself. Greenstreet made Lorenz a many-faceted character and used understated sardonic

Dr. Lorenz (Greenstreet) contemplates the future as (Humphrey Bogart and Mary Astor) look on in Across the Pacific *(1943). Photo courtesy of Gail Greenstreet.*

humor to effect. As Bosley Crowther astutely wrote; "Mr. Greenstreet is entirely an enigma – malefic yet dignified, urbane and full of enviable refinement, yet hard and unpredictable underneath."[5]

Mary Astor recalled the same sense of fun and camaraderie between them all as they had enjoyed on the set of *The Maltese Falcon*. The only one missing was Peter Lorre, who visited the set one day when they were on board the ship;

> "One afternoon, Lorre donned a white coat and walked through a scene in which Sydney, Bogart and I were served breakfast on the ship. He was behind us, so we couldn't see him, and Peter served us – making tiny mistakes – holding a platter a bit too far away, just touching Sydney's arm as he lifted a cup of coffee. Finally, he leaned over and kissed me on the neck and we all broke up. We could always have fun, even though the subtle sense of success was not a part of that picture."[6]

Part way through filming, Huston was called up for war service, and the picture was given over to Vincent Sherman to finish. Sherman did his best at short notice; unfortunately, it is possible to see the join and the last fifteen minutes seem rather disjointed. The ending itself is hurried and quite implausible – Bogart defeats the Japs singlehandedly by blowing up a small plane. It was pure *Boy's Own* stuff, but did not mar the movie as a whole.

It was an excellent role for Greenstreet which played to his strengths. But he indicated in an interview at the time that he was already growing tired of playing the bad guy. "I like those rattlesnake parts for change of pace," he averred, "but not for steady playing. I mean it when I say I am going back to the path of virtue, at least temporarily. Another scoundrel like the Nazi I'm now playing and I won't even be able to get anybody to play golf with me."[7] Greenstreet and Bogie shared some fine scenes on board ship during which Lorenz offers Rick a lot of money to betray his country. At one stage Rick saves his life when he stops an assassin from taking a pot shot at him. Afterwards Rick asks him if he knows the man; "I don't think so," replies Lorenz, "at any rate, he isn't a close friend." But Lorenz is an astute and formidable opponent and begins to suspect Rick is not what he seems. Lorenz' bonhomie contrasts sharply with the viciousness with which he hits Rick with his stick (behind a screen), after drugging him in a similar way as he had Sam Spade in *The Maltese Falcon*. *Across the Pacific* was an enjoyable film but essentially a propaganda effort. As such it could never reach the heights of Huston's debut. Nevertheless, it deserves to be judged on its own merits and ought to be more widely known and appreciated for its many qualities. It had none of the heavy-handedness of the later propagandist *Passage to Marseille* for instance, which suffered from too large a cast.

Incidentally, the story that Bogart, Astor, Greenstreet and Lorre all put in an appearance in Huston's *In This Our Life* (1942) was purely apocryphal. For some time, a rumor circulated that they could be seen during a bar room scene in which Bette Davis plays the jukebox too loud. Although Walter Huston played the bartender in the scene, the others were conspicuous by their absence. It is a fine film anyway and well worth seeing.

Left to right: Humphrey Bogart, Vincent Sherman, Greenstreet, John Huston, Mary Astor. Huston saying goodbye to the cast of Across the Pacific *after being called up for war service. The film was completed by Sherman. Photo courtesy of Gail Greenstreet.*

Conflict, originally known as *The Pentacle*, was an intriguing film noir directed by Curtis Bernhardt. The story concerned an engineer Richard Mason (Bogart) trapped in a loveless marriage who murders his nagging wife Katherine (Rose Hobart) in order to marry her sister Evelyn (the lovely Alexis Smith). He begins to be haunted by reminders of his dead wife and is almost convinced she is still alive. Despite the improbable plot the film had a number of strengths, not least the actors involved and the fine direction by Bernhardt. A London critic hailed *Conflict* as a "cleverly directed film of intelligence," and praised the treatment of the wearing psychological effects of guilt.[8] There were some excellent passages especially in the early part and the scenes between Bogart and his wife utilized some trenchant, well-observed dialogue. The stark contrast between the brittle wife and her carefree sister was apparent in such things as the clothes they wore and even their hairstyles. For example, the wife wears black with her hair swept upwards in

Evocative French poster for Conflict *(1945) an intriguing psychological noir in which Bogart and Greenstreet were ostensibly friends.*

a severe fashion, whereas Smith seems much younger with her hair in a more natural style and wearing brighter-toned clothes. Two key scenes were beautifully done; the dinner party and Bogart's murder of his wife. Bernhardt's skill at suggesting layers of psychological meaning was apparent especially at the dinner party where the sense of bonhomie embodied in the Greenstreet character acts as a thin veil over the obvious tensions in the Mason marriage. "Love and its frustrations are the root of all evil," he declares blithely, as Bogart cannot stop looking at Alexis Smith. It is Greenstreet who introduces the song "Tango of Love" which is used as a memorable *leitmotif* throughout. Writing in *Film Noir*, Bob Porfirio observed that the song was used "to indicate the putative reappearance of Katherine, with the background strings translating the scent of perfume; the opening trucking shot through the rain-soaked night up to the window of the dinner party; and the sinister appearance of Bogart as he steps out of the shadows to murder his wife."[9]

The unusual story was written by Robert Siodmak and Alfred Neumann. Even as a seemingly friendly character, Greenstreet imbued the role with a sinister quality, and his involvement in the case appears more than idle or professional curiosity. Director Bernhardt remarked "Greenstreet was a wonderful actor. I think his strangeness grew more from his own style of acting than out of the story. He had that frightening laugh."[10]

The evocative music was composed by the British-born German composer Friedrich Hollaender who was able to adapt to a wide range of genres. He composed the scores for several films in which Greenstreet appeared including *Pillow to Post* and *Background to Danger*.

Bogart was adamant that he did not want to play the role assigned to him; he didn't like the part or the script. However, Jack Warner reportedly threatened him with suspension if he did not accept.[11] For his role as the psychiatrist, Greenstreet was advised by Dr. Ralph William Pyle, an expert in the field.[12] It was a prominent part and although ostensibly Bogart's friend he was effectively his nemesis. Greenstreet relished the role-reversal; "Bogart's always been top-dog in my pictures," he remarked in jocular fashion, "But *Conflict* is a soul-satisfying experience because the law and I collaborate in bringing Bogart to justice. It's nice for a change to have audiences say 'It serves him right' and mean him, not me."[13] Relaxing on the set one day, Greenstreet and Bogie swapped golfing yarns and in between talked about how successful the films they had made together had been. From *The Maltese Falcon, Casablanca, Passage to Marseille* and *Across the Pacific* Bogart was becoming an immensely popular star. "You know, Bogie, I think I should get the credit," joked Greenstreet, "I'm your good luck charm." "Okay," replied Bogart, "As long as you don't ask me to carry you around."[14]

The Bogart-Greenstreet dynamic always made their films intriguing. Both reached star status in the 1940s and neither were young. Bogart was over forty and Greenstreet over sixty. They were both strong personalities and fine actors who complemented each other in their acting styles. Their work was characterized by intelligence and humor. They also had an ability to create believable characters with an economy of style and movement. They could convey a great deal with their eyes alone. A strong hero figure always needs a first-rate opponent, but what made their performances more interesting was that neither were cut-and-dried stock "hero" or "villain" figures. Bogart was an anti-heroic hero in tune with the age and

A key scene in Conflict *during which the underlying tensions in the Mason marriage become apparent. Left to right: Humphrey Bogart, Rose Hobart, Greenstreet, Charles Drake, Alexis Smith. Photo courtesy of Gail Greenstreet.*

Greenstreet was a curiously appealing villain. Even when they were friends as in *Conflict* they were still on opposite sides. The classic cycle of film noir ushered in by the war and its aftermath introduced the psychological aspect into cinema which set it apart from the prewar era. The sophistication and sense of dislocation in those noir films ensures that they retain their relevance in a fast-changing world and that even now they inform the art of film. The films of Bogart were central to that period circa 1940 to 1956, and helped define the genre. However, he did not work in a vacuum. He needed those other actors around him as much as the writers, directors and cinematographers. Greenstreet was one of the foremost of those who brought out the best in him. On a personal level, it was noticeable that they liked and admired one another. The fruits of their work together on screen is one of classic cinema's abiding joys.

23 Background to Danger

*"Don't let's spoil this delightful evening
with talk of unpleasant things."*

Colonel Robinson to Joe Barton
in *Background to Danger*.

After their successful pairing in *The Maltese Falcon,* it seemed only natural that Greenstreet and Lorre should be teamed again. There was something in their physical and psychological make up that meant they just went together. Perhaps it was no more than that they were complete opposites – but that crucially on screen they just had magic together. They made nine films together in total, but in some they were entirely separate characters who shared few if any scenes. In the best of them they were partners-in-crime.

Their second film together was not one of their best. *Background to Danger* (1943) had its moments but saddled Lorre with a poorly-conceived role as a possible spy who keeps popping up at intervals to rescue George Raft from perilous situations. Raft played an American agent in Ankara who is entrusted with a secret document by a mysterious female on a train. The document is crucial to the efforts of Colonel Robinson (Greenstreet) to drag neutral Turkey into the war. Needless to say, the mysterious female is found dead with Raft the chief suspect. Eric Ambler's *Uncommon Danger* was the promising source material for the film but the finished result was disappointing. Numerous changes were made and Raft insisted that his character should not be an ordinary salesman, as in the novel, but an FBI agent. He declared that he didn't want to play "any ribbon salesman."[1]

Lorre and Greenstreet shared too few scenes and the action became rather repetitive, consisting of Raft dodging in and out of doorways in an atmospheric setting. Greenstreet fared much better and argu-

"A curious touch of the grotesque! A dead man on the floor. A condemned one sitting before me. And a Strauss waltz as a funeral march. What could be more entertaining?" Greenstreet enjoyed himself immensely as the mysterious Colonel Robinson in Background to Danger *(1943). Photo courtesy of Gail Greenstreet.*

ably had the best role on offer by far. He relished the suavity of the curiously-named Colonel Robinson, who was not just another cardboard screen Nazi of the type that was by then altogether too familiar. He outlined his approach to the part; "Too many of us are inclined to underestimate the enemy," he observed, "So I try to portray him as a well-rounded individual and at the same time show him up for what he is."[2] Robinson was a marvelous creation who obviously enjoyed himself as a torturer but who was, like Gutman, able to appreciate a resourceful adversary. "That's right, make yourself comfortable," he says as Raft defiantly lights a cigarette, "I'm all for doing business in comfort." Robinson approaches his profession like a true connoisseur. "The art of persuasion has always interested me," he says ominously as his thugs prepare to beat the truth out of Raft. "The early 1920s brought with them a renaissance of that art that compares in glory of achievement with the Inquisition itself," he eulogizes. He talks about the various merits offered by different methods of persuasion including the effects of rubber truncheons. "For myself I have no special likes or dislikes," he shrugs, as though perusing a menu in a high-class restaurant. The screenplay was adapted by the dependable W. R. Burnett from Eric Ambler's novel. Interestingly, John Huston worked on the script as a polisher and there are some touches of genius in the dialogue, such as when Robinson offers Raft an honorarium for his troubles. The word "honorarium" used in this context sounds delightfully Greenstreetian. Robinson never appears flustered until the moment he is finally defeated and has to suffer the ignominy of being called back to Berlin to account for his failure and almost certain death. At the prospect of facing his superiors the color seems to drain from him. Greenstreet's underplaying ensured that Robinson was all the more chilling. "Hold some of yourself back," he once advised young actors, "If you give everything the audience sees your limitations."[3]

Background to Danger contained some excellent passages and a great study in villainy by Greenstreet. However, as a whole it seemed to lack something. As James Agee remarked; "You could use this film for one kind of measurement of the unconquerable difference between a good job by Hitchcock and a good job of the Hitchcock type."[4] There were several unresolved elements in the storyline; for instance, it was never made clear whether Lorre's character was a Russian spy or not. Lorre had little to work on but made the most of an unsatisfying role. The choice of the lead was a problem; Errol Flynn was the preferred choice of the director and would have been ideal in the role which required someone with spark and agility. Raft has many admirers but for some he does not compare well to Bogart. Greenstreet loved the badinage with Bogart, but when asked if he had the same camaraderie with Raft he replied tactfully that he "didn't think he knew Raft well enough to

French poster for Background to Danger *(1943)*.

exchange many such pleasantries."⁵ Most assuredly, Lorre and Raft didn't get along as has been related often. Bogart would have lifted the film immeasurably and worked so much better with his two old sparring partners so that any deficiencies in the action could have been overlooked. The opening shots of the film when Greenstreet was first introduced made an interesting contrast with the way he had appeared in *The Maltese Falcon*. Rather than the low angle shots which emphasized his bulk, in *Background to Danger* he was seen from a distance in the frame and appears dwarfed by the scale of the rooms, even by the size of Hitler's portrait. This enhanced the impression that Robinson was only a small cog in the Nazi machine. Despite its deficiencies, the film did well at the box office and does not deserve its relative obscurity. Its appeal grows with repeated viewings. Interestingly, writer William Faulkner was employed at that time by Warner Bros. to work on troublesome scripts. On viewing the first version of *Background to Danger* he diagnosed the main problem was that there was "too much running around." He spent two weeks revising the script and creating new scenes. The film made more sense, but Faulkner's ability with dialogue was somewhat less successful. At one stage Greenstreet phoned producer Jerry Wald from the set to tell him that he simply could not deliver a "particularly long and complicated speech as Faulkner had originally written it. The lines were duly modified." Faulkner's dialogue was often altered on set in that way.[6]

Warner Bros. used Greenstreet and Lorre well in all the marketing for their films, even when they hardly shared any scenes. The trailer for *Background to Danger* was narrated by Greenstreet looking sinister highlighted in the darkness, eyes swiveling from side to side. In fact, the trailer made the film look like a bone fide classic. Usually they were billed as "The Fat Man" and "The Little Man," which was an unnecessary and rather crude shorthand. The studio was well aware of the potential for joint Greenstreet-Lorre projects and soon lined up a raft of suggestions. One was a re-working of *The Amazing Dr. Clitterhouse* (1938), one of the most popular films made at the studio. In the new version, the premise had Greenstreet in love with a young girl who treats him contemptuously, with Lorre as a "feebleminded gangster." The idea was soon kicked into touch by the explosive Steve Trilling, Jack Warner's personal assistant.[7]

Passage to Marseille (1944) was yet another attempt to milk the success of *Casablanca*. The cast was headed by Bogart, Lorre, Rains and Greenstreet, with Curtiz again as the director. This time the protagonists were French and Bogart played crusading journalist Jean Marac, sent to Devil's Island on rigged evidence of murder and sedition. Told in flashback he escapes from the penal colony with three others and is picked up by a French ship near the Panama Canal. He lives to fight again as a pilot with the Free French Air Force based in England.

Passage to Marseille was essentially a propaganda film and something of a curate's egg – good in parts. At times stirring, at times slow, it just appeared to lack something; cohesion perhaps, humor certainly. Bogart had marital trouble at the time and was reportedly disinterested in the project; Jean Gabin had been touted as a possible Marac, and would have been an excellent choice, but declined. Greenstreet detested the role he was offered and did all he could to avoid it.[8] Drawing on his experience he made more of Major Duval than appeared to be in the script, but the part was still that of a rather caricatured Vichy Frenchman, lacking even the ambivalence of a Captain Renault as a saving grace. Nonetheless the discussion among the officers during dinner was well observed and enlightening as to attitudes at the early period of the war when the fate of France was still in the balance. This in itself might have been illuminating for an audience that may not have taken much notice of French affairs. Duval, like many of his compatriots, has complete faith in the Maginot Line but when that is breached he loses all patience with his leaders and believes the only salvation for his country lies in co-operating with the Germans. It was a common sentiment at the time. Duval has a lieutenant, a real yes man, and some elements of comedy could have been introduced with this character and their relationship, but this was not developed. The lieutenant appeared so infrequently that the opportunity to lighten the heavy mood was lost. The film was rather grim; Bogart was at his most taciturn and Marac seemed to lack even a streak of sardonic humor to make him appealing. He did have the luminous Michele Morgan who lit up the screen as always during her all-too-brief sequences. As the only woman in the movie more of her would have been a welcome relief. The device of the flashback within a flashback within a flashback might have worked well in the novel but made the film unduly labored. The use of models showed great inventiveness during the opening part of the film set in England. The scenes on Devil's Island were well realized and indeed that was probably the most successful and interesting portion of the film. The scenes on board the ship worked well for the most part, including the action sequences. The

Greenstreet (left) as Major Duval with Charles La Torre as Lieutenant Lenoir in Michael Curtiz' wartime flagwaver Passage to Marseille *(1944)*. Photo courtesy of Gail Greenstreet.

The French officers discuss the political situation in their homeland in Passage to Marseille. *Left to right:* Charles La Torre, Greenstreet, Victor Francen and Raymond St Albin. Photo courtesy of Gail Greenstreet.

ship itself took many months to construct and was testament to the unseen and largely unheralded carpenters and laborers who worked on her. One scene in particular ran contrary to the heroic nature of its characters. When the ship is attacked and the Germans successfully fought off, Marac sees three men from a shot down plane in the water surrendering. With alacrity, he runs to the machine gun and mows them down while the ship's captain shouts for him to stop. This disturbing scene was often omitted for obvious reasons, contravening not only the Geneva Convention but surely undermining the moral high ground on which such flag-waving films were built. "It refused to generate excitement either on screen or at the box office," observed a Warner Bros. historian, "and squandered the talents of its capable cast."[9] The critic of *Punch* was more direct; "Invincibly second-rate," noted Richard Mallett.[10] Bosley Crowther wrote a well-considered piece that highlighted the contrived nature of the film. He also noted with acuity that "the flaring patriotism of the convicts is more apparent than it is convincing."[11]

24 A Star of Tomorrow at Sixty-Four

*"I am comfortable at last - I've done with my travelling.
I'm 64, and I think there is tremendous scope
for fine work here."*

Hedda Hopper, "Looking at Hollywood"
The Hilton Record, October 12, 1944. 31.

It was gratifying to Greenstreet when, at the age of sixty-four, he was voted one of the "Stars of Tomorrow" by the public, the exhibitors and the critics alike in the annual *Motion Picture Herald* poll for 1944.[1] Despite his late entry into cinema he had established himself as a firm favorite of audiences in a surprisingly short time. His star status had been conferred by Warner Bros. the year before and his salary was already higher than that of Peter Lorre and almost on a par with Bogart's.[2]

As a result of his extended stay in Hollywood, Greenstreet bought a house at 1531 Selma Drive, Los Angeles. It was a spacious twelve-room place built in 1929 on a corner plot on a hill overlooking Sunset Boulevard. After a lifetime of hotel rooms and apartments during his peripatetic days of touring, this was the first house he had ever owned. He became attached to the house and its garden despite the slightly hilly location. Ideally, he hoped that he could bring his wife from the hospital to live there with him, but that proved impossible.[3] After avoiding driving for much of his life, he also bought a car, as his granddaughter Gail recalled;

> "In LA, he bought his first and last home. Right off the Sunset Strip. He bought his first car and when he got it home it would barely fit up the steep driveway; he had a gentleman walking by drive it up. When my dad saw the size of the car he took it back to the dealer to get a vehicle that would fit the driveway. Another time he called his son in a panic. Something was wrong with the car. He was stopping

24 A STAR OF TOMORROW AT SIXTY-FOUR

Sydney standing beside his car with "Scotty" Murdock (left), circa 1945. Photo courtesy of Gail Greenstreet.

to make a left turn and there was a big clunk. My dad caught a cab to rush to the rescue; it turned out the noise was made by an umbrella rolling around under the seat. He also had a big problem with the steering wheel rubbing a shine on his nice suits. I believe he solved that problem with a towel he started keeping in the car."[4]

He wanted to return to the theater, his first love, but found the security of Hollywood a blessing after a lifetime on the stage. "All the talent is out here," he remarked, "They naturally come here because of the money. Why, some bit players in Hollywood earn more than most stage stars." He recognized that only a few stage stars could make money purely from theater, including the Lunts, Helen Hayes and Katherine Cornell. "Others gravitated to the easy money in sunny California before achieving box office eminence, he observed."[5] He reflected on his elevated star status; "I signed more autographs in front of the Brown Derby than I ever did in all my years in the theater."[6]

He was one of the best paid stars at Warner Bros. For instance, in 1943-44 he made almost $103,000. He had already overtaken Peter Lorre and was ahead of more well-established character players including Claude Rains ($92,000). In fact, Greenstreet was only a few thousand behind Humphrey Bogart ($107,000).⁷ Sydney always knew his worth and considering his age and vast experience it did not seem an excessive amount when seen in context.

The stage was still close to his heart and he hoped to return to Broadway in a number of projects. After filming *Casablanca*, he came close to reuniting with the Lunts in their production of *The Pirate* by S. N. Behrman.⁸ The play enjoyed a successful six-month run but Greenstreet was not able to devote such time away from the studios as his film contract would not allow it and besides he was in great demand at that time. The Lunts were thrilled by Sydney's tremendous success in movies but at the same time lamented "We wish we could get some of our wonderful people back."⁹

Sydney had many ideas of his own for the stage. One of the closest to his heart was a dramatization of the life of the French writer Honore de Balzac which he had co-authored.¹⁰ It was inspired by George Middleton's *That Was Balzac*. Greenstreet spoke wistfully of the part as "one which I would like to play in spite of both my size and age."¹¹ Another of his cherished projects was a life of Benjamin Franklin. He hoped to get a leave of absence from Warner Bros. and have as his director Otto Preminger who likewise tried to get leave from Twentieth Century Fox.¹² He craved to play the demanding lead role in Shakespeare's great tragedy *King Lear*, and discussed it often with his representatives at around the same time as Orson Welles planned to tour with it. Unfortunately, neither this nor the other ideas were ever realized.¹³ He expressed an interest in reviving a repertory company in London when the war ended and said that he wanted to appear at the opening night, but that idea would also appear to have fallen by the wayside.¹⁴

He retained several habits of behavior from his stage days. For instance, he always carried a small bag containing money which hung from a string around his neck. This went back to his early days and was common practice among actors who would prefer to have their money and valuables with them rather than leave them in their dressing room in case they forgot them or mislaid them.¹⁵

Since 1939 he had a housekeeper, Janet Murdock, to look after him. He always called her Scotty and they had known each other since the days they appeared together as husband and wife in *The*

While home on leave from war service in the Pacific, John (right) visits his father on the set of one of his films, circa 1943. Photo courtesy of Gail Greenstreet.

Magic Ring. "She's a lot of fun," he wrote, "and a great character. John and I are both fond of her."[16] Greenstreet often rehearsed his lines with her. "I try my lines on Scotty Murdock," he said, "When Scotty says I'm okay, that's good enough for me."[17] He enjoyed playing practical jokes on her and she seemed to appreciate his whimsical almost schoolboy humor. One time he phoned her pretending to be from the telephone exchange and asked her to stand away

Greenstreet (far right) chats with Felix Bressart, Greer Garson and unknown actor on the Warner lot. Photo courtesy of Gail Greenstreet.

from the phone and whistle. She informed him that she couldn't whistle and he said she could sing instead, so she gave a rendition of "Loch Lomond" while Greenstreet chortled on the other end of the line.[18] Scotty even made some appearances in small roles in some of Greenstreet's films including *The Verdict* and *That Way with Women*, in which she played a housekeeper.

After graduation from Berkshire School, John went to Hamilton College, New York, in 1939 but left at the end of his freshman year. During the war, he became a Sergeant in the Air Force and at one time was stationed in India. He even flew over to Ceylon once and visited the tea plantation where his father had worked forty-five years earlier.[19] John spent two years as an inspector of armaments for B-29s and later B-52s in Pacific Bomber Command. He was a completely different personality, quiet and retiring where Sydney was ebullient and outgoing. After the war, Sydney tried to get him a job with the production department at Warner Bros.

Greenstreet was set for the leading role in several films which did not transpire. One of the first of these was *The Prison Chaplain* based on Matt Taylor's short story *The Beloved Blackguard* first featured in *Liberty Magazine*.[20] A remake of *The Man Who Played God* was announced by his studio, with Greenstreet in the role that George Arliss had essayed in the original, but that too never came to pass.[21] He was penciled in for a role as a psychiatrist in *One Man's Secret* with Ida Lupino and Paul Lukas. The story by Rita Weiman had first appeared in a newspaper in 1943 but was not filmed until three years later with an entirely different cast. It was released as *Possessed* (1946) starring Joan Crawford and Van Heflin.[22] Another casualty was an adaptation of a successful Broadway play, *Brooklyn, U. S. A.* mooted to star John Garfield. Announced as one of the "most important productions for 1943," the project was abandoned.[23] The much-anticipated series of planned movies of Dashiell Hammett's *The Fat Man* also for producer Jerry Wald, was deliberated over for quite some time. The studio was enthusiastic but Greenstreet appeared reluctant. At one stage Warner Bros. were involved in a legal tussle about the project. Although a series eventually made it onto radio, he did not star in it.[24]

25 THE MASK OF DIMITRIOS

> *"Playing with Sydney is wonderful fun, contagious fun,"*
> said Lorre, *"We bat the ball back and forth*
> *and have a wonderful time."*
>
> "Greenstreet and Lorre Link Popularity to Face-Making"
> The Los Angeles Times, February 25, 1945, 83, 84.

The second adaptation of an Eric Ambler novel in which Greenstreet and Lorre were teamed was *The Mask of Dimitrios* (1944). An atmospheric yarn, the film was unusual for being entirely character driven and built around two character-actors. By far one the strongest of their films together it saw both actors at their best in an enigmatic story.

The film begins with the mystery of a body washed up on a beach in Greece. The dead man is identified from a name in his coat as Dimitrios Makropoulis, a man with a price on his head. Writer Cornelius Leyden (Lorre) meets the local police captain at a party who tells him what he knows about the supposedly dead man. Leyden becomes intrigued and follows the trail of the life of Dimitrios across Europe. As he does so he comes into contact with an elusive Englishman known as Peters or Peterson (Greenstreet) who has a personal interest in the story. An impression of the scoundrel Dimitrios emerges from the different witnesses and at length they come face to face with the man himself.

A highly successful mystery, *The Mask of Dimitrios* was directed effectively by Jean Negulesco, his first feature. Many agreed with the view of one critic who wrote that the film "captures both the cosmopolitan flavor and the sinewy quality of Ambler's novel" *A Coffin for Dimitrios*.[1] Even Ambler was not displeased with the outcome and later presented Negulesco with an autographed copy of his original novel when the two met in London. Negulesco's own appraisal of his debut was somewhat brief and understated in his

Greenstreet (left) and Lorre in a scene from The Mask of Dimitrios *(1944), one of their most satisfying films together. Photo courtesy of Gail Greenstreet.*

memoir; "With Sydney Greenstreet, Peter Lorre and Victor Francen – the dependable regulars – the film was made under budget and brought to the limelight a young stage actor, Zachary Scott. It was an artistic and box office success, and my first break into feature films."[2]

It was a refreshing change that the film was character-led, moreover character actor-led. At that time during the war, the studios were more likely to promote character players to star status and several actors who would not normally be so much to the fore got their chance. Such actors as William Bendix and older ones like Charles Coburn filled the manpower gap. Warner Bros. were keen to find a suitable vehicle for Greenstreet who was one of their most distinct assets. The man himself was in his element; "Look at the parts I snag by being both fat and bad," he declared. "In *The Mask of Dimitrios* I have 724 lines of dialog. I counted them. That's a few more than the slender Hamlet."[3]

Zachary Scott was a fine stage actor and this was his first film. While he was appearing in *Those Endearing Young Charms* on Broadway he was spotted by Jack L. Warner who offered him the part of Dimitrios. Scott was not only handsome but intelligent and talented. He got on well with Lorre and Greenstreet who he credited with helping him to adapt his stage technique to suit that of film.[4] Although he was playing the titular character, he was only seen at intervals throughout in flashback until his final dramatic appearance near the end. He played the role perfectly and the character of Dimitrios remained entirely enigmatic from first to last.

Negulesco knew he was onto a winner early on in filming when Lorre, notoriously disinterested in scripts, not only started learning his lines but also read the scenario too; "I've got the best yarn I've ever had," said Negulesco, "And I'm sure of it because of Peter."[5] However, in their screen test the two actors clowned around so much that the film almost never came to pass, as Lorre's biographer outlined:

> "Let's do a scene, said Negulesco. Lorre and Greenstreet rehearsed their lines. The director heard giggling. "Go to it, boys," he instructed. The actors clowned their way through most of the test. Negulesco said nothing. Anything to be different. "I saw the rushes," [producer] Blanke scolded the next morning. "They are terrible. I want to tell you something, Jean. This is your first chance to make a picture. But if the first day's rushes are as bad as the test I've just seen, you won't be doing the film.
>
> "It was a great gamble," said Negulesco. "They were fooling around, improvising from their characters. It was a test of what they should not do. Fortunately, next day I had a quite a good scene. They liked the rushes of that and the picture progressed smoothly."[6]

Lorre commented on their approach; "The pictures I made with Bogie and Greenstreet were almost always a rewrite of last month's film, but we had such fun making them and we used to work on individual scenes so as to give each picture a hallmark of its own."[7] There were some cleverly constructed scenes such as those on board

Greenstreet (right) discusses a scene with director Jean Negulesco (left) and co-stars Peter Lorre and Zachary Scott on the set of The Mask of Dimitrios. *It was Negulesco's first picture after abandoning a successful career as an artist in Europe. Photo courtesy of Gail Greenstreet.*

the train as Peters reads a book called *Pearls of Everyday Wisdom*, from which he quotes a number of aphorisms. In the scenes where Leyden goes to the Records Office to find out about Dimitrios, the clerk is on a ladder looking through the files as Peters appears in the bottom right hand of the frame but having heard the salient points of their conversation Peters disappears almost immediately. In one almost wordless scene, Peters walks into a hotel lobby and takes a furtive glance down at the register then walks out again. All their shared scenes were a sheer joy; the way they interacted it was clear they were so much at ease together. There was a spontaneity in their conversation that made them appear not to be acting at all. The relationship between Leyden and Peters is closer than in the novel. At the end after Peters has finally got his hands on the money he has always wanted he is wounded but staggers down the staircase to the waiting police. "He is my friend," says Leyden, "Well he is a nice man." As Peters is led away he repeats one of his favorite aphorisms "You see there is not enough kindness in the world."

Peters (Greenstreet, left) finally gets what he always wanted as Van Leyden (Peter Lorre) looks on. A pivotal scene in The Mask of Dimitrios *(1944).*

In *The Mask of Dimitrios* the scene moved across Europe from Greece to Budapest to Sofia. The exotic backgrounds were striking and each atmospheric street scene was drawn in with care. Warner Bros. always used impressive sets and Negulesco's artistic background came to the fore. The studio's designers were among the most inventive. Too seldom are set designers considered, but a great deal of attention went into their work. The sets were cleverly lit and the great use of shadow created a genuine noir look which heightened the sense of menace and intrigue inherent in the characters and situations. Once again, the music of Adolph Deutsch enhanced the drama of the shadowy world in which the characters moved. There was also subtle use made of the popular tunes of the day interwoven into the narrative such as "Perfidia" during the scene in the club.

Once more, Greenstreet had trouble falling in one of the final scenes and was required to do several takes. Negulesco was concerned for his safety and asked if he wanted a double. "Damn the doubles, and full steam ahead," said Greenstreet, "Only haven't you got a couple of pillows for me to land on?"[8]

In those days theater managers had to be inventive and trade publications encouraged all kinds of angles for publicity. For instance, the *Motion Picture Herald* suggested several ways to pique interest in the film. One idea was to instigate a search for Dimitrios by offering a number of cinema tickets or a movie edition of the book for those who could find him when he was due in a certain locale at a certain time. "For lobby attention," offered the *Herald*, "a still of Sydney Greenstreet could be blown up and mounted. Cut a slit in Greenstreet's mouth and fasten a speaker behind cutout. Run wire to a hidden spot and have announcer speak at intervals through mike."[9] It would be interesting to know if any theater managers followed up on these suggestions. The idea for the blown up Greenstreet in the lobby would have been highly effective if the announcer was able imitate his distinctive voice.

Billed as yet another follow-up to *Casablanca*, *The Conspirators* (1944) was set in the favored destination of many in the earlier film – Lisbon. Paul Henreid plus Greenstreet and Lorre were joined by the beautiful Hedy Lamarr in what sounded like an intriguing spy yarn full of stalwart players on the Warner Bros. lot. The dramatic trailer promised much; Greenstreet was the only character who directly addressed the audience; "These are the incredible people in whose lives I deal," he intoned in his inimitable style; "Desperate men and women whose startling mission is to plot and scheme, connive and kill for the world's most guarded secrets." Unfortunately, the disparity between idea and execution was too much. Lorre played one of the Portuguese underground in a group led by Greenstreet. Although both did well in the circumstances their parts were underwritten; Lorre in particular was left with little to do again. Greenstreet had more opportunity as the leader of the gang but the film as a whole did not hang together; nor did it keep the attention. For instance, there was an overlong scene at the end set in a casino when all the suspects are sitting at the roulette table and one is about to be revealed as the traitor among them. The scene seemed to go on too long and little real suspense was built up so that it was difficult to care who the traitor was; especially

Peter Lorre (left) and Greenstreet (right) did their best but despite the cast The Conspirators *(1944) was not a success. Photo courtesy of Gail Greenstreet.*

so because it had already been signposted. Once again, the street scenes and interiors were excellently conceived, and the music of Max Steiner was, as always, a delight.

To begin with Hal Wallis announced Jean Negulesco as the director and filming started well. But then Wallis was fired; seemingly for being too successful on Oscar night. It was after that when the difficulties began, as Negulesco related in his memoir;

> "He [Wallis] was replaced on *The Conspirators* by a minor producer. The Script was changed. The film that had already been shot under the supervision of Wallis was discarded. Location and the pace of the story were changed. Stars took advantage of the situation, especially Hedy Lamarr. Their demands were granted. My job as a young director became a nightmare. Secretly the film became known as *The Constipators*, with "Headache Lamarr" and "Paul Hemorrhoid." The professionals – Greenstreet, Lorre and Victor Francen – gave me their sympathy; but the just valuation of the film was given by Max Steiner, who was called on to do the musical score. We saw the finished product together. After the show,

Left to right: Peter Lorre, Hedy Lamarr and Greenstreet in a scene from The Conspirators. *Photo courtesy of Gail Greenstreet.*

the lights went on. Hopefully I waited for his comment. It was short, just one word: *"Ouch!"* Brief and to the point."[10]

The film was a great disappointment when one considers the cast list alone. Nor was it a harmonious experience for many as Negulesco's assistant Reggie Callow recalled:

"Sydney Greenstreet was a very loveable person. I had a big fight with Hedy Lamar over him. When we were ready for the cast, the first man on set, believe me, was the old man, Sydney Greenstreet. He was always the first. But Hedy liked to make an entrance. She'd always come on the set late. So, I went to her one time and I said "Hedy, you know you're keeping this old man waiting all the time. Why don't you get in when we call you?" She told me to shut my damn mouth. That was her only remark."[11]

The critical reviews were scathing and after the optimism of *The Mask of Dimitrios* the disillusioned Negulesco seriously considered returning to his previous career as an artist. It was when he was at his lowest ebb that he received a letter from director Edmund

Goulding who told him not to take *The Conspirators* to heart. Goulding encouraged him to continue and gave him the soundest advice he ever received; "get the script right."[12]

Few emerged from the experience wishing to remember it, although one observer declared with good reason that the "chief asset of the film is the performance by Sydney Greenstreet."[13]

Greenstreet next shared a wonderful cameo with Peter Lorre in *Hollywood Canteen* (1944) along with a number of other famous faces. It was a well-judged scene which they concocted between them and in which they seemed so at ease.[14] An energetic G. I. dances with Pattie Andrews and declares that he will dance her arms out of their sockets. At which point he encounters Lorre and Greenstreet; "Doesn't that constitute mayhem?" says Lorre innocently; "Definitely, Peter," answers a playfully sinister Greenstreet. Both were frequently to be seen at the real Hollywood Canteen during the war where actresses would dance with servicemen and Greenstreet among others would serve the meals and clear tables. At Christmas, he would dress up as Santa and there was a memorable joke shot of him in character about to be hit by Lorre with a baseball bat.

26 Between Two Worlds

> *"On the stage, there is only one first performance of a play with its nervousness and anxiety. But in a motion picture every scene is a first performance equally trying on the nerves and bringing the same sense of uncertainty. First and last of all, the lens is the actor's severest critic."*
>
> "Sydney Greenstreet Likes to Be Menace"
> *The Brooklyn Daily Eagle*, August 3, 1947, 26.

Greenstreet desired to move away from villainous roles for a change and did so in such films as *Devotion* and *Between Two Worlds*. Later he also made some comedies, but was rarely given enough chances to escape his sinister on-screen persona.

He appeared to effect in *Devotion* another film directed by Curtis Bernhardt, which, like *Conflict* was actually finished in 1943 but for some undisclosed reason was not released until 1946.[1] A curious film, it was allegedly inspired by the lives of the Bronte sisters who famously lived at a remote parsonage in Haworth, Yorkshire. Armed with vivid imaginations they drew their inspiration from the isolation of the spot and the changing seasons in the surrounding moors. Despite the setting few of the actors even attempted a Yorkshire accent. As history, it was risible but as an odd drama it had its moments. Ida Lupino played Anne, with Olivia de Havilland as Charlotte and Arthur Kennedy as their ill-fated brother Branwell. Greenstreet was initially announced as their father but instead played the novelist William Makepeace Thackeray who was instrumental in the sisters' success.[2] The leading players were dismayed at the gulf between the Bronte sisters' real story and Warner Brothers' fiction. For, instance, the typical Hollywood approach even had Anne and Charlotte in love with the same man. Lupino and De Havilland went to the front office to protest, but got nowhere; Jack Warner refused to change anything.[3]

Charlotte Bronte (Olivia De Havilland) is escorted around London by the novelist Thackeray (Greenstreet) in Curtis Bernhardt's curiosity Devotion *(1946). Photo courtesy of Gail Greenstreet.*

The film was well made and there was a distinctive mood maintained by the under-rated Bernhardt. His strength was psychological insight. Especially successful was a sequence in which Anne has a recurrent vision of impending death as a ghostly horseman on the moor whose face she can never see. The scenes of Charlotte's triumphant visit to London after the publication of *Jane Eyre* were a highlight. Indeed, the film brightened up considerably on the appearance of Greenstreet as a foppish and haughty Thackeray.

Publicity still of Greenstreet as The Examiner otherwise known as Reverend Tim Thompson in the mystical drama Between Two Worlds *(1945). Photo courtesy of Gail Greenstreet.*

He was given some choice lines of which he made the most. At one stage Charlotte frets about keeping the gentlemen of the press waiting; "On the contrary," replies Thackeray airily, "Such treatment is meat and drink to their servile souls." When he passes Charles Dickens he mumbles a "Good afternoon," prompting Charlotte to express an interest in meeting the great author and Thackeray's keenest rival. He gives her the priceless response; "I shouldn't like you to get involved with that kind of riff-raff, my dear."

Greenstreet had expressed a desire to play a deeply philosophical role, and found his chance as the Examiner in an updated version of Sutton Vane's metaphysical play *Outward Bound*. Retitled *Between Two Worlds* (1944), the story was transferred to wartime London. It had been filmed in 1930 under its original title.

Several passengers are travelling in a taxi when it is hit and seemingly destroyed by an incendiary bomb in a London street. These people find themselves on an ocean liner along with a young couple who attempted to commit suicide (Paul Henreid and Eleanor Parker). It transpires that all the passengers are dead and being transported to the "other side." In time, their future fates are decided by an Examiner (Greenstreet). The story first came to the author when he was a soldier in France in the First World War, while he was injured and laid up in a hospital bed hovering between life and death. Vane had been unable to interest any producer in his play in London so decided to produce it himself and it proved a remarkable success on both sides of the Atlantic. In the immediate aftermath of the war so many who lost loved ones at such young ages felt an irreparable sense of loss. Death on such an unprecedented industrial scale was impossible to comprehend. Unsurprisingly there was an upsurge of interest in spiritualism, and it is easy to understand why a play like *Outward Bound* would resonate so much at that time in history. The same was still true in 1930 at the time of the first film version, and also to an extent in 1944 and war was again the catalyst. The film proved fairly popular but arguably failed to capture the elusive mystical spirit of the original production. Some of the actors, especially John Garfield, seemed miscast, and the character played by George Tobias was an unnecessary addition. There were some successful scenes and the ensemble playing of all the old troupers such as Sara Allgood was excellent. Edmund Gwenn was memorable as a cheerfully enigmatic steward. Mostly known previously as a singer, the British actor Dennis King proved surprisingly effective as an unworldly vicar. In one scene, he was called on to comfort everyone with a prayer and the only one he could think of was one he used to recite as a child with his nanny. Greenstreet did not appear until some way into the proceedings and brightened it up with his presence but he would have been welcome much

(John Garfield, left) confronts the Examiner (Greenstreet, seated) in Between Two Worlds.

sooner. He was entirely in keeping with the scenario; his Examiner appeared avuncular but resolute. His constant rebuttals of the belligerent arms dealer (George Coulouris) were expertly done. There were some elements of humor in the dialogue such as when a social climber (Isobel Elsom) asks for a particular kind of pink villa in the afterlife. Greenstreet's reaction said everything.

The sets were interesting and well-constructed; the station where the characters are first introduced with their walls adorned with war propaganda posters and the main set on board the ship were all evocative. One scene depicted a banquet and required a table set for eleven people. This necessitated a grand feast consisting of "two dozen buns, 15lb of fresh fruit, 2lb of assorted nuts and two roast chickens." Prop man Budd Friend revealed that he used green fruit because it lasted longer and photographed just as well. The feast was supposed to last through five days of filming but some of the actors couldn't resist tucking in. At the end of shooting there were fifteen buns left, less than half the fruit and two cleanly-picked chicken carcasses. Friend quipped; "If John Garfield and Paul

Henreid didn't like grapes so much I'd have had more fruit left."[4] Director Edward A. Blatt had a brief career at Warner Bros. in the 1940s as a dialog coach on such films as *Now, Voyager* among others. The fine score by the masterful Erich Maria Korngold added immeasurably to the eerie atmosphere.

27 Comedy at Last

"A musician who can play Beethoven wants to play something besides Beethoven once in a while."

Charlotte Kaye, "Big Hit" *Hollywood*, February 1943, 77.

Having long harbored hopes of being offered a screen comedy, Greenstreet made two that were released in 1945. Sadly, they were both disappointing. A couple of years later he made a third, but that was little improvement on the others. This was one area in which cinema missed a trick when the opportunity was lost to see Greenstreet in a first-rate comedy suited to his persona and ability acquired over a lifetime of playing such roles on stage.

The first of the films sounded promising. *Pillow to Post* (1945) was an adaptation of a Broadway play and was to star Ida Lupino in the lead role. What's more it was to be directed by Vincent Sherman who Greenstreet had known since the days they acted together in the Theater Guild. The premise was the usual screwball situation this time the reason behind it was perhaps a more serious one – chronic housing shortages during and after the war. Lupino played a salesman's daughter who wants to prove she can do something for the war effort. She travels the country trying to negotiate deals on behalf of her father, without success. In Dakota, she tries to do a deal with the local oilman Slim, but Slim insists they talk about it over dinner for a few nights. This means she has to stay for several days in the area. She comes across a bungalow in an auto court but in order to stay there she has to be married. Naturally she picks up a lieutenant on his day off and explains her situation, he agrees to act as her spouse for the afternoon. From there the outcome is of course obvious. Greenstreet played a gruff but kindly colonel and the cast included several familiar and much welcome faces including Ruth

Lobby poster for Pillow to Post *(1945) a lesser screwball comedy which starred two of the greats of noir, Ida Lupino and Greenstreet, playing against type. Left to right: Greenstreet, William Prince, Lupino, Willie Best.*

Ida Lupino (left) in Pillow to Post *with Greenstreet (center as Colonel Ottley) and William Prince (right) as a hapless lieutenant.*

Donnelly and Stuart Erwin. Louis Armstrong put in an appearance in a scene in a nightclub with his orchestra and Dorothy Dandridge singing "Whatcha Say?" At one stage Walter Huston was touted as a possible for the role of the colonel.

The director had a good reputation for his popular dramas including *Old Acquaintance* (1943) and *Mr. Skeffington* (1944). Perhaps he did not have such a sure touch with comedies. He described a happy atmosphere on the set of *Pillow to Post*, and said "they were all delightful to work with."[1] According to a Warner Bros. historian the film "laid an egg."[2] However, Sherman reflected otherwise in his autobiography; "audiences laughed long and loud, and the film did good business. I was gratified to learn … the film came as a welcome relief to American soldiers overseas."[3] The subject of housing shortages seemed to be something that struck a chord with many young couples just starting out and the rudimentary facilities in the cabins combined with the close proximity of the neighbors must have been a nightmare to newlyweds. Nevertheless, as a comedy the film has not aged well and it is surprising to learn that Lupino received more fan mail about her role in *Pillow to Post* than she did for any other role in her entire career.[4] She proved she was game for anything and among other indignities had to endure bags of water dropped on her head from a great height and the perils of a makeshift bed in the kitchen comprised of two chairs. Perhaps it was the sight of her in an enticing nightgown that she wore in one of the bedroom scenes that led to the explosion in fan mail.

Greenstreet was called on to be jovial one minute and outraged the next. There was little he could do with the part, although he brought to it a note of pathos when he was told by his superiors that he cannot go into action with his men and must stay behind. He was excited by the chance to do something different and commented at the time "Even I found it hard to believe. A comedy role at last. It worked out beautifully, too."[5]

Despite its title, *Christmas in Connecticut* (1945), was released in August 1945, shortly before the end of the war. Often cited as one of the most perennially popular Christmas films of all time, it was a big hit for the studio and made $3 million at the Box Office.[6] A happy atmosphere on set pervaded and during the making of the

Left to right: Reginald Gardiner, Barbara Stanwyck and Greenstreet in a scene from the charming comedy Christmas in Connecticut *(1945), one of the most popular Christmas perennials. Photo courtesy of Gail Greenstreet.*

Greenstreet (left) with Barbara Stanwyck did well playing against type in Christmas in Connecticut *(1945), which was released just before VJ Day in 1945. Photo courtesy of Gail Greenstreet.*

film one source said that Greenstreet and the director, fellow Englishman Peter Godfrey "had the cast and crew in stitches with … impromptu spoofs."[7]

Not exactly remembered for their comedies, Warner Bros. seemed ill-at-ease in the genre. Bette Davis was first considered for the starring role, but was later replaced by Barbara Stanwyck. It retains the charm of its period and it was the cast that made it worthwhile. Greenstreet contributed a large measure of its value as the seemingly formidable magazine editor Alexander Yardley. The scene where Stanwyck visited him in his Long Island home he handled with finesse. Surely only he could make so much of some of the seemingly banal lines; "Last October when you had breast of guinea hen in madeira – that was perfection!" he declares; "Or in June when you made the strawberry chartreuse with rum and egg-white. You stiffen the egg-white? Of course, it's the only way to do it!" Throughout he entered fully into the spirit of the thing with his familiar laugh and unique knack of characterization. He also displayed his aptitude for physical comedy such as when he followed the two lovers in the sleigh and tumbled down a ditch. There was the rare and welcome sight of him dancing during the festivities at the hall; he was always light on his feet.

The other players suited their parts well, Dennis Morgan was a personable light lead with a pleasant voice and his simple rendition of "O Little Town of Bethlehem" was sincere and quite touching. The stalwarts S. K. "Cuddles" Sakall and Una O'Connor were their reliable selves in the supporting cast, which was just as well because without them the story was so light it might have floated away, it hardly felt tethered to the ground at all. It was all so dream-like, but such escapism was sorely needed in 1945 in a world emerging from unparalleled destruction. Indeed, it was aimed squarely at servicemen and their families. As such it was perfectly attuned to the patriotic mood of the country. Released in early August 1945, special statewide Christmas parties were arranged for re-deployed soldiers. It was an exciting time and almost coincided with V. J. Day on August 21 when everyone was having a party that must have felt like several Christmases had come at once. In addition, there were

Greenstreet (left) showed his comedy skill in That *Way with Women (1947) as a bored millionaire who is constantly forced to take his medicine. Here with the lovely Martha Vickers as his daughter. Photo courtesy of Gail Greenstreet.*

a number of air shows advertising the film which included messages from those serving overseas and those about to return.[8]

A couple of years later, Greenstreet had another chance in a comedy. Fred de Cordoba's *That Way with Women* (1947) was a remake of *The Millionaire* (1931) which had been a hit for George Arliss. Greenstreet was once again delighted at the prospect of returning to comedy, his favorite genre; "It'll be a delight not to have women and children running away from me screaming," he observed wryly.[9] He took the Arliss role as a bored auto millionaire who poses as his own gardener. He goes into partnership with Dane Clark on the quiet to run a gas station and ends up playing cupid for his daughter Martha Vickers. The film was based on a 1921 newspaper story by Earl Derr Biggers, the inventor of Charlie Chan. The emphasis was shifted from the millionaire in the earlier film so that the romance between Clark and Vickers took center stage. Nonetheless, Greenstreet had fun and enjoyed meeting up with fellow trouper Alan

Life begins at sixty-five. A scene at the Smiling Super Service garage from That Way with Women *with Greenstreet driving and Martha Vickers standing by the car. Photo courtesy of Gail Greenstreet.*

Hale many years after they had appeared together in *The Rainbow Girl*. In that show Greenstreet had memorably essayed the role of the butler and Hale had been a handsome leading man. "It has been a long time," reflected Hale, "I guess we're not the men we were in those days." To which Greenstreet replied smartly surveying his bulk and Hale's paunch, "No – we're twice the men."[10] The son of motor magnate Henry Ford visited the set during filming to inspect the cars used in the film. Although Greenstreet happened to mention that his son was on the lookout for a new model T, Ford Jr. just smiled benignly and moved on.

Greenstreet got on well with his young co-stars. Martha Vickers was the girlfriend of the director, Fred de Cordoba, and they used to go over to Greenstreet's house every Saturday for dinner and cards. The redoubtable "Scotty" Murdock would cook the meals.[11]

There were some good scenes between Greenstreet, Fay Bainter and Alan Hale. There was also a memorable encounter between Greenstreet and a timid insurance salesman who ends up buying one of his own policies. There was the memorable sight of him the worse for drink singing the old Irish ditty "Who Threw the Overalls in Mrs. Murphy's Chowder." The Greenstreet barbs about his over-cautious doctor who will not allow him to do anything also hit home, but the general updating of the scenario tended to sideline the old stagers. As a consequence, *That Way with Women* was deemed "just about watchable" in the words of one critic.[12] However, many felt the movie was an improvement on the previous version, and that Greenstreet in the role of the millionaire was more convincing than Arliss had been. Another reviewer felt that Greenstreet's "delightfully poisonous sense of humor" was the film's saving grace. He remarked "His performance marks him as a great comedian, as well as Hollywood's leading 'heavy.'"[13] Such an epithet echoed the verdict of the theater critics of forty years before and must have been music to his ears.

It was a great shame that Greenstreet never had a chance to make a first-rate comedy that played to his strengths. It seems strange that not once was his name suggested for a Shakespearean role of the kind he had played to such acclaim in his stage days. In fairness, Hollywood was not thinking much about the Bard during the 1940s. Among other proposed film projects, he was to have been teamed once again with Dane Clark in *McGuffey the Great*, a backstage yarn which was set to star Greenstreet as a veteran Shakespearian actor who becomes a magician and Clark as a detective posing as his assistant. The promising sounding venture came to naught.[14] Other more obvious comedy projects came along but were not realized, although they were seldom of the quality that suited his talents. One such was for a leading role in a film version of the successful Broadway army comedy *Too Hot for Maneuvers* which was never made.[15]

He felt deeply frustrated and sought a far greater variety of roles; "Next I would like a philosophical part – sort of grumpy – an English lord, happily drunk, or something with edge and authenticity to it," he once said, "Anything human and significant, be it Shylock, Oscar Wilde or Nero Wolfe."[16] Unfortunately, such opportunities were few. Considering his comedic experience in forty years on stage, it was cinema's great loss that Greenstreet was never invited to appear in a decent comedy on screen. Although the three he made had their moments, his dry wit cried out for something more substantial. At times, there were glimpses of his gift for physical and intellectual comedy. Physically one thinks of his dancing and falling about in the snow in *Christmas in Connecticut*. His timing was especially apparent in *That Way with Women*, which was arguably the best of them. However, intellectually there was little to get hold of in the so-called comedy films. Instead it is necessary to look to his performances in dramas. There was a definite sardonic humor in most of the villains he essayed. Sometimes even the turn of phrase he used or the intonation of his voice made one smile even when he was speaking of torture. His beautifully-contained portrait of Thackeray in *Devotion* gave a glimpse of what he could have done had he been able to bring Balzac to life. Arguably his villains would not have been so memorable if he had not spent the best part of his life playing comedy roles because his humor was inherent in everything he did.

28 STILL LEARNING

"I'm still just learning the business. I find it full of exhilarating discoveries that make me feel younger every day."

Sydney Greenstreet interview with Patricia Clary, "Hollywood Film Shops" *Jamestown (N. Y.) Post-Journal*, September 17, 1949, 25.

Greenstreet put a great deal of time and effort into his work. However, he loved to relax too and apart from sports he cultivated other interests including art and antiques. He was an inveterate partygoer and one of the most popular figures in Hollywood whose good humor and sense of good fellowship endeared him to all those he met.

He often spoke about his craft and was acutely aware that the demands of screen acting were far different from the stage. He missed the comfort of rehearsals and recognized the forensic intensity of the camera eye; "In the movies, you are put on an operating table and told to be artistic," he observed, "A performance on screen is like forty New York opening nights."[1] He adapted his technique but approached his work in the same methodical and professional way he always had, as he once explained; "My work in front of the camera is easy compared to the labor pains I go through while developing a characterization. I mull over the character of the man I'm to portray and explore every reason behind his actions in the script. I finally feel comfortable assuming his personality."[2] He loved his work and he put everything into it; indeed, it could be said of him that his work was his life. However, that might appear to imply that he was one-dimensional, which of course he was not. It was only that he cared so much and wanted to maintain his high standard of professionalism.

Greenstreet cycles off to play a round of golf, circa 1945. Photo courtesy of Gail Greenstreet.

Off screen, he continued to enjoy tennis and golf. He retained an interest in all sports with the exception of boxing. He was a member of the Racquet Club of Palm Springs and favored early morning tennis matches.[3] He once said that he had played on most of the major golf courses across America over the years of his theatrical wanderings and continued to play for as long as possible. He had a golf handicap of fourteen and a best score of 78.

Since the early 1930s he spent most of his summers in the Berkshires, even after his son had left the school, and kept a summer house at Great Barrington, Massachusetts for many years.[4] Seaver

Buck remained one of his best friends with whom he loved to play golf; they also played croquet, cribbage and many other games and Greenstreet retained his competitive streak. They were members of the Wyantenuck Country Club and it was said that "witnesses used to maintain that the pool in the men's locker room would rise two inches when Mr. Greenstreet took his pre-round dip."[5] The two friends often competed in the local Governor's Cup competition.[6] His other great friend was J. Sayre Crawley who he had known since 1902 when Sydney had made his professional debut in Ramsgate playing a murderer in *Sherlock Holmes*, and Crawley appeared in the title role.

He amassed a fine collection of books, antiques and *objet d'art* at his comfortable twelve room home in Beverly Hills. "I collect antiques," he said, "Chinese pottery, English china, rare ornaments. I like nice things about me."[7] Among other items he collected canes of all descriptions, gold, silver, Malacca, novelty and some with curiously carved heads; "I've a good fortune's worth of the things," he once observed, "but all I can do with 'em is use 'em for ornaments. I dread to think what would happen if I leaned on one."[8] At one stage he was reported to be considering making an offer for a rare collection of Thackeray's manuscripts.[9] His walls were adorned with many works of art. His other hobbies included oil painting and sculpting which he had done for many years. He had several paintings of himself in his many character roles on stage including King Henry VIII, Falstaff and Caliban.

Many of the articles written about him concerned the subject of his weight, usually presented in jocular fashion. He always saw the funny side and his nickname was 'Tiny.' He was 5' 11" and his weight varied; generally, it was around 260 pounds but sometimes he ballooned to 320. He often tried dieting. A particular film contract once stipulated that he had to lose fifty pounds. He lost sixty pounds in four months by following his own diet plan; "I did not eat any vegetable that grew under the ground," he revealed, "I didn't drink for one hour before meals or during meals and had absolutely no dessert. After every meal, I did not sit down for an hour."[10] Another time his doctor ordered him to lose seventy-five pounds for the sake of his health.[11] Of course he always loved his

Greenstreet at home, with a portrait of him in character on the wall behind him. Photo courtesy of Gail Greenstreet.

food and it was once revealed by Bessie Gant in her weekly newspaper recipe column that his favorite meal was "roast beef, Yorkshire puddings, horseradish and a snappy green salad." The jovial Bessie called him "280 pounds of good nature" and printed his recipe.[12] One doctor ordered him to cut out all proteins, fats and carbohydrates but he found it difficult; "I just eat meat, potatoes, bread and butter – and banana splits!" he joked. "All food is fattening anyway – full of calories – so I might as well eat what I please."[13] This routine was once used on a radio program in which he asked Dorothy Lamour if she had noticed any difference in him; "Why, I've lost half a pound!" he announced.

He was remembered on screen for his white suits, sometimes in a crumpled state depending on the scrupulousness of the character he happened to be playing. Offscreen he was renowned for his sartorial elegance and loved fine clothes. He usually wore tailored handmade suits. A snappy dresser, a typical Greenstreet summer ensemble, for example, saw him in a beige gabardine suit with sport shoes and a bright green tie.[14]

Sydney plays with his dog in the garden of his home, circa 1944. He bought the dog for his son during the war and named it Jog after his son's initials – John Ogden Greenstreet. Photo courtesy of Gail Greenstreet.

He took exception to the doctor who advanced the theory that people who eat too much do so out of romantic disappointment. Dr. George H. Reeves, a physician at the Mount Sinai Hospital in Cleveland, also claimed that joviality was assumed by the overweight as a defense mechanism. "It is well-known that the vast majority of maiden ladies are skinny," remarked Greenstreet, "It is popular widows who are plump. I myself have done some research

Sydney (right) shares a joke with "Scotty" Murdock (left) his housekeeper who he had known since the days they acted together in The Magic Ring *on stage. Photo courtesy of Gail Greenstreet.*

of my own in this field, in a purely amateur way of course." As a parting shot to the good doctor he observed, "As a matter of fact, I can recall some hefty lovers who were hefty. Lord Byron was certainly not frustrated and he always had to watch his weight."[15]

Greenstreet continued to do charity work for such organizations as the Disabled American Veterans National Service Fund.[16] At Christmas he would dress as Santa and visit the Pasadena Hospital where he would distribute presents to the children.[17] Those who came into contact with him invariably spoke of his good humor. The Morris Brothers had a shoe store in Beverly Hills and counted many stars among their customers. They were outspoken in their opinions of all the actors they knew; some they found to be difficult; others treated them with disdain. Greenstreet, however, was one of their favorites; "He's one of the friendliest stars who comes in the store," they remarked.[18]

He maintained all his links to the old country and often visited his sisters in England; they also made several return visits to him.[19] While on tour during the 1930s he usually stayed with his sister Hilda and her husband Fred at their house in Copse Hill, Wimbledon.[20] He kept a financial interest in a hop farm in his native Kent.[21] During the war it was said that his three sisters and both his remaining two brothers were all involved in the war effort despite their age.[22] He lost one brother Guy who died in 1943 at the age of sixty-two. After Sydney's death, it emerged that he had been supporting the family of one of his brothers, (possibly Frank) for many years. Frank had died in 1926 at the age of forty-nine leaving a young widow and at least three children although he left an estate valued at £5754 which was a sizeable sum at that time.[23]

Sydney was once called on in an official capacity by the U. S. War Department to assist two Chinese Officers in perfecting their English.[24] Apart from his brother Harry in Nebraska, Sydney came across another Greenstreet in Washington, who his granddaughter fondly recalled; "Sydney met an actress over here going by the name of Gail Greenstreet. Birth name Dorothy Greenstreet. She and Sydney always kidded around that they were related. In truth, they had no idea. She married Howard Strickling, Louis B Mayer's right-hand man. I was named after her. My unofficial godmother."[25]

He grew attached to his home and because it was built on a hillside the garden was terraced. He instructed the gardener to create a victory garden in one part that happened to be a favored play area for all the dogs of the neighborhood. This meant he had to pay $250 in order to fence off the land.[26]

He thoroughly enjoyed the new lease of life his late-flowering screen career afforded him and even took advantage of the Warner Bros. studio offer of dancing classes. He often danced and once said he was learning the rhumba for exercise.[27] His training must have paid off because he was once snapped by *Look* magazine dancing with Lee Patrick, who said he enjoyed dancing and was often to be seen at Hollywood night spots dancing the night away.[28] He was naturally gallant and loved to help ladies in distress such as the time he changed a tire for "two evening gowned beauties" after their cary had broken down outside a Hollywood restaurant.[29] He entered fully into the spirit of the film capitol, as his granddaughter recalled;

> "He enjoyed the "Hollywood" lifestyle. He loved people and attention. He was a master storyteller and made the

Greenstreet was one of the most diligent of players who not only knew his own lines weeks in advance, but those of his fellow actors. Photo courtesy of Gail Greenstreet.

rounds at parties. There was one story I heard that he had invited people over for a party at his house then got an invite to a party that sounded more interesting. Did he cancel his party? No! But he left his guests and went to the other party."[30]

He frequently attended film premieres and was an immensely popular figure in the film colony. Sometimes at premieres he would be accompanied by a younger actress and once his escort was mistaken for his wife. He found the attention from fans surprising and it was not what he was used to during his years on the stage. He still loved to attend the theater and was among the starry first night audience that witnessed Charles Laughton's return to the stage after fifteen years in *Galileo* at the Coronet Theater in July 1947.[31] In the same year, Sydney was immortalized in a Bugs Bunny cartoon, *Slick Hare*, taking his rightful place among all the other celebrities including his friend Humphrey Bogart who orders fried rabbit. Bugs rebounds off the enormous bulk of the fat man while trying to escape from Elmer Fudd.

He was surprised to find that many in Hollywood did not work as hard as he did. His thoroughly professional approach to his work and insistence on having the script months in advance meant that on the first day of shooting a film he not only knew his own role inside out but had learned everyone's else's part too. Of his fellow players, he rated Bette Davis as a fine artist although sadly never appeared with her onscreen. He often used to visit Phyllis Thaxter, who he had known since the time they appeared together in *There Shall Be No Night*. She recalled that work was never far from his thoughts:

> "Sydney … comes over nearly every Wednesday for dinner and we talk about the house I'm going to have. That is, for a little while we talk about my house. It's pretty hard to keep him off the subject of his work. He strides up and down the room waving his arms and going through scenes. No one could possibly work harder than he does."[32]

29 The Laurel and Hardy of Crime

> *"I'll never forget the movies I made with Sydney Greenstreet. He was one of the great ones."*
>
> Peter Lorre interview by Vernon Scott: "Sees Funny Side of Film Crime: Lorre's a Loveable Villain" *The Press, Binghampton, New York,* January 11, 1962, 18.

Greenstreet and Peter Lorre were one of the most recognizable and well-beloved teams of the 1940s. Polar opposites in some ways they complimented each other perfectly. These two different but highly professional actors came together to create magic on screen, and are still fondly recalled long after their passing from the scene.

They appeared together in nine films but were seen to best advantage as a team in only five of those. The contrast between the two actors was more than physical. Their approaches to acting were different; Lorre seemingly blasé and freewheeling, Greenstreet a professional to his fingertips. The difference in age seemed less important. Lorre was born in 1904 in what was then part of the Austro-Hungarian empire just as Greenstreet was making his American stage debut. Their voices complemented one another; the erudite Greenstreet with his perfect English diction and the curiously soothing Austrian-accented Lorre. They had several things in common, notably their innate intelligence and humor. They had this in common with Bogart which made their films together a natural joy. Crucially all shared the same kind of humor; sideways, sardonic, playful. Their acting always retained the essential spark of spontaneity which made it seem as though they were not acting at all. They were totally at ease on set, comfortable with themselves and each other. Lorre was often mischievous and toyed with the script, but Greenstreet, for all his insistence on being word-perfect,

Lorre and Greenstreet: two inimitable actors who were great individually and magical together on screen. Photo courtesy of Gail Greenstreet.

enjoyed the game of cat-and-mouse that they played. It was clear they thoroughly enjoyed what they were doing and brought out the best in each other. Like many of the strongest on-screen partnerships, for all the depth of their mutual admiration they seldom spent time together off-screen.

Their two last movies together were *Three Strangers* (1945) and *The Verdict* (1946). A great many names were discussed over the years in which *Three Strangers* was being developed. At one time, Bette Davis was earmarked for the leading female role, with Humphrey

29 THE LAUREL AND HARDY OF CRIME

Peter Lorre, Greenstreet and Geraldine Fitzgerald in Three Strangers *(1945). Photo courtesy of Gail Greenstreet.*

Bogart opposite her. In the event neither appeared and the triumvirate consisted of Greenstreet, Lorre and Geraldine Fitzgerald.

The story was set in London in 1938 and concerned the three strangers of the title who wish on a sweepstake ticket for the Grand National horse race in the presence of a Chinese god at the time of the Chinese New Year. They write their names on the ticket but no one sees what the other has written. Each go their separate ways and their individual tales are told. Crystal Shackleford (Fitzgerald) wants to be reunited with her estranged husband who seeks a divorce but she will not acquiesce so he can marry his secretary. Arbutny (Greenstreet) is a solicitor who has been embezzling funds and is about to be found out. West (Lorre) has unwittingly become involved with a gang of thieves and when one of the gang murders a man Lorre gets the blame and faces the hangman's noose.

The intriguing interwoven tale and the way each story panned out made for a curiously compelling film which was quite different and ended more unexpectedly than many. It was brought to life by three excellent actors who carried the audience with them on the journey. The device of three separate stories might have been clumsy in the hands of some, but Negulesco and the actors combined to make the whole thing connect seamlessly. There was none of the disjointedness that often accompanies portmanteau films.

There were many clever touches and it was no surprise to learn that John Huston co-wrote the screenplay. His familiar ironic humor came into play at delightfully unexpected moments. For instance, the scene where West (Lorre) enters the cell awaiting execution and the only record is "I Dreamt I Dwelt in Marbled Halls" which is broken and keeps sticking in one place. The story was based on a tale Huston once heard and at one point he was going to direct it but gave it to Negulesco instead.

Geraldine Fitzgerald was primarily known as a stage actress and made relatively few film appearances but they all had fine quality. Here she played a startling role of a jealous wife to perfection. Several actors were considered for the role of Arbutny, including Claude Rains, Lionel Atwill and Donald Crisp.

The curious bronze pagan Chinese deity seen in the film actually belonged to Greenstreet. He bought it at an antique shop in London with the proceeds of his very first work on stage.[1] Some months earlier it was reported that Greenstreet's image had been discovered at a native shrine on the island of Tinian, one of the Mariana Islands. It was thought that Sydney's resemblance to Buddha was the reason he had become a deity among them.[2]

Once again, Greenstreet introduced the trailer for the film; his face spotlighted in the darkness; "Come closer," he beckons, "I'm going to tell you another astounding story of three dangerous, incredible people drawn together by greed." It was again a highly engaging trailer for one of his best films. He handled all his scenes perfectly and he shared some delicious moments with Rosalind Ivan. The pure comedy of the scene where he asked for her hand in marriage was delightful. It was so subtly done, every nuance of his changing feelings was apparent in his eyes. He was accused of being too emphatic at the climax of the movie but actually that was entirely in keeping with the character and situation.

A scene from Three Strangers. *Left to right: Alan Napier, Peter Lorre, Greenstreet. Photo courtesy of Gail Greenstreet.*

Sydney as Arbutny in Three Strangers *in front of the Chinese deity that the title characters wish upon. Photo courtesy of Gail Greenstreet.*

Sydney (left) with his son John share a joke on set. Photo courtesy of Gail Greenstreet.

Greenstreet and Lorre were again the driving force in *The Verdict* (1946), an atmospheric yarn based on Israel Zangwill's Victorian novel *The Big Bow Mystery*. It was a classic locked door mystery. Superintendent Grodman (Greenstreet) of Scotland Yard has an excellent reputation and is about to retire with a spotless record. However, it is proved to him that he sent an innocent man to hang and he is forced to make way for his subordinate Buckley (George Coulouris), who he despises. Grodman recruits the help of his artist friend Victor Emmric (Lorre) to solve a murder and discredit Buckley so gaining his revenge.

The film marked the feature debut of Don Siegel who became one of the most influential directors of modern times. He had started in the film library at Warner Bros. and was responsible for the opening montage of *Casablanca*. He directed two short documentary films, *Star in the Night* (1945) and *Hitler Lives,* which both won Oscars. In an interview, he once said that Greenstreet had been partially instrumental in his elevation to features: "Both Walter Huston and Sydney Greenstreet went to Jack Warner and recommended to Jack that he give me a picture to direct, which was possibly one of the reasons why I got *The Verdict*," he said.[3]

There was a strike on at the time during filming which made life difficult for the cast and crew. Sometimes the director had no idea

Peter Lorre, George Coulouris and Greenstreet waiting to exhume a body in The Verdict *(1946). Photo courtesy of Gail Greenstreet.*

who was going to turn up on a given day. The lack of personnel and the unavailability of some sections of the studio meant that some of the sets used were not of the correct Victorian period. To help hide this fact abundant use was made of the fog machine. This certainly created atmosphere but there was rather too much fog at times and it tended to deaden an already somber feeling. In addition, it caused

Greenstreet to suffer badly from an attack of bronchial trouble. His condition was so dire that he needed to be put in an oxygen tent and filming was halted for two weeks without pay.[4] Lorre and the director were also reportedly ill, but whether that was the effect of the fog was not stated. In the meantime, they took off for a short break in Palm Springs.

In many ways, *The Verdict* was rather a disappointing note on which to say farewell to two of the greats of cinema. In prospect it sounded promising, but ultimately left one wanting more. There were some highlights, notably a spirited turn from Rosalind Ivan as an over-imaginative landlady. Such touches brought much needed humor to the proceedings. Ivan had known the author Zangwill personally and was an excellent stage actress with a great sense of comedy. She was first lured to Hollywood for a role as a housekeeper in *The Corn is Green* and stayed. This was her second film with Greenstreet and they had first met many years earlier when they were with the Greet Woodland Players together in *A Midsummer Night's Dream*. At that time Greenstreet was Flute, the Bellows Mender and Ivan played Hippolyta, Queen of the Amazons. She greatly enjoyed working with him again; "He's such a fine actor – and a nice person," she declared. Music had been her first love and she shared Sydney's love of the theater, and of Shakespeare in particular. "Shakespeare is such wonderful training," she remarked, "Basic, really. He is, you know, the Beethoven and Bach of the theater. He teaches you rhythm and timing and the differences between poetry and prose, and so many other things."[5] She felt that young up-and-coming actors and actresses were not benefitting from such training.

There were several successful scenes in *The Verdict*, not least the opening sequence when Grodman attends the hanging. The melancholy toll of the bell, Greenstreet with a deadly serious face and the irony of the brief conversation with the policeman on the beat congratulating him. As the black flag goes up and he is told it's all over now, he walks somberly away to the news that the man was innocent. The scene in the café with Joan Lorring worked well and the gathering of friends at Grodman's retirement party was another successful sequence. As always, the scenes between

Greenstreet (right) as Superintendent Grodman in The Verdict *with Joan Lorring as Music Hall singer Lottie Rawson. Photo courtesy of Gail Greenstreet.*

Lorre and Greenstreet showed their great empathy together. There just seemed to be something missing, something even intangible and perhaps the main weakness was the story which felt curiously stagey and dated. Some of the subsidiary characters were not well sketched in. At the first showing, Jack Warner was surprised by the ending and insisted changes be made to signpost the real killer. The film was neatly summarized by one reviewer who commented; "Mr. Peter Lorre, as an artist, trots along, a small mongrel of uncertain temper and dubious habits, beside the mastiff dignity of Mr. Greenstreet's inspector, a man whom Sherlock Holmes would have been proud to work with, and who gives a hint of substance to a box of otherwise shadowy and unsatisfying tricks."[6]

Many other projects were considered with Greenstreet and Lorre together, including *Private Eye*, a parody of the detective genre starring Bob Hope for Paramount. The film was re-titled *My Favorite Brunette* (1946), and although it featured Lorre, Greenstreet was sadly missing.[7] Jerry Wald hoped to make a version of *The Smiling*

Corpse, a satire of the mystery genre, based on a 1935 novel by Bernard Bergman and Philip Wylie. The story centered on a writer who invites a number of guests to his house and the host is murdered. The proposed cast consisted of Messrs. Lorre, Greenstreet and Bogart, augmented by Basil Rathbone and Sidney Toler. Unfortunately, this tantalizing idea was never brought to life on screen.[8] Greenstreet was in the running to play the lead role in the Warner Bros. horror film *The Beast with Five Fingers* (1946), a part which famously went to Lorre instead, marking his final appearance for the studio.[9]

With the release of *The Verdict* in November 1946, the screen partnership of Greenstreet and Lorre ended. Such was the larger-than-life personality of both men on screen that it appears they were together for far longer. But it was a mere five years and nine films they made together. They made many films apart from each other but generally they are thought of as being together. There was just something irresistible about them as a team. Perhaps this over familiarity was what caused them to go their separate ways. Lorre left Warner Bros. shortly afterwards looking for new challenges. He once declared "Sydney and I made so many pictures together we were becoming Abbott and Costello."[10] They were thought of so often together in the mid-1940s that it made headlines when Greenstreet did not feature with Lorre in *Hotel Berlin* (1945).[11] There is often a tension in most successful screen partnerships – they are usually opposites physically and philosophically – and they usually want different things. But Greenstreet and Lorre were always more than the sum of their parts because they were not a double act. They were both excellent actors in their own rights – and both had a sure gift for comedy, even seeing humor in the dark roles they played. Both wanted to explore their art further in different kinds of projects. Both were sadly frustrated with the way their careers developed. Lorre left Warner Brothers in 1946 and increasingly he was designated some poor roles as the years went by. In addition, he had problems with his weight. Later on, he badly missed Greenstreet, Bogart and his glory days at Warner Brothers. Greenstreet always hoped to be given decent comedy roles and dramatic parts away from stereotyped villains. Although they were both disappointed they will always be remembered for the roles they played together. Those films contained some of their finest work on screen and the serendipity of their meeting was one of the blessings of the age.

30 Prelude to Night

> *"I'm an emotional actor. And I've got to get the feel of a part before I let the cameraman start in. After that you get that all the gestures and expressiveness and lines come automatically. But it's a terrible strain. And it takes a lot out of you."*
>
> Virginia Macpherson, "Sydney Greenstreet is a Practical Joker at Home" *The Schenectady Gazette*, August 1, 1945, 23.

In the late 1940s Greenstreet played some intriguing roles in films. He was especially memorable in a strong supporting role in *Ruthless*. He was not officially the lead in *The Woman in White* but he dominated the screen as Wilkie Collins' complex literary creation Count Fosco.

Based on the novel *Prelude to Night* by Dayton Stoddart, Edgar G. Ulmer's *Ruthless* (1948) was an atmospheric drama which featured Greenstreet in a key role. The suavely caddish Zachary Scott played Vendig, an ultra-ambitious businessman. Louis Hayward had a good part as Vic, one-time friend of Vendig who charts his rise and fall. The film begins with Vendig addressing a meeting of a conference for peace. Knowing him as he does, Vic suspects Vendig's motives from the first. The film was a telling indictment of the business mind and had fine performances from a good cast.

Scott especially enjoyed working again with Greenstreet, who he cited as his biggest influence in acting terms. Scott reflected; "I always felt, and still feel, that my beginning in Hollywood was so auspicious for the simple reason that I was surrounded by some of the great talent in the business. Sydney Greenstreet was my real teacher as far as movies went."[1]

Stoddart's original novel was fiercely anti-capitalist in tone and criticized politicians of all hues. However, the film goes further in

A strained atmosphere during dinner at the Mansfield house in the underrated noir Ruthless *(1948): Left to right: Lucille Bremer, Zachary Scott and Greenstreet. Photo courtesy of Gail Greenstreet.*

many ways and probes into the psychology of the central character of Vendig so that the audience understands why he is the way he is. A perceptive interpretation of *Ruthless* is contained in the book *Edgar G. Ulmer: Detour on Poverty Row*. In his chapter "Beyond *Citizen Kane: Ruthless* as Radical Psychobiography," Tony Williams offers an illuminating analysis of the film in Freudian terms. He compares and contrasts it with Orson Welles' *Citizen Kane* and makes a cogent case for the elevation of Ulmer's underrated drama in the pantheon of cinema. "In *Ruthless*," writes Williams, "Ulmer combines the novel's political critique with a subversively radical psycho-analytic approach developing features implicit within its linear narrative structure."[2] There are no flashback scenes in the novel but, as Williams points out, they are essential to the film and provide a depth of insight into the motivations of all the characters, especially the protagonist Vendig. Ulmer had an intriguing career and displayed a remarkable but often overlooked imagination albeit one mostly consigned to working on B-movies. His *oeuvre* encompassed an atmospheric horror, *The Black Cat* (1934); a stark noir, *Detour* (1945) and a curiously memorable science fiction drama *The Man from Planet X* (1951), with perhaps the most melancholy-looking alien ever seen on screen.

Greenstreet found one of his most satisfying roles as Buck Mansfield. When first introduced he is already a ruined man, the worse for drink and needing to be held back from attacking Vendig. In flashback, his tale is told. At first when they meet, Mansfield is in total control; he has advance information with which he outmaneuvers Vendig in his business deals when the latter visits him at his home. The visitor is young and determined not to be intimidated. Mansfield is expansive and relaxed. Greenstreet tosses out his lines in his inimitable style; "Energy like yours, Mr. Vendig, is much to be admired in Wall Street between ten and three," he observes while walking over to the large colonial style window, "But in this house and in this climate, well, if you'll allow me to say, it approaches the vainglorious." In time Vendig brings him down, and these scenes were again well-handled with dramatic economy. The scene where Mansfield is besieged by creditors and his own board members contained a pithy comment on the business mind. Mansfield's underlings tell him that he is finished and that he has no alternative but to sign over power of attorney to them to salvage something from the debacle. "The touch of happiness in your voice is all the proof I need," he comments as he signs everything over to them.

There was an especially memorable sequence which begins with Mansfield admiring himself in a wardrobe mirror. He then goes to his wife's room but she is not in a playful mood. By this stage, she is already besotted with Vendig and taunts Mansfield with his age. It was a telling scene, wonderfully handled by the actors. Mansfield visibly aged when forced to see himself as his wife saw him in the mirror. The scene spoke volumes for their relationship; the self-delusion of an older man and the bitterness of a deeply unhappy younger wife. He made the powerful businessman curiously human and vulnerable. The veteran actor refused the make-up man's offer to make him look younger for the scene; "It's no use," he remarked, "If I feel younger I'll look younger, and no amount of make-up will help if I don't."[24] He also handled the

Marital trouble: Christa (Lucille Bremer, left) and Buck Mansfield (Greenstreet) shared a memorable scene in Ruthless. *"I like to think a role," commented Sydney, "I never just act it. I've never looked in a mirror to study acting. That's why I enjoy making motion pictures. I can see what I was thinking, something I could never do on stage."³ Photo courtesy of Gail Greenstreet.*

scenes at the party well. Mansfield has been drinking; he is broody then belligerent and finally vengeful. Greenstreet captures the changing moods of the character, memorably quoting lines from the Bible; "Though you set your nest among the stars, from there I will bring you down." The allusion to a minor prophet of the Old Testament was apt for the depth of feeling on Mansfield's part.

The flashback scenes were especially well done. Bobby Anderson and Ann Carter were two of the most natural child actors ever. Anderson was especially memorable as the young George Bailey in *It's a Wonderful Life* (1946) and Carter was wonderful as Amy in

Val Lewton's eloquent parable of loneliness, *Curse of the Cat People* (1943). In *Ruthless*, the flashback begins with the three friends in a boat singing the evocative ballad "Pretty Red Wing" which immediately establishes the era. The potency of music should never be underestimated. The scenes of Vendig's youth were illuminating; his weak and absent father (Raymond Burr), his embittered class-conscious mother (Joyce Arling). There is a stark contrast with the warmth of the home of Amy and her parents (Edith Barrett and Dennis Hoey). On first viewing the feeling is that the opening scenes are too long, but actually they are just right. The film has a unity of purpose sometimes missing from those that rely heavily on the flashback device. At the end of the first sequence when Vendig leaves the small town of his childhood and youth behind, he also breaks off the engagement with long-time sweetheart Martha. He tells her that he is going places; "I can see the road I have to take and the sacrifices I have to make." Martha asks him "Am I the first?" To which he replies, tellingly, "No. I am." It is an effective scene that could be overlooked but is essentially a key to the character. From here on Vendig loses his humanity, to such an extent that the words that end the film summarizes what he becomes; "He wasn't a man, he was a way of life."

Critical reaction at the time was unsurprisingly negative in tone but Williams and others have made more considered appraisals of the film that have deservedly raised its reputation over recent years. A reviewer of the fine Blu-ray version release brought attention to the film's "quietly subversive" quality which encapsulates its curious appeal.[5] It was reported that Greenstreet refused a double for the scenes where he struggles with Scott on the pier at the climax.[6] The scenes Greenstreet played with Bremer provoked much comment at the time, so much so that it was reported that producer Arthur Lyons hoped to co-star them once more if a suitable story could be found.[7] An attractive brunette, Bremer was a dancer who appeared in only a few films, notably *Meet Me In St Louis* (1944) and *Ziegfeld Follies* (1946); in the latter she danced with Fred Astaire. She showed to effect in *Ruthless* but it turned out to be her penultimate film. She lost interest in Hollywood and settled down to marriage and family life.

31 "Most unfortunate!"

> "I'm positively the meanest and most ruthless character in this one than I've ever been. I'm so cruel, in fact, that I think audiences will simply love me."
>
> Greenstreet talking about *The Woman in White* in an interview: "Meanest Man in Films is Most Congenial Actor" *The Star Press* (Muncie, Indiana), December 8, 1946, A-19.

A natural for works of literature, Greenstreet was announced as co-star with Nigel Bruce in a version of *The Moonstone* by Wilkie Collins, to be produced by John Collier with a screenplay by Arnold Albert. Alas, this version was never made. However, Sydney had a leading role in Collins' other most famous novel *The Woman in White* (1948), and it proved to be one of his finest.[1]

Collins had links to Greenstreet's home county of Kent having lived for a while in Margate for sake of his health. It was while there indeed that he became addicted to laudanum which he thought might be a cure for his ailments but which proved calamitous to him. His highly-detailed mystery novels were popular in Britain and the United States. Several versions of his stories were turned into successful stage plays. Although his work would seem to be ideal for cinema, few of the films inspired by his books have captured them successfully. In a similar way to Henry James, only occasionally has the unique atmosphere and spirit been transferred in any satisfactory sense to the big screen. There had been five previous versions of *The Woman in White*, including two British films; there have been several since. However, the 1948 film arguably comes closest to capturing the novel's elusive spirit.

The complicated story concerned arch schemer Fosco's attempts to secure the fortune of Laura Fairlie (Eleanor Parker). Having already driven one sister half way to madness he then plans the

Count Fosco, one of literature's most intriguing villains was vividly brought to life on screen by Sydney in The Woman in White *(1948). Photo courtesy of Gail Greenstreet.*

same fate for the other. Parker played both sisters. Alexis Smith played the unsuspecting cousin with Gig Young as a drawing master who is suspicious of Fosco. Agnes Moorehead appeared as Fosco's put-upon wife.

The film was well-received at the time in Britain; "Hollywood here has passed a formidable test with honors," said *The Times* of

London.[2] The low-key lighting and use of shadow showed a definite noir sensibility and was apt for the complex psychological nature of the work. English-born director Peter Godfrey began as a clown and conjuror in a circus before becoming a stage actor and director. Perhaps it was his experience in repertory theater or his British background that made him a sympathetic choice for *The Woman in White*. He had a varied career on screen as an actor and appeared in such diverse fare as a Will Hay comedy, *Good Morning Boys* (1937) and the Universal horror, *The Hunchback of Notre Dame* (1939). He turned to directing with mixed results. *Christmas in Connecticut* was perhaps typical of his comedy output and was arguably more successful than *That Hagen Girl* (1947) which was once voted one of the worst films of all time. However, along the way he made some interesting noir dramas, such as *The Two Mrs. Carrolls* (1947) in which he also featured in a small role as a racetrack tout. By the time he made his final film, *Please Murder Me* (1956), he was already well-established as a television director.

A good cast was assembled with some especially eye-catching character studies. John Abbott was a standout as the weak and foppish Uncle Frederick Fairlie, with his wayward hair, laudanum and coin collection, constantly berating his silent manservant. There were some priceless exchanges between Fosco and Fairlie, when the former expounds on his hatred of murder; "I detest violence … so clumsy." "Yes," replies Fairlie, "and noisy. Oh, no violence please! Police, bodies! My nerves could never stand it." The lugubrious-faced Abbott was a fellow Englishman who settled in Hollywood and played numerous small roles in a long career, but none as satisfying as Fairlie. In the 1960s, he popped up on television in some guest spots in such beloved programs as *The Munsters*, *Land of the Giants* and *Star Trek*.

Greenstreet had full mastery of the character and situation; even the way he handled the menagerie of animals, such as the cinnamon monkey with the ring tail known as Junior, perched on his shoulder. In the film, it was called Iago and added to the disconcerting reappearance of Fosco at intervals, especially when silhouetted in the French windows. No one would have guessed that the animal was somewhat testy and actually bit him at one stage.[3] In a curious

Italian poster for The Women in White.

statistic, the wardrobe department made sixteen suits for Greenstreet to wear during the course of the film.[4] The director had taken many soundings to ensure the accuracy of the period feel, and Greenstreet was consulted on the script, costumes and sets, to which he gave his hearty approval.[5]

Once again, he had problems dying. Death was always a tricky business for him to negotiate. His demise in *The Woman in White* was intensely dramatic; he was required to crash to the floor – no easy thing for a man weighing 260-plus pounds. On his first attempt, he missed his chalk marks on the floor and accidentally knocked into Alexis Smith on the way down. They ended up in a heap together but Greenstreet was soon on his feet to help her up. "So sorry, my dear," he said, "I seem to have made a complete mess of my death. I swear I won't take you with me next time." The next attempt he smashed into an antique table. It took a number of goes before one of the technical staff brought some better padding for him to fall on, which did the trick. "Through it all," reported an onlooker, "Greenstreet never lost his sense of humor. Ribbed by everyone on the set, he taunted right back." He eyed the padding. "They really didn't put that down to protect me," he joked, "The floor was taking a terrific beating."[6]

There had been the prospect of a stage version of *The Woman in White* even before the film was finished. Greenstreet discussed the idea with the British playwright Terence Rattigan. Director Albert de Courville expressed an interest in producing the play, but unfortunately it was another project which was not realized.[7]

Count Fosco was a tour-de-force for Greenstreet whose presence is continually felt throughout. He also had some of the best lines. When Emery talks of murder, Fosco tells him that murder is the last resort of imbeciles. "What, on the other hand, is so complete, so exquisitely final as well-arranged natural death," he purrs. There was a well-judged scene when his wife was introduced at the dinner table and he displays the bejeweled necklace to the assembled guests. One day it will be hers he says, taunting her with it, "We're waiting for that supreme moment when her thoughtfulness completely overwhelms me," he says sarcastically, turning to her, "Aren't we, my dear?" Throughout, he made exquisite use of one of his favorite phrases; "Most unfortunate," who no one else ever made so loaded with such ambiguity. A typically English understatement full of irony. The correspondent of *Picturegoer* considered it to be his finest role, commenting "Fat, sophisticated, polished and yet given to odd moments of unleashed fury, this rich scoundrel gave Sydney a rare opportunity which he savored lovingly, like a connoisseur of old brandy."[8]

Among the cast, Alexis Smith was especially fascinated by the old trouper; "Alexis was mesmerized by Sydney Greenstreet," said [Craig] Stevens, "He memorized the entire script. He knew everyone's role. She just thought he was fascinating to be around."[9] Towards the end of filming Smith broke her ankle but went against doctor's orders to finish shooting her scenes so that Sydney could get away in time for his next assignment in *The Hucksters*.[10]

32 The Velvet Touch

> *"There's something about an empty theater. Memories, lingering images, echoes of all the emotions these windowless walls have seen."*
>
> Captain Danbury to Valerie Stanton
> in *The Velvet Touch*.

In 1947 Greenstreet sought his release from Warner Bros. and eventually succeeded in going freelance. In the meantime, he made some films on loan to MGM. He appeared in a good variety of roles including the most uncouth character he had ever been called on to portray, but made a fine contrast in *The Velvet Touch* as a gentlemanly police captain.

The Hucksters (1947) was based on Frederick Wakeman's caustic novel about radio advertising. Clark Gable starred as Victor Norman, a returning war veteran trying to re-establish his way in the world of the hard sell. The novel had spent over half a year at the top of the bestseller lists and raised much controversy, not least because Norman was in love with a married woman. Gable insisted that this be changed to a war widow in the film, in a role played by Deborah Kerr.[1] It was the great British actress' first Hollywood movie and a part she later admitted she detested. The supporting cast featured a good turn from Adolphe Menjou as a harassed executive, and an eye-catching Ava Gardner as a nightclub singer.

In the process of transferring the novel to Broadway and after that to the screen, some of its strength of purpose was diluted in favor of a more standard romantic yarn with an advertising background. However, one personality that was brought to life much as he appeared in the novel was Evan Llewellyn Evans, ably portrayed by Greenstreet. Evans was by far the crudest character he ever essayed and the scene where he spits on the table to prove a point was one of the most startling and memorable in the film. "You have

The cast of The Hucksters *(1947): Left to right: Greenstreet, Deborah Kerr, Clark Gable, Ava Gardner and Adolphe Menjou. Photo courtesy of Gail Greenstreet.*

Lobby card showing Victor Norman (Clark Gable, left) confronting the domineering soap king Evan Llewellyn Evans (Greenstreet) in The Hucksters.

seen me do a disgusting thing," he declares to his astonished board members, "But you'll never forget it." Later he poured water on the table to prove a point and at the end he was doused with a carafe of water by Clark Gable. That did not happen in the book. But it was well worth Greenstreet's while to suffer such ignominies; he was paid $50,000 for his four days' work on *The Hucksters*, reportedly one of the highest salaries ever paid to an actor at that time.[2] It was a suitably theatrical portrayal which captured much of the spirit of the book. The critic Herbert Cohn wrote a perceptive piece about the film and the vagaries of adapting a work of fiction for the screen. He pointed out the deficiencies of the screen version, the introduction of a conventional romance, the softening of the biting satire of the novel. However, he delighted in Greenstreet's performance. "One character is drawn as acidulously and unforgettable as Wakeman drew it straight off the printed page – straw hat, bandana, spit and all. He has never had a more spectacular part, never played with more striking effect."[3] The vulgar Evans "thinks of America as a blank space between New York and Hollywood where people buy soap." His minions are there merely to say yes to everything. "A figure of speech," he says, tossing his straw hat away, "a straw in the wind. Check?" All the yes-men echo in unison "Check!" The character was a gift to an experienced player such as Greenstreet who featured extensively in a preview of the film in *Life* magazine in December 1946. The article noted the resemblance of the character to the Lucky Strike cigarette tycoon George Washington Hill, described as "an egocentric genius with a flair for the dramatic."[4] The film was ably directed by veteran Jack Conway, his penultimate movie. It earned over $4 million at the U. S. box office but failed to ignite in the rest of the world.[5] On its release it received a critical mauling. However, what praise was on offer went to Greenstreet. Bosley Crowther lauded his "entertaining and fascinating" portrait of the soap magnate.[6] *Variety* declared that he gave "the performance of the picture."[7]

In complete contrast, *The Velvet Touch* (1948) was an unusual crime drama set in the world of the theater. Rosalind Russell played a leading Broadway actress who accidentally kills her producer but whose conscience constantly plagues her. Sydney appeared as the

Captain Danbury (Greenstreet, right) with Valerie Stanton (Rosalind Russell, left) in a scene from The Velvet Touch *(1948). Photo courtesy of Gail Greenstreet.*

detective, Captain Danbury, who suspects her from the first but who leaves her to make all the running, astutely realizing the kind of woman she is. Although somewhat overlong, the intriguing game of cat and mouse between Russell and Greenstreet was the chief delight. The two were able to convey the many subtleties in their dialogue and the denouement used scenes from *Hedda Gabler* to good effect. Claire Trevor was excellent in the supporting role of another actress who loved the dead man and is soon lined up as chief suspect.

Much of the earlier part of the film was told in flashback and so Danbury did not appear until some way into the action. Nonetheless, he made an impression the minute he was first seen framed in the door way from the wings of the stage. His familiar figure, paradoxically menacing yet reassuring, smartly-dressed, holding his stick and wearing a flamboyant hat. It was a suitably theatrical entrance in a screenplay that was imbued with a fine understanding of the stage and all its workings. Russell had a great love of the theater which showed in clever ways in the film. After testing his rickety-looking chair which creaks noticeably under his weight, Danbury disarms the assembled witnesses on the stage with his familiar laugh; "Ladies and gentlemen," he announces, "I trust you'll all bear with me in what may seem a long and sometimes discourteous process."

Danbury was an appealing personage, the polar opposite of Evans. He was deemed too gentlemanly to convince as a New York police captain by some critics, although perhaps the NYPD might have begged to differ. After all, no one ever complained about the not dissimilar characters played by Barry Fitzgerald in *The Naked City* (1948) and *Union Station* (1950). One could easily imagine the character would have made a popular recurring figure perhaps in a series of films. Danbury's courtesy and old-world charm made a refreshing change from the stereotyped bull-nosed no-frills policemen that often peopled so many films of the era and beyond. Greenstreet was ideally cast as the theater-loving detective who, during a performance, is to be found in his usual place in the audience "Row E, on the aisle." Few noir films have had the theater as background; the one that springs to mind most readily is *A Double Life* (1948). With its jealousies, temptations and insecurities it seems the ideal territory to explore noir themes.

Producer Freddie Brisson had found the greatest difficulty in making the film was tracking down the literary heirs to Henrik Ibsen in order to obtain permission to use scenes from *Hedda Gabler* as the play within the play. Eventually an agent in Norway was discovered who owned the rights. It was the first time the play had been seen on screen in any form. Incidentally the sumptuous theater set complete with majestic sweeping staircase was constructed entirely in the studio and based on the design of the old Empire Theater in New York. William Flannery, previously the unit director at Paramount studios, was the art director who captured exactly the opulent look and atmosphere of an old theater.[8] It was a curious irony that it was one of the few theaters in which Greenstreet had not played during his illustrious career.[9]

Greenstreet influenced the portrayal of the character in subtle ways. For instance, he joined Russell and Brisson for dinner one

Sydney visited by his son John (second from left) and daughter-in-law Beverly (right) on the set of The Velvet Touch *(1948), with star Rosalind Russell, left. Photo courtesy of Gail Greenstreet.*

night and she was impressed with the nonchalant way he mixed a salad and kept up a discussion at the same time, without so much as glancing at the table. Subsequently this was used in one sequence in the film where Danbury questions a witness at a restaurant. The creaking chair routine was another instance where art imitated life. On every film, he made certain that all chairs were scrutinized beforehand to see if they would bear his weight. In the scene when he is about to question all the witnesses on the stage he first checks the chair and gingerly positions himself in it as it creaks, chuckling as he does so. Such adroit touches make one think that Russell could have directed if she had so wanted; she was inventive and observant.[10] She enjoyed working with Greenstreet, so much that he was on board for her next scheduled production, *New Model*, a comedy by Harry Kurnitz and Collier Young.[11] Warner Bros. arranged a lucrative deal with Russell's production company worth $75,000.[12] It is not clear if the comedy *Lucky Penny* which Russell and Greenstreet had also discussed was one and the same as *New Model*, but in the event neither title was ever made.[13]

Sydney (seated right) gave an engagement party for his son John (left) and daughter-in-law Beverley (second from left), 1948. Photo courtesy of Gail Greenstreet.

On February 19, 1948, Sydney's son John was married to Beverly Harvey, a model and secretary of a dance studio; Sydney acted as best man.[14] Beverly's father was a doctor who originally hailed from England.

At this stage of his career Greenstreet was often suggested for roles but was unable to take them on because of his increasingly perilous state of health. The opportunity arose to play Cardinal Richelieu in MGM's rollicking all-star swashbuckler *The Three Musketeers*, however he was too ill and the role went to Vincent Price instead.[15] Nor was he able to accept the part of the Mayor in the Danny Kaye comedy *The Inspector General* based on the novel by Nikolai Gogol.[16] The film was known at one stage as *The Happy Times*, and the role devolved to Gene Lockhart. Richard Rovere's *Howe & Hummel* told the story of the lives of two notoriously crooked lawyers in nineteenth century New York who represented many theatrical celebrity clients. In 1948, there was a proposal to make a drama based on the book and Greenstreet's was one of the names put forward by the producer to play the role of Howe. However, the plans were abandoned.[17]

33 Flamingo Road

"Motion picture makers saw fit to shift my talents to the ways of evil and I don't suppose I'll ever know why."
"Sydney Greenstreet Was Shakespearean Comedian"
South Coast Times & Wollongong Argus (Australia),
March 7, 1950, 10.

In 1948 Greenstreet's health began to fail and he was able to make just a few more appearances on screen. He enjoyed a prominent role in political melodrama *Flamingo Road* as a corrupt sheriff in a Southern town which reunited him with director Michael Curtiz. In his final film role, he played an enigmatic saloon owner in the adventure *Malaya* and in the process arguably stole the show from two of the biggest stars of the era.

Flamingo Road (1949) was based on the novel by Robert Wilder written in 1942. In 1946, a successful stage production was mounted by Wilder in collaboration with his wife. It seemed eminently suitable for adaptation to the screen, but it took some time to come to fruition. According to reports it was in the planning stage for two years and went through a number of cast and script changes *en route*. Ann Sheridan was first announced for the lead role of the carnival dancer, but when she read the script she turned it down on the grounds that it had strayed too far from the original novel. At that stage, Wilder was brought in and wrote the screenplay. There were other casting headaches and at one point, Burt Lancaster was touted for the part that eventually went to David Brian, handing the latter his screen debut. Claude Rains had first been considered for the role of Sheriff Titus Semple and, although interested, was unavailable, so the part went to Greenstreet instead.[1] Few of Wilder's novels were filmed but he also worked as a screenwriter on later movies such as *The Big Country* (1958).

Greenstreet in character as the seedy, corrupt Sheriff Titus Semple in Flamingo Road (1949), one of the most loathsome characters he ever played. Photo courtesy of Gail Greenstreet.

The scene was set early with the voiceover of the jaded Crawford describing how everyone wants to reach Flamingo Road in Boldon City, "a small town with people of big dreams." The sly Semple is first introduced swinging on his porch. He turns to his manservant and observes "You know there was a time when if my hat fell on the floor I had to pick it up myself." He imbued the character with a distinct seediness, and surely no one ever glowered over a glass of milk with such intent.

It was rather a strenuous part for Greenstreet who was frankly not in the best state of health and was working against doctor's orders. He was required to climb a lot of stairs, smash windows and many other things and the exertion tired him out. "Haven't exercised so much since my childhood days," he joked.[2] It was trying for the old stager who was approaching seventy and suffering from diabetes but he was ever the perfectionist and was determined to do his best. He always put so much into his roles and this was no exception. It was curious that Curtiz chose two Englishmen for the part of Semple considering that the character is such an essentially American personality. Especially so bearing in mind how well-spoken Rains and Greenstreet were. However, Greenstreet caught the southern accent just right which was a major key to understanding the character. The other actors were ideal for their roles; David Brian made an effective debut and despite criticism of her, it is hard to imagine anyone else in place of Crawford. Much of the emphasis of the novel was shifted to Crawford's character, but in cinematic terms that probably made more sense. There were some fine vignettes from familiar faces including Fred Clark as a philosophical newspaperman. Lula Mae, the madam at the "roadhouse" was brought to life in inimitable style by Gladys George, one of the finest unsung actresses of her time. "I don't read the papers," she declares, "If I don't know what's happening I don't need to worry about it." This sentiment aptly sums up the attitude of 90% of the population then and now and was a comment on how such men as Semple were able to come to such prominence.

Once again, Greenstreet ended up dead, and had to negotiate the tricky business of dying. This time he was not required to hit the floor with a wallop as he did in *The Woman in White*. He explained his difficulty in finding a suitable way to die; "I have to sort of fold up," he said, "I need to be near a bed, a chair or a table to give me leverage while I slide to the floor gently and sideways." In *Flamingo Road*, he was shot by Joan Crawford and leant on her slightly as he slid to the ground; "Softest death I've ever had," he later remarked. Reporters joked that there was no possibility of any retakes because "Miss Crawford wasn't up to it."[3]

Joan Crawford (right) confronts Sheriff Titus Semple (Greenstreet) in Flamingo Road *(1949), his third film for director Michael Curtiz.*

He said of Crawford that she was "a tough professional, and a better actress than a lot of people realize," he continued, "Her gifts may not have been natural, her talents may have been carefully nurtured or even manufactured over the years, but however she learned, she learned." For her part, Crawford commented; "Sydney was a really fine actor, and it was a pleasure to have someone on that level to play in our scenes together. He certainly gave me a run for my money. What a presence! And that girth of his!"[4]

The scene where he threw the telephone at Crawford was suitably dramatic. Those old telephones were heavy, although of course Greenstreet was not the one who actually threw it. That was done by Herbert Plews who practiced for six weeks to make certain he didn't hit his target. "I finally made her change her hairdo," commented Plews, "She put a puff of hair out in front that the telephone would move when it brushed her forehead. Makes it more real."[5] The film was highly improbable, as its numerous critics are only too eager to point out, but the actors made it thoroughly enjoyable. It is never likely to be universally loved anytime soon but is a rare treat to those who appreciate the larger-than-life approach of the film's makers. A critic remarked; "Greenstreet as the corrupt sheriff gives a masterly performance. Vast reserves of power are well contained in his every word and act."[6] Curtiz' biographer considered Semple to have been Greenstreet's best performance of the three he did for the director.

The film was telling in its political satire and Wilder appeared to have retained as much as possible of the spirit of his original novel. The character of Semple may or may not have been based on a specific person, but his approach to politics was eminently believable. The cynicism of the political leaders who cooked up deals over card games in smoke-filled backrooms was well-captured. When Greenstreet blackmails the recalcitrant kingmakers into backing his campaign for governorship he declares "The public are all so used to you eating at the same trough. I wonder what they'll think when they find you've eaten the trough too." The pure greed of those in positions of power seems never to be sated which Semple defines as well as anyone. "He's the only man I know who can make a sow's ear out of a silk purse," comments the cornered Brian when thinking perhaps of the effect Semple has had on his deputy (Zachary Scott). Indeed, Semple's ruination of his own deputy was one as easily accomplished as his rise. At one point, the deputy tells Semple that he has been thinking; "Well you can stop thinking now," replies Semple swiftly, "I did it for you." The atmosphere of the carnival was well captured; the bored expression on Crawford's face under a thin veil as she does an afternoon shimmy dance before a few equally bored spectators for the umpteenth time spoke volumes. There were some highly effective set-piece scenes and good use was made of the old song "If I Can Be with You One Hour Tonight." Some of the dialogue raised a smile. At one stage Scott says to Crawford when they are in a romantic embrace "I love you. What's your last name?" The film has often been dismissed because of its implausibility, but if every film was dismissed on that basis the vast majority of Hollywood's output would have to go with it. Some films are so well made and acted that they transcend all their apparent limitations. *Flamingo Road* is arguably one such that deserves to be seen by all those interested in politics and those who hate the subject. *The Showmen's Trade*

Greenstreet (left) as the ambiguous Dutchman watches as James Stewart and Spencer Tracy get tough with a rubber planter (Roland Winters) in Malaya *(1950).*

Review concluded "Sydney Greenstreet, in a harrowingly villainous portrayal of a grasping, power-seeking politician adds another finely-drawn characterization to the gallery of memorable screen menaces."[7] The film marked the end of Greenstreet's contract with Warner Bros. He hoped to make twice as much money at other studios than what they were offering.[8]

There was little left for Greenstreet on screen. He was now suffering for the intensive work he had done in his last few films and was only able to complete two more assignments. He was one of many who made a fleeting appearance in the Doris Day vehicle *It's a Great Feeling* (1949). Day played a waitress who gets her chance in movies in this colorful musical comedy. There was a perfectly pitched performance by the wonderful Jack Carson, along with a host of familiar faces. Audiences relished the behind-the-scenes glimpses of their favorite stars. A highlight among the cameos came from Joan Crawford splendidly sending up her own on-screen image. Greenstreet's scene consisted of Day almost running into him with a tray after which he passes a few *bon mots* with her, exiting with his trademark guffaw.

Described by the London critics at the time as "exciting hokum," *Malaya* (1950) had a stellar cast involved in highly improbable adventures on the MGM backlot.[9] Set during the Japanese occupation of the Malay peninsula, it starred Spencer Tracy as a soldier of fortune and James Stewart as a journalist who join forces on a mission to smuggle 150,000 tons of rubber to a waiting U. S. frigate. Posing as Irishmen, not only do they make one trip, but three, with the help of a shady saloon owner simply known as The Dutchman (Greenstreet). In reality, most Dutchmen were imprisoned at Changi; however, reality was not allowed to intrude too much into proceedings. For instance, it stretched the credulity of those in the know that it would be logistically possible to transport so much rubber under the noses of the highly alert enemy even with Messrs. Tracy and Stewart leading the operation. To make matters worse they all wore white suits throughout the whole covert nighttime operation. Such slips apart, the film did decent business in the United States and more pertinently the rest of the world. It was popular in Britain and its Commonwealth where it was sometimes known under the title *East of the Rising Sun*. It was strictly the Hollywood version of the peninsula where the locals dress as pirates and call each other "amigo," and more like South America than South East Asia. "Malayans who see *Malaya*," wrote a far east newspaper, "will not easily recognize their own country nor themselves as others see them."[10]

Greenstreet had one of the best roles in the supporting cast. Without even so much as a name to latch onto, he created yet another memorable character study as the keeper of a saloon which was surely the Malay equivalent of the Blue Parrot in *Casablanca*. He looked somewhat more disheveled than Senor Ferrari but with the help of a laughing cockatoo and the enticing Valentina Cortese singing "Blue Moon," the allusion was obvious. This time he had to contend with the Japanese commander, who he managed to sidestep and bamboozle with his usual admixture of guile and amiability. He also enjoyed some of the best lines, such as when his guests (Tracy and Stewart) are about to meet the Japanese for the first time; Greenstreet turns to them and says nonchalantly, adding his trademark chuckle, "You'd better let me do the talking. Probably the only thing that stands between you and eternity is my vocabulary." There was a good scene when he rescues the hot-headed Tracy from the wily Japanese commander. Even when faced with interrogation the Dutchman was benignly equivocal; "You have access to facts," he tells the general blandly with a roll of the eyes, "I am merely a saloon keeper, I only have access to gossip." At one stage, the earnest Stewart turns to him and asks him if a German planter is a Nazi; Greenstreet shrugs "Who knows a man's politics?" It was a good role for him and he was fourth billed in a fine cast which included Lionel Barrymore and John Hodiak in much smaller roles. The movie was unsuited to the talents of Tracy and Stewart who both appeared to be adrift. Their roles were not well conceived and the romance between Tracy and Cortese never seemed convincing. At the time it was promoted, at least in Britain, with the byline "Tracy's Most Exciting Hit Since Northwest Passage."[11] Indeed, Tracy had requested an action role but lost interest part way through, and made it known he was in a walking mood. Stewart attempted to cajole him the rest of the way, with the notion that they would travel the world together.[12]

The only woman in the film, the beautiful Cortese, was unfortunately wasted in a badly underwritten part. Greenstreet did not look well, and seemed tired. This tiredness underlined the world-weary nature of the character he played and his apparent age added an elusive pathos. The Dutchman was philosophical and not a little wistful. "It's an inexplicable world," he says at one stage. Sadly, it was Greenstreet's last appearance on screen and although not a great film it was better than some and entertaining in its way, especially when he appeared. Most observers agreed that it was an appropriate role for him and that the old stager stole the show from the ostensible stars.

34 Radio Swansong

Greenstreet in a publicity still for the series The New Adventures of Nero Wolfe *(1951). Photo courtesy of Gail Greenstreet.*

Apart from a brief interview over a New York network in 1926, Greenstreet did not make his radio debut until 1941 and made his last appearance in 1951. He played in numerous versions of *The Maltese Falcon* along with mysteries and comedy shows with and without Peter Lorre. However, perhaps Greenstreet's best-remembered radio contribution was as the orchid-loving detective Nero Wolfe which was his final work in any medium.

He started his career in earnest in 1941 in a tryout for the NBC soap opera, *Our Boarding House,* mooted as a possible replacement for the hugely popular and long-running saga *Big Town.* Greenstreet was given a prominent role as a Major. However, the option for the series was not taken up by the station. There followed a first recording of *The Maltese Falcon* with the same stellar cast of Bogart, Astor and Lorre. Nor was this the final time Dashiell Hammett's perennial classic was heard because there were two further presentations in 1946 and 1950. Thereafter for the Screen Guild Theater he reprised two more of his film roles for *Across the Pacific* and *The Mask of Dimitrios*. A further Hollywood Star Time presented a version of *Conflict* with George Brent taking the Bogart role.

Greenstreet often featured as a guest of the popular stars of the day mostly appearing as himself – or at least the version of himself which Hollywood expected. He appeared to breeze through with the same nonchalance with which he had waved to Miss O'Shaughnessy at the denouement of *The Maltese Falcon*. In the process, he enhanced and happily sent-up his own image. The combined efforts of Bob Hope, Abbott & Costello and Edgar Bergen merely cemented his standing in the eyes of the listening public; he was game for anything. For one-off guest appearances, his fee was reportedly $2,000. Radio was a well-paid medium and this was slightly less than the average, but it put him on a par with Lucille Ball and $500 ahead of John Wayne.[1]

Much more suited to his métier were the occasional readings of Edgar Allan Poe and the stories of Nathaniel Hawthorne, whose dark romanticism appealed to him greatly. One of his favorite Hawthorne tales was *Rappaccini's Daughter*, a short story about a young student, Giovanni, who falls in love with Beatrice. But Beatrice has been contaminated by her father's garden which is poisonous and if he should ever touch her he would die. Greenstreet was also heard in an assortment of roles as shady agents and mysterious strangers. His distinctive voice had a great timbre that made him ideal for the medium. He actually went one better than his film career when he recited a speech by Shylock from *The Merchant of Venice* for the panel show *Which is Which?* Oddly, only one of his recordings was released on record, Poe's *The Cask of Amontillado* on the Decca label. The sleeve notes commented "No better man could have been chosen to feature in this gruesome tale … His voice can strike terror into even the strongest hearts with its steely, sinister implications."[2]

He was excellent in an early episode of the much-loved mystery series *Suspense* as Dr. Gideon Fell in John Dickson Carr's "The Hangman Won't Wait," of which unfortunately only the first half has known to have survived. In *The Fabulous Mr. Manchester* he played a mysterious kingpin ensconced in a fictional island somewhere off the coast of Italy. The story involved a U. S. newspaperman, O'Hara, who asks too many questions for his own good. Manchester was an ambiguous and menacing character with global influence. It was an eminently suitable role for the veteran actor who even got to quote Shakespeare at times when he spoke of "the dead vast middle of the night." The program sounded like the start of a promising series but no other episodes have come to light. Around the same time, Greenstreet made a pilot show for a whodunit announced by ABC entitled "The Key."[3]

For some time, there was much discussion about a mystery series called *The Fat Man*, based on the detective created by Dashiell Hammett. Warner Bros. wanted this to be an exclusive vehicle for Greenstreet and first envisaged it as a film and radio series. When the option lapsed, others took an interest and after much wrangling the series appeared on radio starring the relatively unknown Jack Smart. The lack of a star name made it difficult for the franchise to gain momentum and the show did not last long. However, Greenstreet essayed a similar kind of role when he played Rex Stout's armchair detective Nero Wolfe. This was perhaps the actor's most abiding radio contribution. An entertaining series, Greenstreet sounded hoarse at times but the voice was still recognizable and he had lost none of his timing or mastery of words. Experts on Stout's fictional character felt that the radio version as played by Greenstreet was some way removed from the original. No doubt much of this was down to the adaptors who decided that changes were needed to suit the format. For instance, several characters from the books were missing, and orchids were mentioned far less. Greenstreet was also considered to be much more jovial than the original. The author was enthusiastic at the choice of actor but disappointed with the scripts. He reputedly listened to one episode but stopped the tape after five minutes saying "he could take no more."[4] Even so, he commented that Greenstreet had captured the wryness of his character, unlike his two predecessors in the role on radio. The show also struggled because it could not find a suitable sponsor. It was a curious fact that five actors appeared in the role of sidekick Archie over the course of the six-month run.[5]

The shows stands up quite well today and the feeling remains that any deficiencies in the script were made up for by the actor himself, who brought a lifetime of acting knowledge and knowhow to bear on his portrayal of what would prove to be his final performance in any medium. It was fifty years since he had first entered Ben Greet's Academy as a hopeful twenty-one-year-old, and as he left the studio after recording the final episode of *The New Adventures of Nero Wolfe*, Greenstreet's long career was over.

35 Finis

*"I plan to start another career, be I 80, 90 or
a round 100 ... I am going to start a school of the drama;
spend the rest of my life teaching youngsters
how I got this way."*

"Screen's Noted 'Fat Man' Follows Serene Policy"
The Pittsburgh Press, August 5, 1945, 30.

When he was approaching seventy in 1949, Greenstreet had disdained any notion of retirement; "Pure rubbish, the whole idea," he declared, "What would I find to do except go mad from inactivity."[1] He really had no desire to retire because he was having the time of his life. Unfortunately, he had been unwell for some time and was ultimately forced to take it easier.

One of his oft-stated ambitions was to start a drama school when he retired and help another generation of actors.[2] He had always helped younger players, taking his cue from the ones who had helped him when he was just starting out. He had always maintained an optimistic outlook on life; "Look to the future for youth," he once said, "Look in the past and it does nothing but multiply."[3] He also spoke about writing his memoirs which he intended to call "The Diary of a Fat Man." "I'm old enough now to spare a little time to remembering," he reflected.[4] Unfortunately he never got around to completing the task.

As early as 1947 he was being ordered by his doctors not to work, but still continued until he was just too exhausted to do so. After 1949, he received offers for film roles and other interesting projects. One was a proposed British stage version of *The Maltese Falcon*, which W. J. Rosenberg hoped to mount in London. Among those suggested for the role of Sam Spade were Burt Lancaster, Richard Conte and Howard Duff.[5] However it never transpired. The prospect of a film version of the mystery series *The Fat Man* re-emerged yet again.

Sydney at home playing with his granddaughter Gail, circa 1952. Photo courtesy of Gail Greenstreet.

This time Columbia were interested in the idea and lined up Hunt Stromberg as the putative director, but the film was never made.[6] Greenstreet was pursued by MGM for a role in the colorful adventure *Ivanhoe*, but by the time it was made he was no longer available.[7]

In June 1948, he revealed to a columnist that he had had a complete breakdown; "That is why you haven't seen me around town," he said, "I made too many pictures last year and that was stupid of me. I shan't do anything this year until September. I just won't make so many this year that's all."[8] That same year he was greatly cheered by a visit from his brother Arthur and his young wife Gwendoline. It was Arthur's first ever visit to America.[9]

As time passed his health improved a little, but never for long enough for him to consider returning to work – unless it was something that really captured his imagination. In terms of his film career Greenstreet said that he was tired of playing villains; "Until I get a comedy part on the screen I'm just not making any more movies," he declared.[10] He was still able to work on radio which extended his career into the 1950s with *The New Adventures of Nero Wolfe*

Sydney at home with his son John (left) and daughter-in-law Beverly, circa 1953. Photo courtesy of Gail Greenstreet.

as previously discussed. In February 1951, he came close to making a return to the screen. His agent Arthur Lyons announced that Sydney was feeling better and would make his comeback in *Three on a Match*, a remake of a 1932 drama.[11] However the film was not made. John Huston wanted him to play the missionary brother of Katherine Hepburn in *The African Queen* (1951) but he was not well enough at the time. Huston also hoped he could play the flustered

Peterson in *Beat the Devil* (1953), but by then there was no question of his return. Both of those roles went to Robert Morley instead.[12] For all his ability Morley was ill-at-ease in the latter, something which he readily admitted. He had no time for Lorre with whom he did not get along and just did not seem to fit in to the ensemble. It was a role which was more suited to Greenstreet and his particular brand of nonchalant menace and inherent gift of comedy. There were many weak links in this curious enterprise not least the story and the lack of direction; 'Tiny' would have improved the situation immeasurably and the triumvirate of Bogart, Lorre and Greenstreet would have provided a distinct cachet at the box office.

The playwright Tennessee Williams wrote the one-Act play *The Last of My Solid Gold Watches* with him in mind and dedicated it to him. Elegiac in tone it concerned an aging shoe salesman who reminisces to a disinterested young man in a Mississippi hotel room about the world he once knew that has long since passed. It was written in about 1943 and a television version was made in 1958 for the *NBC Kraft Theater* along with two other plays, directed by Sidney Lumet. A young Williams had seen the Lunts' production of *The Seagull* in 1938 in which Greenstreet had appeared. The author wrote in his dedication; "This play is inscribed to Mr. Sydney Greenstreet, for whom the principal character was hopefully conceived."[13]

Sydney was deeply saddened by the deaths of his best friends within two years of each other. John Sayre Crawley, his friend for forty-six years, died in March 1948 in New York at the age of eighty.[14] A valued stage actor he had continued working until the last few years and had appeared several times in productions in the Berkshires. Dr. Seaver Buck died in May 1950 aged eighty-one, eighteen years after he and Greenstreet had first met.[15]

As time went on he was not able to accept any further offers as he grew increasingly debilitated by his illnesses. In addition to diabetes he suffered from Bright's disease, also known as Nephritis, which is a progressive problem of the ability of the kidneys to function correctly. He also suffered three mystery viruses and his weight dropped from 268 pounds to 215 pounds. His absence from the screen was noticed. There were several obvious Greenstreet roles that devolved to his various replacements, but the man himself was sorely missed. A number of Hollywood columnists including Sheilah Graham called him up again in 1952 and asked if he would be returning anytime soon. His answer echoed much of what he had said four years before; "I had a bit of a breakdown," he said, "and after fifty years acting it's too much of a strain."[16] To another reporter, he remarked "I was ordered by my doctor to take a long rest, and I'm doing it. I'm not making any plans."[17] Apart from his housekeeper, the redoubtable Janet "Scotty" Murdock who had been with him for many years since the late 1930s, he also had a maid. Unable to play any competitive sport any longer – he especially missed his beloved golf – he related how much he still enjoyed playing bridge after dinner. One of the final reports about him revealed that he had lost about 100 pounds and was unrecognizable.[18]

Sydney died on January 18, 1954 at his home, 1531 Selma Drive, at the age of 74. He was interred at the Great Mausoleum in the Forest Park Memorial Park, Glendale in a section not open to the general public.[19] Surprisingly, he did not leave a will and it also emerged after he died that he had been supporting the family of one of his brothers for many years. An earlier will was discovered dated June 24, 1948 in which he left the bulk of his estate, which was valued at $150,000, to his widow Dorothy and his son John. Dorothy was living in Oconomowoc, Wisconsin, and John was working at that time as a tobacco salesman and living in Oakland, California. Sydney left $2000 to "Scotty" Murdock, and $1000 each to his sisters.[20] His furniture was put up for sale in September 1954.[21]

Sydney's widow Dorothy died in Oconomowoc, Wisconsin in April 1972 at the age of eighty, almost forty years after being first admitted to the sanatarium.[22] John later moved to Tucson, Arizona and became a furniture buyer for Levy's Department Store at the El Chi mall until he retired in 1984. He died at Tucson on March 4, 2005 aged 84. He was married twice; he had two children with his first wife Beverly Harvey; Gail Harvey Greenstreet (b. 1951) and James Ogden Greenstreet (b. 1955). After his first wife's death he married Mary Cochran, who survived him. Like his father, John was a keen tennis player and an excellent golfer who won numerous trophies in the latter.[23]

At the time of his death, Sydney's brother Arthur Venn Greenstreet was still alive and all three of his sisters. Arthur sadly lost his wife in 1957 at the age of only forty-two; he died two years later in Birmingham at the age of 80. Hilda and Margery both died in 1972 in their eighties. His favorite sister Olive outlived all her siblings and died in Brighton, Sussex in 1981 at the age of 100.[24]

Epilogue

> "There is a powerful attraction about his smooth rogues. Unctuous as Uriah Heep, polished as William Powell, as brutal mentally as Bogart is physically, he offers an irresistible line in villainy."
>
> Leonard Wallace, "The Film Fat Man: Sydney Greenstreet" *Picturegoer*, January 21, 1950, 39.

> "Sydney Greenstreet was not only one of the nicest men and gentlemen I've ever known, I think he was one of the truly great, great actors of our time."
>
> Peter Lorre (Quoted in *The Lost One*, 220.)

In many ways Greenstreet's film career was a disappointment to him. He never found a good comedy role for instance, nor an ideal sympathetic dramatic role. Despite his unparalleled stage experience he was never called on to appear in any film version of a Shakespeare play. His debut in *The Maltese Falcon* ensured that he was cast as a suave and erudite villain for the most part. It suited him but he was not a one-note player. Apart from the problems of his size and age, he was saddled with other limitations including unimaginative casting directors and increasingly as he aged, serious health issues.

Nevertheless, his late-flowering film career ought to be celebrated for what it was and not for what it was not. After all, it happened against the odds. If he had not accepted Huston's film offer in 1940 he would, in all likelihood, have seen out his life on stage with the Lunts. Had he done so he would no doubt have been successful, but he would have been entirely forgotten.

The films he made were not all classics but most were excellent and he enhanced the less good ones like the trouper he was. His first was undoubtedly his best, but a close second was *The Mask of*

Dimitrios. Of the others, he was outstanding in *Conflict, Across the Pacific, Three Strangers, Ruthless, The Woman in White* and *Flamingo Road*. He even shone in smaller roles, such as the immortal *Casablanca*. At those times when the film was not so strong he still did remarkably well and lifted the material; one thinks especially of his saloon keeper in *Malaya*.

Greenstreet contradicted many of the pre-conceived notions that the fat man could only be a figure of fun on screen. It was an irony that one of the stage's foremost comedians should became one of the screen's greatest villains. As he once observed "There's no reason in the world why a fat man shouldn't have evil ideas. He can be as mean as anybody else. It's just that he's been typed, I suppose, as the pleasant fellow who ripples his belly as he laughs and laughs."[1] He set the trend but few if any of those that followed reached the same star status as he did. It's impossible to imagine anyone of similar appearance enjoying such a career today.

Greenstreet challenged the familiar dictum that inside every fat man was a thin man trying to escape. *Au contraire*, he appeared to be entirely at ease with himself and the world. If there was a thin man inside then he was obviously too content to want to escape. He breezed around as though it was the rest of the world that was missing out on something. "I've got a pretty good shape, even if I do say so myself," he once observed, "A stylish stout." One can hear the chuckle.[2]

For all that, Greenstreet would have been just as memorable whatever his physical appearance. He was an actor of rare intelligence and humor. It was also important that he was an Englishman in what might have been the golden age of the type. The advent of Talkies brought forward many an English stage actor to prominence; Claude Rains, Basil Rathbone, Ronald Colman et al. In common with most of them Greenstreet was cast as a villain; a tradition which, for Hollywood, continues to the present day. The idea of a specifically English villain appears to be a cliché these days. It did not begin with Greenstreet but he was one of the best. Perhaps it is the use of irony and understatement, two particularly English qualities, which are so little understood in the United States. Perhaps it goes back to cultural and historic roots. However, in the

1940s it was not just the English who were the bogeymen. Europeans were often given shady roles; one has only to think of Bela Lugosi and Peter Lorre who were driven into a career cul-de-sac by virtue of their accents and appearance.

In terms of his villainous screen persona Greenstreet was much imitated both at the time and ever since. In the world of comic books for instance, he was the prototype for a number of villains. In 1945, he was the inspiration for the leader of a band of crooks in the Batman newspaper comic strip, according to the artist who drew him. He was the inspiration for Spiderman's evil foe Wilson Fisk otherwise known as Kingpin. A supervillain and crime boss of New York he is pictured as a white-suited heavy-set man who carries a cane. Since he first appeared in the 1960s, Kingpin has gone on to menace other heroes such as Daredevil.[3] Greenstreet was surely the precursor to many a James Bond villain including Goldfinger, or indeed of any cultured gang boss with a nice line in suits and a sneaking admiration for his enemy. Greenstreet's cultural significance was even recognized by the cult writer Richard Brautigan in his poem *The Sydney Greenstreet Blues* and in a chapter of *A Confederate General from Big Sur* (1965) in which the author images a scene in a plush hotel apartment with Greenstreet and Lorre. The duo was also fondly recalled in the song "The Friends of Mr. Cairo" by Jon and Vangelis on the 1981 album of the same name, a homage to bygone Hollywood.

Perhaps if he had made his debut twenty years earlier Greenstreet would have enjoyed a greater reputation latterly than he now does. But there was a kind of symmetry to his career which effectively shows the history of popular art on stage and screen, only narrowly missing out on the television age. Beginning with Ben Greet's pastoral vision embodied by his Woodland Players Greenstreet enjoyed a career like no other. When he finally progressed to the screen he had so much experience behind him that showed in his every performance and assured him his place among the immortals of the silver screen. As film historian William K. Everson observed: "There were other fat men in pictures, but not with that suavity or the depravity underneath the smile. Even those who preceded Greenstreet in movies seem now to fit into what must be termed 'a Greenstreet category.'"[4]

In many ways, it is not possible to assess him fully because few if any alive now ever saw him on stage. He was one of the finest screen villains but he was far more than that. At the time of his death there were many glowing tributes to him that spoke of his work in the cinema of the 1940s. Such was only a part of his life and for all his achievements on screen it was left to *Life* magazine to astutely point out that he was "one of the most skillful Shakespeare players of modern times."[5] As an old music hall comedian used to say, "There'll never be another."

Publicity still of Greenstreet circa 1946. Photo courtesy of Gail Greenstreet.

Appendix

Films

Note: The name of the character Greenstreet played is in italics at the end of each entry.

The Maltese Falcon. Warner Brothers. 1941. Dir.: John Huston. Scr.: John Huston, based on novel by Dashiell Hammett. Cast: Humphrey Bogart, Mary Astor, Peter Lorre, Gladys George, Lee Patrick, Elisha Cook, Jr., Ward Bond. *Kaspar Gutman.* (Nominated for Academy Award as Best Supporting Actor, 1942) (DVD)

They Died with Their Boots On. Warner Brothers. 1941. Dir.: Raoul Walsh. Scr.: Wally Klein & Aeneas MacKenzie. Cast: Errol Flynn, Olivia de Havilland, Arthur Kennedy, Charlie Grapewin, Gene Lockhart, Walter Hampden, Anthony Quinn. *Lt. Gen. Winfield Scott.* (DVD)

Across the Pacific. Warner Brothers. 1942. Dir.: John Huston. Scr.: Richard Macauley, based on the *Saturday Evening Post* story "Aloha Means Goodbye" by Robert Carson. Cast: Humphrey Bogart, Mary Astor, Charles Halton, Sen Yung, Roland Got, Lee Tung Foo. *Dr. H. F. G. Lorenz.* (Winner of the National Board of Review Award for Best Acting, 1942). (DVD)

Casablanca. Warner Brothers. 1942. Dir.: Michael Curtiz. Scr.: Julius J. & Philip G. Epstein and Howard Koch, based on the unproduced play *Everybody Comes to Rick's* by Murray Burnett & Joan Allison. Cast: Humphrey Bogart, Ingrid Bergman, Paul Henreid, Claude Rains, Conrad Veidt, Peter Lorre, Dooley Wilson. *Senor Ferrari.* (DVD)

Background to Danger. Warner Brothers. 1943. Dir.: Raoul Walsh. Scr.: W. R. Burnett adapted from the novel *Uncommon Danger* by Eric Ambler. Cast: George Raft, Brenda Marshall, Peter Lorre, Osa Massen, Kurt Hatch, Daniel Ocko, Pedro de Cordoba. *Colonel Robinson.* (DVD)

Passage to Marseilles. Warner Brothers. 1944. Dir.: Michael Curtiz. Scr.: Casey Robinson & Jack Moffitt from the novel *Men Without a Country* by Charles Nordoff & James Norman Hall. Cast.: Humphrey Bogart, Claude Rains, Michelle Morgan, Peter Lorre, George Tobias, Philip Dorn, Helmut Dantine. *Major Duval.* (DVD)

Between Two Worlds. Warner Brothers. 1944. Dir.: Edward A. Blatt. Scr.: Daniel Fuchs adapted from the play *Outward Bound* by Sutton Vane. Cast: John Garfield, Paul Henreid, Eleanor Parker, Edmund Gwenn, George Couluris, George Tobias, Sara Allgood. *The Examiner.* (DVD)

The Mask of Dimitrios. Warner Brothers. 1944. Dir.: Jean Negulesco. Scr.: Frank Gruber adapted from the novel *A Coffin for Dimitrios* by Eric Ambler. Cast.: Peter Lorre, Zachary Scott, Faye Emerson, Victor Francen, Steven Geray, Eduardo Cianelli, Florence Bates. *Mr. Peters/Peterson.* (DVD)

The Conspirators. Warner Brothers. 1944. Dir.: Jean Negulesco. Scr.: Vladimir Pozned & Leo C. Rosten adapted from the novel by Frederic Prokosch. Cast.: Hedy Lamarr, Paul Henreid, Peter Lorre, Victor Francen, Joseph Calleia, Vladmir Sokoloff, Eduardo Cianelli. *Ricardo Quintinilla.* (DVD)

Hollywood Canteen. Warner Brothers. 1944. Dir.: Delmer Daves. Scr.: Delmer Daves. Cast: Joan Leslie, Dane Clark & guest stars including Bette Davis, Jack Benny, Eddie Cantor, Barbara Stanwyck, Peter Lorre. *Himself.* (DVD)

Pillow to Post. Warner Brothers. 1945. Dir.: Vincent Sherman. Scr.: Charles Hoffman adapted from the play *Pillar to Post* by Rose Simon Kohn. Cast: Ida Lupino, William Prince, Stuart Erwin, Ruth Donnelly, Frank Orth, Barbara Brown, Johnny Mitchell. *Colonel Ottley.*

Conflict. Warner Brothers. 1945. Dir.: Curtis Bernhardt. Scr.: Arthur T. Horman & Dwight Taylor, adapted from a story by Robert Siodmak & Alfred Neumann. Cast: Humphrey Bogart, Alexis Smith, Rose Hobart, Charles Drake, Grant Mitchell, Patrick O'Moore, Ann Shoemaker. *Dr. Mark Hamilton.* (DVD)

Christmas in Connecticut. Warner Brothers. 1945. Dir.: Peter Godfrey. Scr.: Lionel Hauser & Adele Comandini adapted from a story by Aileen Hamilton. Cast: Barbara Stanwyck, Dennis Morgan, Reginald Gardiner, S. Z. Sakall, Una O'Connor, Frank Jenks, Robert Shayne. *Alexander Yardley.* (DVD)

Three Strangers. Warner Brothers. 1946. Dir.: Jean Negulesco. Scr.: John Huston & Howard Koch. Cast: Geraldine Fitzgerald, Peter Lorre, Joan Lorring, Rosalind Ivan, Arthur Shields, Alan Napier, Peter Whitney. *Jerome K. Arbutny.* (DVD)

Devotion. Warner Brothers. 1946. Dir.: Curtis Bernhardt. Scr.: Keith Winter adapted from a story by Theodore Reeves. Cast: Ida Lupino, Olivia de Havilland, Paul Henreid, Nancy Coleman, Arthur Kennedy, Montague Love, Dame May Whitty. *William Makepeace Thackeray.* (DVD)

The Verdict. Warner Brothers. 1946. Dir.: Don Seigel. Scr.: Peter Milne adapted from the novel *The Big Bow Mystery* by Israel Zangwill. Cast: Peter Lorre, Joan Lorring, George Coulouris, Rosalind Ivan, Paul Cavanagh, Arthur Shields, Morton Lowry. *Superintendent George Edward Grodman.* (DVD)

That Way with Women. Warner Brothers. 1947. Dir.: Frederick de Cordova. Scr.: Leo Townsend adapted from the short story *Idle Hands* by Earl Derr Biggers. Cast: Dane Clark, Martha Vickers, Alan Hale, Craig Stevens, Barbara Brown, Don McGuire, Charles Arnt. *James P. Alden.*

The Hucksters. MGM. 1947. Dir.: Jack Conway. Scr.: Luther Davis, adapted by Edward Chodorov & George Wells from the novel by Frederic Wakeman. Cast: Clark Gable, Deborah Kerr, Adolphe Menjou, Keenan Wynn, Ava Gardner, Edward Arnold, *Evan Llewelyn Evans.*

Ruthless. Producing Artists Production released by Eagle Lion. 1948. Dir.: Edgar G. Ulmer. Scr.: S. K. Lauren & Gordon Kahn adapted from the novel *Prelude to Night* by Dalton Stoddard. Cast: Zachary Scott, Louis Hayward, Diana Lynn, Lucille Bremer, Martha Vickers, Edith Barrett, Raymond Burr. *Buck Mansfield.* (DVD)

The Woman in White. Warner Brothers. 1948. Dir.: Peter Godfrey. Scr.: Stephen Morehouse Avery based on the novel by Wilkie Collins. Cast: Eleanor Parker, Gig Young, Alexis Smith, Agnes Moorehead, John Abbott, John Amery, Curt Bois. *Count Alessandro Fosco.* (DVD)

The Velvet Touch. RKO Pictures. 1948. Dir.: John Gage. Scr.: Leo Rosten, adapted from Walter Reilly's adaptation of an original story by William Mercer & Annabel Ross. Cast: Rosalind Russell, Leo Genn, Claire Trevor, Leon Ames, Frank McHugh, Walter Kingsford, Dan Tobin. *Captain Danbury.* (DVD)

Flamingo Road. Warner Brothers. 1949. Dir.: Michael Curtiz. Scr.: Robert Wilder from his play co-written with his wife Sally. Cast: Joan Crawford, Zachary Scott, David Brian, Gladys George, Fred Clark, Gertrude Michael, Virginia Huston. *Sheriff Titus Semple.* (DVD)

It's A Great Feeling. Warner Brothers. 1949. Dir.: David Butler. Scr.: Jack Rose & Mel Shavelson from a story by I. A. L. Diamond. Cast: Doris Day, Jack Carson, Dennis Morgan, Bill Goodwin, Irving Bacon and many guest stars including Joan Crawford and Gary Cooper. *Himself.* (DVD)

Malaya. (Also known as *East of the Rising Sun.*) MGM. 1950. Dir.: Richard Thorpe. Scr.: Frank Kenton from an original story by Manchester Boddy. Cast: Spencer Tracy, James Stewart, Valentina Cortesa, John Hodiak, Lionel Barrymore, Richard Loo, Gilbert Roland. *The Dutchman.* (DVD)

Theater

Sherlock Holmes. Mystery drama by Arthur Conan-Doyle and William Gillette, Marine Theater, Ramsgate, Kent, & Tour, September 1902. *Jim Craigan.*

The Eternal City. Historical drama by Franz Werfel, London & Tour, 1903. Known itinerary & dates: Grand Theatre, Hull, East Riding, February 14, 1903; Royal County Theatre, Bedford, February 26 to 28, 1903; Opera House, Margate, Kent, March 26, 1903; Opera House, Tunbridge Wells, Kent, March

28 to 31, 1903; Theatre Royal, Dover, Kent, April 16, 1903; Theatre Royal, Gloucester, May 4 to 6, 1903; Pleasure Gardens Theatre, Folkestone, Kent, May 8, 1903; Theatre Royal, Worthing, Sussex, June 1, 1903; Theatre Royal, Ryde, Isle of Wight, August 3 to 5, 1903; Royal Aquarium, Great Yarmouth, Norfolk, August 23 to 25, 1903; Subscription Rooms, Dartmouth, Devon, August 31, 1903; Drill Hall, Falmouth, Devon, November 5, 1903; Public Rooms, Camborne, Cornwall, November 6 & 7, 1903; St John o'Ball, Penzance, Cornwall, November 9 to 10, 1903. *Bruno Rocco.*

The Merry Wives of Windsor. Comedy by William Shakespeare, Lyric Theater, London, 1904. *Sir John Falstaff.*

Kentucky. Comedy musical, circa 1905, London. *Jockey.*

Ben Greet's players made annual tours of the United States and England from 1903. Greenstreet was on every tour between 1904 and 1908/9. What follows is a partial list of the places they appeared. In England they played at the following venues in addition to those on the regular theater circuit:

Worcester College, Oxford & Downing College, Cambridge (Every year).

Jesus College, Cambridge & St John's College, Cambridge.

Royal Botanical Gardens, Regent's Park, London. (For five seasons).

Lowther Lodge, Kensington, London.

Witham Park, Ashbridge, Royston, Worcestershire; Warwick Castle, Stratford-on-Avon, Warwickshire; Stafford House, London.

In Canada: University of Toronto, Ontario; McGill University, Montreal, Quebec.

In the United States: Columbia University, New York; Harvard College, Cambridge, Massachusetts; Yale University, New Haven, Connecticut (4 years), Wellesley, Boston, Massachusetts; Princeton, New Jersey (6 years); Vassar, Poughkeepsie, New York; Smith, Northampton, Massachusetts; Bryn Mawr, Pennsylvania (for 3 years); University of Chicago, Illinois; University of Michigan, Ann Arbor; Converse College, Spartanburg, South Carolina; U. S. Military Academy, West Point, Orange County, New York; University of Pennsylvania, Philadelphia; University of Minnesota, Minneapolis & St Paul; East Aurora High School, Erie County, New York; Lake Placid Club, New York; Onwentsia Golf Club, Lake Forest, Illinois; Tuxedo Club, Tuxedo Park, New York; Oberlin College, Ohio; University of Illinois, Urbana; University of California, Berkeley; Brown University, Providence, R. I. ; Mills College, Benicia, California; Lenox College, Hopkinton, Iowa; Lake Minnetonka, Minnesota; Stockbridge, Massachusetts; University of Virginia, Charlottesville, Virginia (for 6 years); University of the South, Savant, Tennessee; University of Tennessee, Knoxville; Bar Harbor, Maine; Culver Military Academy, Indiana (4 years running).

Between 1904 and 1906-07 the Greet repertory of plays included: *Everyman, The Merchant of Venice, Macbeth, As You Like It, Hamlet, Julius Caesar, Twelfth Night, Much Ado About Nothing.* These were given at the Garden Theater, New York, March 4, 1907. Cast lists were not provided for most of these performances.

As You Like It. Carisbrooke Castle, Isle of Wight, in the presence of King Edward VII, King Alfonso XIII of Spain & members of royal family, August 1907.

Repertory of plays: *She Stoops to Conquer.* Comedy by Oliver Goldsmith, *The Merchant of Venice, Macbeth. Masks and Faces.* Drama by Charles Reade & Tom Taylor; *Wonder Tales.* Fantasies by Nathaniel Hawthorne; *Pandora and the Mysterious Box, Midas & the Golden Touch, Philomen & Baucis* and *The Mysterious Pitcher.* Tour, August 1908 to February 1909.

Pandora and the Mysterious Box and *Midas and the Golden Touch.* White House Lawn, Washington, D. C., October 16 & 17, 1908. *Shepherd.*

The Goddess of Reason. Tragedy by Mary Johnston, Majestic Theatre, Boston, Massachusetts, December 21, 1908; Daly's

Theater, New York, February 15 to March 18, 1909, & Tour. *Melipars de L'Orient.*

A Midsummer Night's Dream. August 8, 12 & 14, 1909; ***As You Like It.*** August 10 & 14; ***Hamlet.*** August 12, 1909; ***Twelfth Night.*** August 13; ***The Tempest.*** August 13, 1909, Columbia University Campus; ***The Taming of the Shrew.*** August 11, 1909, Gymnasium, Columbia University.

The Road to Yesterday. Drama by Beulah Marie Dix & Evelyn Greenleaf Sutherland, Duquesne Theater, Pittsburgh, PA, September 27, 1909.

The Little Minister. Drama based on the novel by J. M. Barrie, The Duquesne Theater, Pittsburgh, October 1, 1909.

Are You a Mason? Comedy by Leo Ditrichstein, The Duquesne Theater, Pittsburgh, October 12, 1909. *Grand Master.*

A Lady of Quality. Romantic drama based on the novel by Frances Hodgson Burnett, The Duquesne Theater, Pittsburgh, October 15, 1909.

Rose of the Rancho. Adventure drama by David Belasco, The Duquesne Theater, Pittsburgh, October 19, 1909.

The Two Orphans. Melodrama by Adolphe d'Ennery & Eugene Cormon, The Duquesne Theater, Pittsburgh, October 24, 1909.

Sherlock Holmes. Mystery drama by William Gillette, The Duquesne Theater, Pittsburgh, November 3, 1909.

Prince Chap. Drama by Edward Peple, The Duquesne Theater, Pittsburgh, November 10, 1909. *Marcus Runion, the butler.*

When Knighthood Was In Flower. Comedy by Paul Kester from the novel by Charles Major, The Duquesne Theater, Pittsburgh, November 15, 1909. *King Henry VIII.*

When We Were Twenty-One. Comedy drama by Esmond V. Esmond, The Duquesne Theater, Pittsburgh, November 21, 1909.

Mrs. Temple's Telegram. Comedy by Frank Wyatt, The Duquesne Theater, Pittsburgh, December 1, 1909.

Leah Kleschna. Drama by C. M. S. McClellan, The Duquesne Theater, Pittsburgh, December 4, 1909.

Secret Service. Mystery drama by William Gillette, The Duquesne Theater, Pittsburgh, December 7, 1909.

Divorcons. Comedy adapted by Margaret Mayo from the French original by Victorien Sardou, The Duquesne Theater, Pittsburgh, December 12, 1909.

Romeo and Juliet. The Duquesne Theater, Pittsburgh, December 26, 1909.

What Happened to Jones? Farce by George H. Broadhurst, The Duquesne Theater, Pittsburgh, December 28, 1909.

Ranson's Folly. Drama by Richard Harding Davis, The Duquesne Theater, Pittsburgh, January 11, 1910. *Colonel Bolland.*

Saint Elmo. Drama by Augusta Jane Evans, The Duquesne Theater, Pittsburgh, January 18, 1910.

The Merchant of Venice. The Duquesne Theater, Pittsburgh, January 25, 1910. *Launcelot Gobbo.*

My Friend from India. Farce comedy by Henry A. du Souchet, The Duquesne Theater, Pittsburgh, January 31 to February 4, 1910. *Erastus Underholt.*

A Temperance Town. Satire by Charles Hoyt, The Duquesne Theater, Pittsburgh, March 28, 1910.

As You Like It. Comedy by William Shakespeare, The Duquesne Theater, Pittsburgh, April 5, 1910.

The Dairy Farm. Drama by Eleanor Merron, The Duquesne Theater, Pittsburgh, April 12, 1910. *Squire Hurley.*

East Lynn. Melodrama based on the book by Mrs. Wood, The Duquesne Theater, Pittsburgh, April 17, 1910.

The Climbers. Drama by Clyde Fitch, The Duquesne Theater, Pittsburgh, April 22, 1910.

Camille. Romantic drama by Alexandre Dumas, *fils,* The Duquesne Theater, Pittsburgh, April 27, 1910.

My Cinderella Girl. Musical comedy by Richard Walton Tully, Robert Baker, C. P. McDonald & Edmond Stevens; music & lyrics by Frederick William Peters & Harold Atteridge; Tour September to November 1910; Known dates & venues: The Auditorium, South Bend, Indiana, September 13, 1910; Nelson Theater, Logansport, Indiana, September 15, 1910; Temple Theater, Alton, Illinois, September 21, 1910; Empire Theater, Quincy, Illinois, September 24, 1910; Ebinger Grand Theater, Fort Madison, Indianapolis, September 25, 1910; Auditorium, Galesburg, Illinois, September 27, 1910; Burtis Opera House, Davenport, Indiana, October 1, 1910; Auditorium, Morrison, Indiana, October 3, 1910; Academy, Sterling, Illinois, October 4, 1910; Derthick's Opera House, Belvidere, Illinois, October 6, 1910; Plumb Opera House, Streator, Illinois, October 8, 1910; Chatterton Theater, Bloomington, Illinois, October 11, 1910; Elks' Theater, Taylorville, Illinois, October 13, 1910; Pattee Opera House, Monmouth, Illinois, October 29, 1910; Zimmerman Opera House, La Salle, Chicago, Illinois, November 1, 1910.[1]

The Nest-Egg. Drama by Anne Caldwell, Plainfield Theater, New Jersey, November 12, 1910.

Mankind. Morality play, The Hackett Theater, New York, December 9, 1910. *Nought.*

The Second Shepherd's Play. Miracle play, The Hackett Theater, New York, December 9, 1910. *Shepherd.*

The Duchess of Suds. Historical drama by Miriam Michelson, Tour, December 1910 to January 1911. *Captain Bustamaenty.*

Thais. Allegorical drama by Paul Wilstach based on the book by Anatole France, with music by Massanet, Criterion Theater, Manhattan, March 13, 1911; Ford's Grand Opera House, New York, December 11, 1911. *Cephanes, cook to Thais.*

Soldiers of Fortune. Drama by Augustus Thomas, West End Theatre, New York, May 1, 1911. *MacWilliams.*

The Liars. Comedy by Henry Arthur Jones, West End Theater, New York, May 6, 1911. *Archibald Coke.*

Strongheart. Drama by William C. de Mille, West End Theatre, New York, May 10, 1911.

Paid in Full. Drama by Eugene Walter, West End Theatre, New York, May 21, 1911.

The Great Divide. Drama by William Vaughn Moody, West End Theatre, New York, May 27, 1911. *Lon Anderson.*

The Lion and the Mouse. Drama by Charles Klein, West End Theater, New York, June 11, 1911.

Rose the Circus Girl. Drama, West End Theater, New York, June 15, 1911.

Ingomar. Drama by Eligius Franz Josef Munch-Bellinghausen & Maria Lovell, West End Theater, New York, June 18 to 22, 1911.

Secret Service. Drama by William Gillette, Savoy Theater, Asbury Park, New Jersey, June 26 to June 30, 1911. *General.*

The Merchant of Venice. Public School 64, New York, July 29, 1911. *Gratiano.*

Speed. Satiric comedy by Lee Wilson Dodd, Collier's Comedy Theater, New York, September 9 to September 18, 1911. *Billy Podmore.*

Excuse Me. Farce by Rupert Hughes, Tour, December 1911 to April 1912; November 1912 to April 1913. *"Little" Jimmy Wellington.*

What Ails You? Farce by Rupert Hughes, Criterion Theater, New York, November 18 to December 12, 1912. *Archibald Petherbridge, Esq.*

Pomander Walk. Comedy by Louis N. Walker, Crescent City Athletic Club, Bay Ridge, New York, June 12, 1913. *Jerome Brooks-Hoskyns, Esq.*

The Romancers. Drama by Edmond Rostand, Grove Park School, Danville, Virginia, May 5, 1913; Country Club, Richmond, Virginia, May 8, 1913; Alexandria Hospital Grounds, Richmond, Virginia, May 12, 1913; Fort Myer Hall, Washington, D. C., May 15, 1913; Catonsville Country Club, Maryland,

May 30, 1913; Country Club, Scranton, Pennsylvania, June 7, 1913; Sylvania Country Club, Ohio, June 12, 1913; Trophy Point, West Point Academy, June 16, 1913; Knickerbocker Club Grounds, New York, June 25, 1913. *Straforel.*

Twelfth Night. Tour including Avenue Theatre, Vancouver, British Columbia, Canada, October 29, 1913. *Sir Toby Belch.*

As You Like It. Hudson Theater, New York, March 16 to 18, 1914. *Touchstone.*

The Taming of the Shrew. Hudson Theater, New York, March 19, 1914. *Biondello.*

Twelfth Night. Hudson Theater, New York, March 22 to March 27, 1914. *Sir Toby Belch.*

Lady Windermere's Fan Comedy by Oscar Wilde, Hudson Theater, New York, March 30 to April 10, 1914; Liberty Theater, New York, April 13 to June 1914. *Lord Augustus Lorton.*

Pomander Walk. Comedy by Louis N. Walker, Ocean Avenue & Lincoln Road, Prospect Park, Brooklyn, New York, June 6, 1914; Queen's Campus, Rutger's College, New Jersey, June 13, 1914. *Jerome Brooks-Hoskyns, Esq.*

Twelfth Night. Chautauqua Circuit tour, with The Ben Greet Players: 56-date eleven-week tour of Pennsylvania & West Virginia; (Known dates and venues): Monessen, Pennsylvania, July 20, 1914; Charleroi, Pennsylvania, July 21, 1914; Monongahela City, Pennsylvania, July 22, 1914; Homestead, Pennsylvania, July 23, 1914; McKeesport, Pennsylvania, July 24, 1914; Braddock, Pennsylvania, July 25, 1914. *Sir Toby Belch.*

She's In Again. Farce by Thomas J. Gray, adapted from the English play *My Aunt* by Sidney Blow & Douglas Hoare, which was adapted from the French original *Ma Tante de l'Honfleur* by Paul Gavault; Gaiety Theater, New York, May 17 to June 15, 1915. *Anthony.*

A World of Pleasure. Musical revue; Book & lyrics by Harold Atteridge; Music by Sigmund Romberg, Winter Garden Theater, New York, October 14, 1915 to January 22, 1916; Opera House, Providence, R. I., January 24 to 26, 1916. *V. Gates.*

A King of Nowhere. Historical drama by J. & L. du Rocher MacPherson, Collingwood Opera House, Poughkeepsie, New York, February 19, 1916; Maxine Elliott's Theater, New York, March 20 to March 26, 1916; 39th Street Theater, New York, March 27, 1916 to circa June 1916; & Tour: Academy Theater, Baltimore, October 9, 1917. *King Henry VIII.*

The Merry Wives of Windsor. Comedy by William Shakespeare, New Amsterdam Theater, New York, May 25 to circa June 1916. *Landlord of the Garter Inn.*

A Pair of Queens. Farce by Otto Hauerbach, A. Seymour Brown & Harry Lewis, Cort Theater, Chicago, July 2 to 26, 1916.

Give and Take. (Previously known as *Standards*). Mystery by John Howard Lawson, Wieting Opera House, Syracuse, New York. November 23 to 25; Hudson Theater, Albany, New York, November 27 to 29, 1916; Van Curler Opera House, Schenectady, New York, November 30, 1916. *Daniel Drum.*

Here Comes the Bride. Farce by Max Marcin & Roy Atwell, Van Curler Theater, Schenectady, New York, February 10, 1917; Star Theater, Buffalo, New York, February 19 to 20, 1917. *Judge Huselton.*

King Henry VIII. Drama by William Shakespeare, National Theatre, Washington, March 6 to 10, 1917; Nixon Theater, Pittsburgh, Pennsylvania, March 12 to 17, 1917; Lyceum Theater, Rochester, New York, March 19, 1917; Star Theater, Buffalo, New York, March 22 to 24, 1917; His Majesty's Theatre, Montreal, Quebec, Canada, March 26 to 31, 1917. *King Henry VIII.*

Colonel Newcombe. Drama by Michael Morton adapted from *The Newcomes* by William Makepeace Thackeray, New Amsterdam Theater, New York April 10 to May 12, 1917. *Fred Bayham.*

As You Like It. Chautauqua Circuit tour of Eastern United States and Eastern Canada with a Ben Greet company: (Known dates and venues): Cortland High School Grounds, Fulton, New York, July 3, 1917; Brockport, New York, July 4, 1917; Honeoye Falls, New York, July 5, 1917; Geneseo, New York, July 6, 1917; Cazenovia, New York, July 11, 1917; Cooperstown, New York,

July 17, 1917; Cobleskill, New York, July 18, 1917; Newark, New York, July 31, 1917; Oswego, New York, August 4, 1917; Riverside Park, Ogdensburg, August 9, 1917; Gouverneur, New York, August 10, 1917; Potsdam, New York, August 11, 1917; Malone, New York, August 14, 1917; *Touchstone.*

Friend Martha. Drama by Edward Peple, Booth Theater, New York, August 17 to September 1, 1917. *Elder Aaron Quane.*

The Rainbow Girl Musical comedy; book and lyrics by Rennold Wolf, New Amsterdam Theater, New York, April 1, to June 30, 1918; Gaiety Theater, New York, July 6, to August 17, 1918. *Martin Bennett, a butler.*

Twelfth Night. Garden Theater, Sleepy Hollow Country Club, Scarborough, New York, May 30, 1919. *Sir Toby Belch.*

Lady Billy. Musical comedy; book & lyrics by Zelda Sears, music by Harold A. Levey, Liberty Theater, New York, December 14, 1920 to May 21, 1921. *Bateson.*

Her Happiness. Drama by Paul Wilstach, Garrick-Shubert Theater, Washington, D. C., October 2 to 7, 1922; Lyric Theater, Allentown, Pennsylvania, October 9; The Playhouse, Wilmington, Delaware, October 13 to 14, 1922. *Max Mazarine.*

The Whole Town's Talking. Farce adapted by John Emerson & Anita Loos from the German original by Francis Arnold & Ernest Bache. Hempstead Theater, Long Island, November 13, 1922; The Grand Opera House, Wilkes-Barre, Pennsylvania, November 20 to 21, 1922; Academy Theater, Scranton, Pennsylvania, November 24 to 25, 1922. *Mr. Simmonds.*

The Magic Ring (Originally known as **Minnie & Me**). Musical comedy by Harold A. Levey, book & lyrics by Zelda Sears, Liberty Theater, New York, October 1 to December 22, 1923. *Henry Brockway.*

The Student Prince. Operetta, with music by Sigmund Romberg, lyrics by Dorothy Donnelly, based on *Alt Heidelberg* by Wilhelm Meyer-Foerster, Jolson's Theater, 59th Street, New York, October 1, 1925 to May 18, 1926. *Lutz, valet to the prince.*

The Humble. Drama adapted by Laurence Irving from the novel by Feodor Dostoyevski, Greenwich Village Theater, New York October 13 to 29, 1926. *Bezack, Examining Magistrate.*

Junk. Comedy by Edwin B. Shelf, Garrick Theater, New York January 5, to 14, 1927. *Ernest John.*

A Lady in Love. Comedy by Dorrance Davis, Lyceum Theater, New York, February 21, 1927 to March 1927. *Sir Jeremy.*

The Madcap. Musical comedy by Gertrude Purcell; music by Maurice Rubens, lyrics Clifford Grey, book by Gladys Under, based on French farce by Regis Gignoux & Jacques Thery, Tour: Lyric Theater, Allentown, Pennsylvania, April 16 to 19, 1927; Majestic Theater, Brooklyn, New York, May 2 to 5, 1927; Olympic Theater, Chicago, May 9 to August 13, 1927; Great Northern Theater, Chicago, August 15 to September 3, 1927; Metropolitan Theater, Minneapolis, Minnesota, September 5 to 26, 1927; Royale Theater, Brooklyn, New York January 31, to February 18, 1928; Casino Theater, New York, February 20, to April 28, 1928. *Lord Henry Steeple.*

Much Ado About Nothing. Broad Street Theater, Newark, New Jersey, November 9, 1928; Hollis Theater, Boston, Massachusetts, November Parson's Theater, Hartford, Connecticut, December 6 to 8, 1928; Capitol Theater, Albany, New York, December 14, 1928; Van Curler Theater, Schenectady, New York, December 17, 1928; Broad Street Theater, Philadelphia, Pennsylvania, December 25, 1928 to January 6, 1929. *Constable Dogberry.*

Marco's Millions. Satire by Eugene O'Neill, Liberty Theater, New York, March 1930. *Kublai Khan.*

Volpone. Comedy by Ben Jonson, Liberty Theater, New York, March 10, to March 17, 1930. *Volpone.*

R. U. R. Fantasy drama by Karel Capek, Liberty Theater, New York, March 1930. *Beck.*

Lysistrata. Drama by Aristophanes, Philadelphia, June 1, 1930; 44th Street Theater, New York, June 5 to August 14, 1930;

Revival: Majestic Theater, Brooklyn, February 8 to March 1932. *President of the Senate.*

The Admirable Crichton. Drama by J. M. Barrie, Erlanger Theater, Buffalo, New York, October 15 to 17, 1931. *The Earl of Loam.*

Berlin. Drama by Valentine Williams & Alice Crawford, George M. Cohan's Theatre, New York, December 30, 1931 to January 1932. *Dr. Grundt.*

Olivia Bows to Mrs. Grundy. Satiric comedy by Roland Bottomley, Great Neck, Long Island, March 26, 1932; Shubert-Belasco Theater, Washington, March 28 to April 1, 1932; Playhouse, Wilmington, Delaware, April 3 to April 5, 1932; Parson's Theater, Hartford, Connecticut, April 8 to 10, 1932. *Colonel Bumperley.*

The Good Earth. Drama adapted by Owen & Donald Davis from the novel by Pearl S. Buck, Guild Theater, New York, October 17 to December 3, 1932. *Wang Lung's Uncle.*

Roberta. Musical comedy; music by Jerome Kern, book & lyrics by Otto Harbach adapted from the novel *Gowns By Roberta* by Alice Duer Miller; New Amsterdam Theater, November 18, 1933 to July 21, 1934; & Tour; Strand Theater, Ithaca, New York, November 7, 1934. *Lord Henry Delves, the friend of Roberta.*

The Taming of the Shrew. Drama by William Shakespeare, Guild Theater, New York, September 30, 1935 to January 1936. *Baptista.*

Idiot's Delight. Drama by Robert E. Sherwood, Shubert Theater, New York, March 24 to December 1936. *Dr. Waldesee.*

Amphytron 38. Satiric drama adapted by S. N. Behrman from the original play by Jean Giradoux, Shubert Theater, New York, November 1, 1937 to March 1938, & tour of Britain, June to August, 1938. *Trumpeter.*

The Seagull. Drama by Anton Chekhov, Shubert Theater, New York, March 28 to May 1938. *Peter Sorin.*

Tour of *Idiot's Delight, Amphytron 38* and *The Seagull* 1938 to 1939: Partial itinerary of route from Chicago: American Theater, St Louis, Missouri, January 23, 1939; Municipal Hall, Kansas City, Missouri, January 28, 31 & February 1, 1939; The Forum, Wichita, Kansas, February 2; Shrine Auditorium, Oklahoma City, Oklahoma, February 3 & 4; Majestic Theater, Fort Worth, Texas, February 6 & 7; Majestic Theater, Dallas, Texas, February 8, 9 & 10; Waco Hall, Waco, Texas, February 11; Paramount, Austin, Texas, February 13; Majestic, Houston, Texas, February 14, 15 & 16; Majestic, San Antonio, Texas, February 17 & 18, 1939.

The Taming of the Shrew. Washington, D. C., October 1939; New Theater, University of Madison, Madison, Wisconsin; Milwaukee, Wisconsin; St Paul, Lyceum Theater, Minneapolis, Minnesota; Shrine Auditorium, Des Moines, Iowa; Sioux City, Iowa; Technical High School Auditorium, Omaha, Nebraska; American Theater, St Louis, Missouri; Alvin Theater, New York, February 5 to 10, 1940. *Baptista.*

There Shall Be No Night. Drama by Robert E. Sherwood, Alvin Theater, New York, April 29 to August 9, 1940 & September 9 to November 2, 1940 & Tour, 1940-41. *Uncle Waldemar.*

Radio

Sydney Greenstreet interviewed by Terese Rose Nagel, broadcast on station WGBS, New York, November 1926. *Guest.*[1]

Our Boarding House. NBC Small-town soap opera audition show as possible replacement for *Big Town* by Ruthrauff & Ryan, June 1941. *Major Hoople.*[2]

Vallee Varieties. NBC comedy/variety show hosted by Rudy Vallee, January 14, 1943. *Guest.*

Lady Esther Screen Guild Theater. CBS Drama. "Across the Pacific," with Mary Astor, Humphrey Bogart, January 25, 1943. *Dr. Lorenz.* "The Maltese Falcon" with Humphrey Bogart, Mary Astor, September 20, 1943. *Kaspar Gutman.* "The Mask of Dimitrios" with Peter Lorre, Zachary Scott, April 16, 1945. *Mr. Peters/Peterson.* "The Velvet Touch" with Rosalind Russell, January 10, 1949. *Captain Danbury.*

Suspense. CBS Mystery drama series. "The Hangman Won't Wait" by John Dickson Carr, with Ian Martin, February 9, 1943. *Dr. Gideon Fell.*

The Charlie McCarthy Show. NBC Comedy show, with Edgar Bergen, Bill Thompson, Ray Noble & His Orchestra, March 7, 1943. *Guest.*

The Abbott & Costello Show. ABC Comedy series, with Connie Haines, Freddie Rich, February 24, 1944. *Guest.*

The Amos and Andy Show. NBC Comedy variety serial, with Freeman Gosdell, Charles Correll, Harlow Wilcox (announcer), September 29, 1944. *Hotel House Detective.*

The Dinah Shore Show. "Birds Eye Opera House" NBC Variety show, with Peter Lorre, November 23, 1944. *Guest.*

Which is Which? CBS quiz show, with Dick Nelson, Frances Langford, Richard Himber & His Orchestra, Greenstreet recites a speech by Shylock from *The Merchant of Venice*, December 6, 1944. *Guest.*

Duffy's Tavern. CBS Comedy Variety show, with Ed Gardner, December 15, 1944. *Guest.*

The Andrews Sisters' Eight-to-the-Bar Ranch. NBC-Blue Network, with Gabby Hayes, Peter Lorre, January 21, 1945. *Guest.*

Command Performance. AFRS Variety show, (1) "A Visit to the Stars" with Peter Lorre, Jack Carson, Jack Oakie, April 19, 1945; (2) with Myrna Loy, Jimmy Durante, Dick Haymes, June 7, 1945; (3) with Jim Backus, Billie Burke, Miklos Rozsa, Dr. Samuel Hoffman playing the Theremin, June 8, 1946. *Guest.*

G. I. Journal AFRS Comedy, with Marie McDonald, Arthur Treacher, Jack Carson, May 18, 1945. *Guest.*

Baby Snooks Show. CBS variety show, with Peter Lorre (substitutes for Fanny Brice), Robert Benchley, September 23, 1945. *Guest.*

Request Performance – The Hour of Mystery Drama. CBS Variety show, with Mary Astor, Jack Benny, November 11, 1945, Greenstreet reads "The Tell-Tale Heart" by Edgar Allan Poe. *Narrator.*

The Alan Young Show. ABC Comedy series, with Jean Gillespie, Jim Backus, January 22, 1946. *Guest as "The Fat Man" in The Maltese Falcon satire.*

The Bob Hope Show. NBC/AFRS Comedy variety show, with Shirley Ross in skit, *The Case of the Missing Nylons or See How They Run*, April 2, 1946. *Guest.*

The Fred Allen Show. NBC Comedy variety show, "Cairo" with Kenny Delmar, the De Marco Sisters, May 12, 1946. *Guest as "The Fat Man" in Casablanca skit.*

The Radio Reader's Digest. CBS Drama, "Nazi Spies and the FBI" with Gilbert Mack, May 19, 1946. *Agent.*

Favorite Story of Sydney Greenstreet. KFI Los Angeles, drama, "Rappaccini's Daughter" by Nathaniel Hawthorne, with Ronald Colman (Host), Howard Duff, Janet Waldo, July 16, 1946.

Hollywood Star Time/Hollywood Star Theater. CBS Mystery drama; "Conflict" with George Brent, August 17, 1946. *Dr. Mark Hamilton.*

The Man from Below. CBS Mystery drama, April 2, 1947. *Detective.*[3]

Hollywood Star Theater: Sydney Greenstreet Presents Richard Basehart. CBS Drama; "Home for Christmas" with Richard Basehart, December 25, 1948.

Sealtest Variety Theater. NBC Variety show, with Eddie Bracken, Dorothy Lamour, Henry Russell and His Orchestra, May 5, 1949. *Guest.*

Louella Parsons. CBS Variety/Interview show, with Joan Crawford, Dorothy Lamour, at the Farmer's Market discussing Thanksgiving shopping, November 28, 1949. *Guest.*[4]

The Key. ABC Mystery Drama pilot, April 1950.[5]

The Fabulous Mr. Manchester. ABC Mystery Drama by William Cozlinko, "The Investigation" with Howard Culver, Jay Novello, Nestor Paiva, May 6, 1950. *Mr. James Manchester.*

Hollywood, USA. CBS Variety show, May 15, 1950. *Guest.*

The New Adventures of Nero Wolfe. NBC Detective Series based on the stories by Rex Stout, with Lawrence Dobkin, Gerald Mohr, Harry Bartell, October 20, 1950 to April 27, 1951. *Nero Wolfe.*

"Stamped for Murder" October 20, 1950; "The Careworn Cuff" October 27, 1950; "The Dear, Dead Lady" November 3, 1950; "Headless Hunter" November 11, 1950; "The Careless Cleaner" November 17, 1950; "The Beautiful Archer" November 24, 1950; "The Brave Rabbit" December 1, 1950; "The Impolite Corpse" December 8, 1950; "The Girl Who Cried Wolfe" December 15, 1950; "The Slaughtered Santas" December 22, 1950; "The Bashful Body" December 29, 1950; "Deadly Sell-Out" January 5, 1951; "The Killer Cards" January 12, 1951; "The Calculated Risk" January 19, 1951; "The Phantom Fingers" January 26, 1951; "The Vanishing Shells" February 2, 1951; "The Party for Death" February 16, 1951; "The Malevolent Medic" February 23, 1951; "The Hasty Will" March 2, 1951; "The Disappearing Diamonds" March 9, 1951; "The Midnight Ride" March 16, 1951; "The Final Page" March 23, 1951; "The Tell-Tale Ribbon" March 30, 1951; "A Slight Case of Perjury" April 6, 1951; "The Lost Heir" April 20, 1951; "Room 304" April 27, 1951.

Recordings

The Cask of Amontillado by Edgar Allan Poe, with Victor Young & Orchestra, LP Decca Records DA-479 [1946] 7" EP Brunswick Records OE 9171 [1955] *Montressor.*

Humphrey Bogart in The Maltese Falcon with Mary Astor & Sydney Greenstreet; B/w *Love's Lovely Counterfeit* by James M. Cain, with Lurene Tuttle. Green transparent vinyl LP exclusively produced for members of the Humphrey Bogart Memorial

Society, Command Performance Records LP-1. [Circa 1975]. *Kaspar Gutman.*

The New Adventures of Nero Wolfe: *"The Case of the Careless Cleaner"* (Originally broadcast November 17, 1950). Side B: *The Adventures of Ellery Queen* (Broadcast January 1944). Radiola Records MR – 112S [circa 1976] *Nero Wolfe.*

Adventure Series No. 12: The Maltese Falcon. (A) CBS Lady Esther Screen Guild Players, recorded September 20, 1943; (B) CBS Academy Award Theater, recorded July 3, 1946; with Humphrey Bogart, Mary Astor, Peter Lorre. Radiola Records MR-1091 [1978] *Kaspar Gutman.*

Joan Crawford – Live. Short excerpts from her films including *Flamingo Road* with Greenstreet. DPA Records (2 x 12" records) DPA 2-1402 [1978] *Sheriff Titus Semple.*

The Maltese Falcon/The Front Page. A: *The Maltese Falcon* CBS Academy Award Theater, recorded July 3, 1946; B: *The Front Page* with Adolphe Menjou, Pat O'Brien, June 22, 1946. Nostalgia Lane Records NLR 1503. [1979] *Kaspar Gutman.*

Casablanca & The Maltese Falcon. Hollywood Playhouse Series recorded April 26, 1943 & September 20, 1943 respectively. CD issued free with *Sight & Sound* magazine (UK). Mr. Punch (Audio) Limited 020 7368 0088 [1997]. *Senor Ferrari; Kaspar Gutman.*

Bibliography & Suggested Further Reading

Aeker, Everett *George Raft: The Films* (Jefferson, NC: McFarland & Co., Inc., 2013)

Astor, Mary *A Life on Film* (London: W. H. Allen, 1973)

Barringer, Millie *Margaret Webster: A Life in the Theater* (Ann Arbor, Michigan: The University of Michigan Press, 2007)

Behlmer, Rudy *Shoot the Rehearsal! Behind the Scenes with Assistant Director Reggie Callow* (Lanham, MD: Scarecrow Press, Inc., 2010)

Bernhardt, Curtis & Kiersch, Mary *Curtis Bernhardt: A Director's Guild of America Oral History* (Berkeley, CA: University of California Press/Director's Guild of America, 1986)

Binns, Archie *Mrs. Fiske and the American Theater* (New York: Crown Publishing, Inc., 1955)

Bogar, Thomas A. *American Presidents Attend the Theater: The Playgoing Experience of Each Chief Executive* (Jefferson, NC: McFarland & Co, Inc., 2006)

Bogdanovich, Peter *Who the Devil Made It? Conversations with Legendary Film Directors* (New York: Ballantine Books, 1997)

Bordman, Gerald *A Chronicle of American Comedy and Drama 1914-1930* (New York: Oxford University Press, 1995)

Bordman, Gerald & Norton, Richard *American Musical Theater: A Chronicle* (New York: Oxford University Press, 2010)

Bosworth, Patricia *Montgomery Clift: A Biography* (New York: Harcourt Brace Jovanovic, 1978)

Brown, Jared *The Fabulous Lunts: A Biography of Alfred Lunt and Lynn Fontanne* (New York: Atheneum, 1986)

Bubbeo, Daniel *The Women of Warner Brothers: The Lives and Careers of 15 Leading Ladies* (Jefferson, NC: McFarland & Co, Inc., 2002)

Capua, Michelangelo *Deborah Kerr: A Biography* (Jefferson, NC: McFarland & Co, Inc., 2010)

Cecil, David *Max: A Biography* (London: Constable & Co, Ltd., 1964)

Chaplin, Charles *My Autobiography* (London: The Bodley Head, 1964)

Clunn, Harold P. *The Face of the Home Counties* (London: Spring Books, 1960)

Cobrin, Pamela *From Winning the Vote – To Directing on Broadway: The Emergence of Women on the New York Stage 1880-1927* (Newark, NJ: University of Delaware Press, 2009)

Conner, Lynn *Pittsburgh in Stages: Two Hundred Years of Theater* (Pittsburgh, PA: University of Pittsburgh Press, 2007)

Cowie, Peter *Joan Crawford: Enduring Star* (New York: Rizzoli International Publications, 2009)

Cowsill, Alan *Spider-Man Chronicle: A Year By Year Visual History* (London: DK Publishing, 2012)

Croall, Jonathon *Sybil Thorndike: A Star of Life* (London: Haus Publishing, 2008)

Cullen, Frank, Hackman, Florence & McNeilly, Donald *Vaudeville Old and New: An Encyclopedia of Variety Performers Vol. 1* (New York; Routledge, Taylor & Francis Group, 2007)

Curtis, James, *Spencer Tracy: A Biography* (London: Hutchinson, 2011)

Davis, Ronald L. *Zachary Scott: Hollywood's Sophisticated Cad* (Jackson, Mississippi: University of Mississippi Press, 2009)

DeForest, Tim *Radio by the Book: Adaptations of Literature and Fiction on the Airwaves* (Jefferson, North Carolina: McFarland & Co, Inc., 2008)

Dewey, Donald *James Stewart: A Biography* (Atlanta, GA: Turner Publishing, Inc., 1996)

Donati, William, *Ida Lupino: A Biography* (Lexington, Kentucky: The University of Kentucky Press, 1996)

Dugas, Don-John *Shakespeare for Everyman: Ben Greet in Early Twentieth Century America* (London: Society for Theatre Research, 2016)

Dwerlcotte, Carolyn Regina *Mrs. Minnie Maddern Fiske: The First Stage Director in the American Interpretational Style, Vol. 1* (Berkeley, CA: University of California, 1990)

Eames, John Douglas *The MGM Story* (London: Octopus Books, 1979)

Eco, Umberto *Travels in Hyper-Reality* (London: Picador, 1986)

Fisher, James & Londre, Felicia Hardison *The A-Z of American Theater: Modernism* (Lanham, Maryland: The Scarecrow Press, Inc., 2008)

Gabbard, Krin & Luhr, William [Eds.] *Screening Genders* (New Brunswick, New Jersey: Rutgers University Press, 2008)

Gaines, Jane M. *Contested Culture: The Image, the Voice and the Law* (Chapel Hill, NC: The University of North Carolina Press, 2000)

Gelman, Howard *The Films of John Garfield* (New York: Citadel Press, 1975)

Gobel, Laurence *The Hustons: The Life and Times of a Hollywood Dynasty* (New York: Scribner, 1989)

Guide to Margate, Broadstairs, Ramsgate, Herne Bay, Canterbury & North-East Kent (London: Ward, Lock & Co., Ltd., Tenth Edition, circa 1950)

Hadleigh, Boze *Leading Ladies* (London: Robson Books, 1992)

Halliwell, Leslie *Halliwell's Film Guide: Fourth Edition* (London: Guild Publishing, 1983)

Harmetz, Aljean *Round Up the Usual Suspects: The Making of Casablanca: Bogart, Bergman & World War II* (New York: Hyperion, 1992)

Harris, Warren G., *Clark Gable: A Biography* (London: Aurum Press Ltd., 2002)

Higham, Charles, *Olivia & Joan: A Biography of Olivia de Havilland and Joan Fontaine* (New English Library, 1984)

Hirschhorn, Clive *The Warner Bros. Story* (New York: Octopus Books, 1979)

Hirschhorn, Clive *The Universal Story* (New York: Octopus Books, 1983)

Hischak, Thomas S. *The Jerome Kern Encyclopedia* (Lanham, Maryland: The Scarecrow Press, 2013)

Hischak, Thomas S. *Broadway Plays & Musicals: Descriptions & Essential Facts of More Than 14,000 Shows Through 2007* (Jefferson, NC: McFarland & Co, Inc., 2015)

Isaac, Winifred F. E. C. *Ben Greet and the Old Vic: A Biography of Philip Ben Greet* (London: Published by the author, 1964)

Isenberg, Noah *We'll Always Have Casablanca: The Life, Legend and Afterlife of Hollywood's Most Beloved Movie* (New York: W. W. Norton & Company,)

Isenberg, Noah William *Edgar G. Ulmer: A Filmmaker on the Margins* (Berkeley, CA: University of California Press, 2014)

Jacobs, Steven & Colpeart, Lisa *The Dark Galleries* (Ghent, Belgium: Aramer, 2013)

Jewell, Richard B. & Harbin, Vernon *The RKO Story* (London: Octopus Books, 1982)

Katz, Jeffrey M. *Plie Ball: Baseball Meets Dance on Stage & Screen* (Jefferson, NC: McFarland & Co, Inc., 2016)

Lebo, Harlan *Casablanca: Behind the Scenes* (New York: Simon & Schuster, 1992)

Le Vay, John *Margaret Anglin: A Stage Life* (Toronto, Canada: Simon & Pierre, 1989)

Levine, Sanford *Best Movie Scenes: 549 Memorable Bank Robbers, Car Chases, Duels, Haircuts et al* (Jefferson, North Carolina: McFarland & Co, Inc., 2012)

Luhr, William [Ed.] *The Maltese Falcon, John Huston, director* (New Brunswick, New Jersey: Rutgers University Press, 1996)

Luhrssen, David *Mamoulian: Life on Stage & Screen* (Lexington, KY: The University of Kentucky Press, 2010)

Macksoud, Meredith C. *Arthur Kennedy, Man of Characters* (Jefferson, North Carolina: McFarland & Co. Inc., 2003)

McBride, O. E. *Stout Fellow: A Guide Through Nero Wolfe's World* (Lincoln, NE: IUniverse, 2003)

McClelland, Doug *Eleanor Parker: Woman of a Thousand Faces: A Bio-Bibliography & Filmography* (Lanham, Maryland: The Scarecrow Press, Inc., 1989)

McGilligan, Patrick [Ed.] *Backstory: Interviews with Screenwriters of Hollywood's Golden Age* (Berkeley, CA: University of California Press, 1986)

McGrath, Patrick *John Garfield: The Illustrated Career in Films & on the Stage* (Jefferson, NC: McFarland & Co, Inc., 1993)

Maltby, Richard et al, *Going to the Movies: Hollywood and the Social Experience of Cinema* (Exeter, England: University of Exeter Press, 2007)

Morley, Sheridan *The Great Stage Stars* (London: Angus & Robertson, 1986)

Morley, Sheridan *Robert My Father* (London: Weidenfeld & Nicholson, 1993)

Moss, Marilyn Ann *Raoul Walsh: The True Adventures of Hollywood's Legendary Director* (Lexington, Kentucky: University of Kentucky Press, 2011)

Negulesco, Jean *Things I Did and Things I Think I Did: A Hollywood Memoir* (New York: Linden Press/Simon & Schuster, 1984)

Nissen, Axel *The Films of Agnes Moorehead* (Lanham, Maryland: Scarecrow Press, Inc., 2013)

Parish, James Robert & Bowers, Ronald L. *The MGM Stock Company* (London: Ian Allan, 1973)

Parker, John (Compiler & Editor) *Who's Who in the Theatre: A Biographical Record of the Contemporary Stage: Tenth Edition* (London: Sir Isaac Pitman & Sons, Ltd., 1947)

Pearson, Hesketh *Beerbohm Tree: His Life and Laughter* (London: Greenwood Press, 1971)

Peary, Danny, *Close-Ups: The Movie Star Book* (New York: Workman Publishing, 1978)

Peters, Margot *Design for Living: Alfred Lunt and Lynn Fontaine: A Biography* (New York: Alfred A. Knopf, 2003)

Phillips, Gene D. *Fiction, Film & Faulkner: The Art of Adaptation* (Knoxville, Tennessee: University of Tennessee Press, 1988)

Pontuso, James F. [Ed.] *Political Philosophy Comes to Rick's: Casablanca and American Civic Culture* (Lanham, MD: Lexington Books, 2005)

Porter, Darwin, *Humphrey Bogart: The Making of a Legend* (New York: Blood Moon Productions Ltd., 2010)

Quirk, Lawrence J., *The Passionate Life of Bette Davis* (London: Robson Books, 1990)

Quirk, Lawrence J. & Schoell, William *Joan Crawford: The Essential Biography* (Lexington, KY: University Press of Kentucky, 2002)

Reaney, P. H. *A Dictionary of British Surnames* (London: Routledge & Keegan Paul 1958)

Rhodes, Gary *Edgar G. Ulmer: Detour on Poverty Row* (Lanham, MD: Rowman & Littlefield, 2009)

Robertson, Dr. James C. *The Casablanca Man: The Cinema of Michael Curtiz* (New York: Routledge, 1993)

Russell, Charles Edward *Julia Marlowe: Her Life and Art* (New York: D. Appleton & Co, 1926)

Santas, Constantine *The Essential Humphrey Bogart* (Lanham, MD: Rowman & Littlefield, 2016)

Sante, Luc & Pierson, Melissa Holbrook *OK You Mugs: Writers on Movie Actors* (New York: Pantheon Books, 1999)

Sennett, Ted *Masters of Menace: Greenstreet & Lorre* (New York: E. P. Dutton, 1979)

Sennett, Ted *Warner Brothers Presents: The Most Exciting Years – From The Jazz Singer to White Heat* (New York: Arlington House, 1971)

Sherman, Vincent *Studio Affairs: My Life as a Film Director* (Lexington, Kentucky: University of Kentucky Press, 2015)

Shipman, David, *The Great Movie Stars: The International Years* (London: Angus & Robinson, 1974)

Silver, Alain & Ward, Elizabeth *Film Noir* (London: Secker & Warburg, 1980)

Skal, David J. & Rains, Jessica, *Claude Rains: An Actor's Voice* (The University Press of Kentucky, 2008)

Sperber, A. M. & Lax, Eric *Bogart: The Biography* (New York: Harper Collins, 1996)

Spicer, Andrew *Historical Dictionary of Film Noir* (Lanham, MD: Scarecrow Press, Inc., 2010)

Spoto, Donald, *Possessed: The Life of Joan Crawford* (London: HutchinArtson, 2011)

Stephens, Michael *Art Directors in Cinema: A Worldwide Biographical Dictionary* (Jefferson, NC: McFarland & Co, Inc., 2008)

Stubblebine, Donald J. *Early Broadway Sheet Music: A Comprehensive Listing of Published Music from Broadway & Other Shows 1843-1918* (Jefferson, NC: McFarland & Co, Inc., 2010)

Terrace, Vincent *Radio Openings and Closings, 1931-1972* (Jefferson, North Carolina: McFarland & Co, Inc., 2003)

Thompson, David *Great Stars: Humphrey Bogart* (London: Penguin Books, 2009)

Tree, Sir Herbert Beerbohm *Thoughts & After Thoughts* (London: Cassell, 1913)

Trewin, J. C. *The Edwardian Stage* (Oxford, England: Basil Blackwell, 1976)

Turk, Edward Baron *Hollywood Diva: A Biography of Jeanette MacDonald* (Berkeley, California: University of California Press, 1998)

Walker, Alexander, *Joan Crawford: The Ultimate Star* (New York: Harper & Row, 1983)

Webster, Margaret *Don't Put Your Daughter on the Stage* (New York: Alfred A. Knopf, Inc., 1972)

Wells, Stanley & Stanton, Julia [Ed] *The Cambridge Companion to Shakespeare on Stage* (New York: Cambridge University Press, 2002)

Williams, Tennessee *27 Wagons Full of Cotton & Other One-Act Plays* (Ann Arbor, Michigan: New Directions, University of Michigan, 1946)

Wills, Brian Steel *Gone with the Glory: The Civil War in Cinema* (Lanham, Maryland: Rowman & Littlefield, 2011)

Wodehouse, P. G. & Bolton, Guy *Bring on the Girls! The Improbable Story of Our Life in Musical Comedy, With Pictures to Prove it* (New York: Simon & Schuster, 1953)

Young, Jordan R., *Reel Characters* (Beverly Hills, CA: Moonstone Press, 1986)

Youngkin, Stephen D., *The Lost One: A Life of Peter Lorre* (Lexington, KY: The University Press of Kentucky, 2005)

Notes

1 Man of Kent

1. "UK Census: Sandwich St Mary, Kent, 1881."
2. Clunn, Harold P. *The Face of the Home Counties* (London: Spring Books, 1960), 281.
3. *Guide to Margate, Broadstairs, Ramsgate, Herne Bay, Canterbury & North-East Kent* (London: Ward, Lock & Co., Ltd., Tenth Edition circa 1950), 94.
4. Reaney, P. H. *A Dictionary of British Surnames* (London: Routledge & Keegan Paul 1958), 145.
5. "UK Census: John Greenstreet et al, Sandwich, Kent, 1881, Margate, Kent, 1891, Deal, Kent, 1891."
6. "UK Census: William Greenstreet & family, Broad Alley, Chatham, Gillingham, Kent, 1841, 1851; William Cooper & family, Chalkwell Road, Milton, Kent, 1841-61."
7. "UK Census: White Hart Inn, Sittingbourne, Kent, 1871"
8. William Cooper, Tanner, died February 14, 1871 aged 83, leaving estate valued at around £12,000. His son Venn Cooper died November 25, 1872, Effects £2,000. "UK Probate Calendars."
9. "Henry Baker, Bookseller & Stationer, of Sandwich, Kent, died July 28. 1867. Effects less than £1,500." "UK Probate Calendars."
10. "UK Census: Sandwich St Mary, Kent, 1861; William Greenstreet & family, Eastchurch, Kent, 1841-61; Hannah Pratt, wid, Eastchurch, Kent, 1871.
11. "Nice Thought" *Reno Gazette-Journal*, April 28, 1938, 4.
12. Jimmie Fidler, "In Hollywood" *Joplin Globe* (Missouri), June 17, 1944, 3.
13. "Duquesne Stock Company is announced by Mr. Davis" *The Pittsburgh Press*, September 19, 1909, 25.
14. "Shakespearian Star Now on Musical Stage" *New York Morning Telegraph*, November 18, 1923, 8.
15. "Sydney Greenstreet" *The Oregon Daily Journal*, February 9, 1913, 39.
16. "Asbury Tennis Player Now on the Stage" *Asbury Park Press*, October 15, 1919, 7. The Davis Cup was inaugurated in 1900 in the United States and was held most years in various countries until the outbreak of war in 1914, resuming in 1919.
17. Gail Greenstreet, email to the author, June 5, 2017.
18. "Shakespearian Star Now on Musical Stage" *New York Morning Telegraph*, November 18, 1923, 8.
19. "Speaks Singhalese" *The Lincoln Star* (Lincoln, Nebraska), March 30, 1947, 38.
20. Gail Greenstreet, email to the author, June 5, 2017.
21. Harold Heffernan, "Movieland" *The Baltimore Sun*, November 22, 1942, 116.

2 An Actor's Life for Me

1. "Shakespearean Star Now On Musical Stage" *New York Morning Telegraph*, November 18, 1923, 8.

2. Charlotte Kaye, "Big Hit" *Hollywood*, January 1943, 62.
3. "He Never Should Have Seen It" *The Pittsburgh Press*, May 18, 1949, 18.
4. Charlotte Kaye, "Big Hit" *Hollywood*, January1943, 77.
5. Barringer, Millie *Margaret Webster: A Life in the Theater* (Ann Arbor, Michigan: The University of Michigan Press), 38.
6. Trewin, J. C. *The Edwardian Theatre* (Oxford, England: Basil Blackwell, 1976), 144.
7. "English Actor Dies" *The Winnipeg Tribune* (Manitoba, Canada), March 8, 1948, 2.
8. Promotional material: "The Ben Greet Players of London & New York: 1904-32," 2.
9. "Dover Theatre Royal" *Dover Express* (Kent, England), April 17, 1903, 7.
10. "About Mitzi and Others Who Are Soon to Appear in Indianapolis" *The Indianapolis News*, January 14, 1928, 9.
11. "Gossip of the Rialto" *The Duluth Evening Herald*, September 29, 1906, 7.
12. "From Our Stageland Scrapbook: Sydney Greenstreet" Casino, Broadway & 39th Street, New York, *Mitzi the Madcap Playbill*, 1928, 31.
132. "The Stage Door" *The Evening Journal* (Wilmington, Delaware), June 21, 1913, 8.

3 American Adventure

1. "United States Incoming Passenger Lists, 1904."
2. "Amusements: 'Everyman'" *Daily Capital Journal* (Salem, Oregon), December 13, 1904, 8.
3. W. B. Chamberlain, "At the Theaters; Auditorium – "Everyman"" *The Minneapolis Journal*, April 25, 1905, 4.
4. "Student Players to Aid Ben Greet in "Hamlet"" *The San Francisco Call*, October 1, 1904, 6.
5. Hadleigh, Boze *Leading Ladies* (London: Robson Books, 1992). 169-170.
6. Dugas, Don-John *Shakespeare for Everyman* (London: Society for Theatre Research, 2016), 136.
7. Dugas, Don-John *Shakespeare for Everyman*, 139.
8. "Ben Greet and Company Here" *Rock Island Argus*, March 15, 1905, 4.
9. "Montreal" *The New York Dramatic Mirror*, June 17, 1905, 5.
10. "Mr. Henry George" *The Era*, April 15, 1905, 4.
11. UK Incoming Passenger Lists, July 1905.
12. "Woodlawn Players at Lawn Club" *Yale News*, June 1, 1906, 1.
13. Dugas, Don-John *Shakespeare for Everyman*, 163-65.
14. Dugas, Don-John *Shakespeare for Everyman*, 129.
15. "Lord and Lady Alvin Bring New Players" *The San Francisco Call*, October 11, 1904,5.
16. "Drama Outdoors: Ben Greet Woodland Players on the Stephens Lawn" *Detroit Free Press*, June 13, 1906, 3.

17. "Twelfth Night and Tempest: Ben Greet Concludes Engagement at Catonsville" *The Baltimore Sun*, May 23, 1906, 7.
18. "Twelfth Night and Tempest: Ben Greet Concludes Engagement at Catonsville" *The Baltimore Sun*, May 23, 1906, 7.
19. "The Ben Greet Players of London & New York: 1904-32," 2.
20. "Ben Greet Players Seen in 'She Stoops to Conquer'" *The Washington Times*, February 8, 1908, 6.

4 A Pastoral Idyll

1. Bogar, Thomas A. *American Presidents Attend the Theater: The Playgoing Experience of Each Chief Executive* (Jefferson, NC: McFarland & Co, Inc., 2006). 1.
2. Hedda Hopper, "Sydney Greenstreet Busy, But Maintains Perfection" *Argus Leader* (Sioux Falls, South Dakota), September 10, 1944, 14.
3. "Everyman A Success: Benefit Performance Greeted By Large Audience" *Evening Star* (Washington), April 30, 1907, 14.
4. "Woodland Players" *Geneva Daily Times*, June 14, 1909, 12.
5. "Drama in the United States" *The Times* (London), December 26, 1906, 8.
6. "Professor Ben Greet" *Evening Star, Washington, D. C.*, April 22, 1905, 18.
7. "Actor Told by Boy He Was the "Big Noise"" *The Pittsburgh Press*, November 7, 1909, 35.
8. "Screen's Noted Fat Man Follows Serene Philosophy: No Matter What Happens, Sydney Greenstreet Takes it All in His Stride" *The Pittsburgh Press*, August 5, 1945, 30.
9. "Ben Greet Players in Open Air Productions at Hotel Champlain" *Plattsburgh Daily Press*, August 19, 1908, 3.
10. "Real Tempest Drives "The Tempest" Indoors" *New York Herald*, August 16, 1905, 2.
11. "Woodland Players in "Merry Wives"" *New York Herald*, August 8, 1908, 11.
12. Mollie Meddle, "Some Chat & Chatter" *The New York Press*, June 28, 1914, 2.
13. "Prominent Actor Tells Good Story" *The Morning News* (Wilmington, Delaware), March 31, 1932, 10.
14. *The Michigan Alumnus Quarterly Review Volume 65* (Ann Arbor, Michigan: The Alumni Association of the University of Michigan, 1958-59), 206.
15. "Society, the Stage and Personal Chat: Playgrounds Benefit Play Triumph" *The Washington Times*, October 18, 1908, 4.
16. "Society in Force Sees Greet Plays: President Smiles on Greet Crowds" *The Washington Times*, October 17, 1908, 4.
17. "Society in Force Sees Greet Plays: President Smiles on Greet Crowds" *The Washington Times*, October 17, 1908, 4.
18. Bogar, Thomas A. *American Presidents Attend the Theater: The Playgoing Experience of Each Chief Executive* (Jefferson, NC: McFarland & Co, Inc., 2006), 196.

19. Anthony J. Scantlen, "Sydney Greenstreet Found Movies A Far Tougher Master Than Stage" *The Kansas City Times* (Missouri), January 27, 1954, 24.
20. "Outdoor Play Good: All Society Throngs to White House Lawn" *Evening Star*, October 17, 1908, 4.
21. "Society, the Stage and Personal Chat: Playgrounds Benefit Play Triumph" *The Washington Times*, October 18, 1908, 4.
22. Walter Anthony "Ben Greet – Pessimist: Mrs. Phipps – Optimist" *The Call* (San Francisco), May 9, 1909, 27. For a thorough analysis of Ben Greet's tours and his influence on drama in the United States see Dugas, Don-John *Shakespeare for Everyman: Ben Greet in Early Twentieth Century America* (London: Society for Theatre Research, 2016)

5 Happy Days in Pittsburgh

1. "In the Playhouses" *The Auburn Citizen*, October 31, 1908, 12.
2. "The Goddess of Reason Opens with Julia Marlowe" *The Billboard*, January 2, 1909, 4.
3. Morley, Sheridan *The Great Stage Stars* (London: Angus & Robertson, 1986), 261.
4. "Columbia University – The Ben Greet Players" *The New York Dramatic Mirror*, August 14, 1909, 5.
5. Conner, Lynn *Pittsburgh in Stages: Two Hundred Years of Theater* (Pittsburgh, PA: University of Pittsburgh Press, 2007), 79.
6. Conner, Lynn *Pittsburgh in Stages: Two Hundred Years of Theater* (Pittsburgh, PA: University of Pittsburgh Press, 2007), 79.
7. "Duquesne Stock Company is announced by Mr. Davis" *The Pittsburgh Press*, September 19, 1909, 25.
8. "The Duquesne Theater" *Pittsburgh Daily Post*, October 12, 1909, 6.
9. "The Duquesne" *The Pittsburgh Press*, October 19, 1909, 5.
10. "The Duquesne" *Pittsburgh Daily Post*, April 12, 1910, 7.
11. "The Duquesne" *The Pittsburgh Press*, April 12, 1910, 9.
12. "The Duquesne" *The Pittsburgh Press*, March 8, 1910, 7.
13. "Mrs. Temple's Telegram – Pittsburgh, December 13" *The New York Dramatic Mirror*, December 18, 1909, 11.
14. "Entertainments: The Duquesne" *The Pittsburgh Press*, December 28, 1909, 5.
15. "The Duquesne Theater" *Pittsburgh Daily Post*, March 29, 1910, 6.
16. "The Duquesne" *Pittsburgh Daily Post*, November 16, 1909, 23.
17. "Theater Gossip: The Duquesne" *The Pittsburgh Press*, February 20, 1910, 34.
18. "The Duquesne" *The Pittsburgh Press*, March 27, 1910, 50.
19. "The Duquesne Theater – "The Merchant of Venice"" *Pittsburgh Daily Post*, February 8, 1910, 5.
20. "The Place to Succeed" *The Pittsburgh Press*, December 3, 1909, 6.

6 Dissension in Harlem

1. "Auditorium (Harry G. Sommers) My Cinderella Girl" *The New York Dramatic Mirror*, September 28, 1910, 21.
2. Sennett, Ted *Masters of Menace: Greenstreet & Lorre* (New York: E. P. Dutton, 1979), 11.
3. "Sidney's First Appearance on Stage" *The Wilkes-Barre Record*, October 9, 1922, 13.
4. "Pre-Elizabethan Revivals" *The New York Dramatic Mirror*, December 14, 1910, 6.
5. Parker, John (Compiler & Editor) *Who's Who in the Theatre: A Biographical Record of the Contemporary Stage: Tenth Edition* (London: Sir Isaac Pitman & Sons, Ltd., 1947), 670.
6. "'Thais' A Dreary Play, Poorly Staged and Acted" *New York Press*, March 11, 1911, 10.
7. "Haines Organizes Company" *The Billboard*, April 29, 1911, 8.
8. Jolo, "West End Stock" *Variety*, May 23, 1911, 21.
9. "At Other Playhouses – West End" *The New York Dramatic Mirror*, May 10, 1911, 7.
10. "Local Offerings for the Week: West End (J. K. Cookson, Mgr.)" *The New York Clipper*, May 6, 1911, 14.
11. "Change for Beatrice Morgan" *Variety*, May 20, 1911, 17.
12. "The Other – Or Haines' Side" *Variety*, May 27, 1911, 15.
13. "At the Theaters: West End – The Lion and the Mouse" *The New York Dramatic Mirror*, June 14, 1911, 10.
14. "Theatrical Notes" *The New York Times*, May 17, 1911, 13.
15. "Haines Through with Stock" *Variety*, July 15, 1911, 19.
16. "'Secret Service' Presented Before Large Audience at the Savoy" *Asbury Park Press*, June 27, 1911, 6.
17. "Leading Lady in Suit for Salary" *Asbury Park Press*, July 7, 1911, 1.
18. "Patronage Poor, Haines Company Gives Up Ghost" *Asbury Park Press*, July 6, 1911, 6.
19. "Obituaries: Robert T. Haines Dies; Leader in Actor Groups" *Motion Picture Herald*, May 15, 1943, 63.

7 Enter, Colonel Savage

1. Vanderheyden Fyles, "Gotham's Season Opens With Artillery Bombardment in a Bowery Melodrama Emporium" *The Los Angeles Herald*, August 6, 1911, 3.
2. "Drama for the East Side: The Merchant of Venice" *The Brooklyn Daily Eagle*, August 2, 1911, 7.
3. "Drama for the East Side: "The Merchant of Venice"" *The New York Dramatic Mirror*, August 2, 1911, 7.
4. "Theater Topics: "Speed" Proves a Farce with a Moral at Collier's Comedy" *The Brooklyn Daily Eagle*, September 11, 1911, 7.
5. "Speed" *The Evening News* (Wilkes-Barre, Pennsylvania), October 14, 1911, 14.

6. "Excuse Me!" A Great Show" *The Daily Enquirer, Carlinville, Illinois,* January 8, 1912, 7.
7. "The Kempner – Dark" *Arkansas Democrat,* December 13, 1911, 10.
8. "Amusements Notes" *The Duluth Herald,* May 9, 1912, 14.
9. "Amusements – "Excuse Me" *El Paso Herald,* January 1, 1913, 11.
10. "Excuse Me" Good Farce at the Grand" *The Times* (Shreveport, Louisiana), December 29, 1912, 19.
11. "Coming Events at the Local Theaters: "Excuse Me"" *The San Francisco Call,* January 26, 1913, 29.
12. "Excuse Me!" A Great Show" *The Daily Enquirer, Carlinville, Illinois,* January 8, 1912, 7.
13. "Ann Greenstreet et al," 1911 Census, 62 Nevern Square, South Kensington, London.
14. "Frederick William Daniel Davis, (38), & Margery Greenstreet, (26), Married September 5, 1912, St. Cuthbert's Church, Kensington, London."
15. "Arthur Dashwood Hayward, 29, & Hilda Greenstreet, 30, Married August 5, 1913, St Cuthbert's Church, Kensington, London."
16. "Deaths: Strand, March Quarter, 1913, John J. Greenstreet, 65.
17. "What Ails You?" *The New York Dramatic Mirror,* November 20, 1912, 7.
18. "What Ails You?" *Variety,* November 22, 1912, 23.
19. "'Cart Wheels' and 'Skin the Cat' Help in 'What Ails You?'" *The Evening Telegram – New York,* November 19, 1912, 6.
20. "Excuse Me" *Arkansas Democrat,* December 18, 1912, 5.

8 Margaret Anglin

1. "Rostand's "Romancers" at Marine and Field Club" *The Daily Standard,* Brooklyn, June 12, 1913, 9.
2. "The Romancers at West Point: (Special Dispatch to the Herald)" *New York Herald,* June 17, 1913, 9.
3. "Open Air Show at Country Club" *The Times Dispatch* (Richmond, Virginia), May 9, 1913, 10.
4. "Crescent Club Play "Pomander Walk" Given on Lawn of the Bay Ridge Summer Home" *The Brooklyn Daily Eagle,* June 19, 1913, 7.
5. "Crescent Club Play "Pomander Walk" Given on Lawn of the Bay Ridge Summer Home" *The Brooklyn Daily Eagle,* June 19, 1913, 7.
6. "Suffragists See "Pomander Walk" Fine Performance in the Open of Frank Lea Short Players Delights Audience" *The Brooklyn Daily Eagle,* June 7, 1914, 10.
7. "Sydney Greenstreet to Play" *The Brooklyn Daily Eagle,* June 6, 1914, 3.
8. "Suffragists See "Pomander Walk" Fine Performance in the Open of Frank Lea Short Players Delights Audience" *The Brooklyn Daily Eagle,* June 7, 1914, 10.
9. "Mrs. Notman is Held" *The Brooklyn Daily Eagle,* June 16, 1914, 1.
10. "Columbia Theater" *The San Francisco Dramatic Review,* September 27, 1913, 9.

11. "Columbia Theater" *The San Francisco Dramatic Review*, September 20, 1913, 10.
12. "Miss Anglin Charms in Role of Viola" *New York Herald*, March 24, 1914, 10.
13. Arthur Ruhl, "A Delightful "Twelfth Night" Miss Anglin and Her Company at Their Best In Fine Old Comedy" *New York Tribune*, March 24, 1914, 9.
14. "Plays & Players: Lady Windermere's Fan" *Brooklyn Life*, April 4, 1914, 23.
15. "From Shakespeare to Musical Comedy" *The Evening Telegram, New York*, November 14, 1923, 14.
16. "Montreal" *The New York Dramatic Mirror*, January 21, 1914, 8.
17. "Margaret Anglin a Pleasing Rosalind: As You Like It at Hudson" *The Brooklyn Daily Eagle*, March 17, 1914, 26.
18. "Twelfth Night" *The New York Dramatic Mirror*, March 25, 1914, 14.
19. "Miss Anglin Scores in Brilliant Revival" *The Brooklyn Daily Eagle*, March 24, 1914, 26.
20. "Miss Anglin Seen in Twelfth Night" *The New York Press*, March 24, 1914, 12.
21. "Gave Beautiful Rendering of Viola" *Vancouver Daily World*, October 30, 1913, 20.
22. "Whisperings in the Wings" *The San Francisco Call*, September 30, 1913, 4.
23. Walter Prichard Eaton, "The Theater" circa 1914, *Greenstreet Family Archive*, by courtesy of Gail Greenstreet.
24. "Plays & Players: Lady Windermere's Fan" *Brooklyn Life*, April 4, 1914, 23.
25. "Anglin Players Wedded" *The New York Clipper*, October 4, 1913, 15.
26. "Actor Here in "Grumpy" Dead" *Ithaca Daily News*, January 4, 1917, 3. Eric Blind died December 31, 1916 about a week after becoming ill while appearing in *Grumpy*. At the time of his illness, Frances was working in the East in *Daddy Long Legs*. She took a train to Reading, Pennsylvania, but when she reached Baltimore she was met by friends at the station to tell her that her husband was dead. She was carrying flowers for his bedside which were put on his coffin instead.

9 A Farceur

1. "The First Nighters: She's in Again" *The New York Dramatic Review*, May 19, 1915, 8.
2. "New Plays: She's in Again" *Billboard*, May 29, 1915, 4.
3. "A World of Pleasure" *Variety*, October 15, 1915, 16.
4. "Old Favorites at Winter Garden" *The New York Press*, October 15, 1915, 12.
5. Burns Mantle, "The Nakedest of the New York Shows" *Chicago Tribune*, October 24, 1915, 55.
6. "A Pair of Queens Cast Substitutions Chicago," *Variety*, June 30, 1916, 1.
7. "Here Comes the Bride!" *The Brooklyn Daily Eagle*, September 27, 1917, 7.
8. Dugas, Don-John *Shakespeare for Everyman* (London: The Society for Theatre Research, 2016), 280
9. Paula Sperdakos "Dora Mavor Moore Before the New Play Society" *Theatre Research in Canada*, Volume 10, No. 1, Spring 1989.

10. "Redpath Chautauqua: Superior Attractions Draw Large and Delighted Audiences" *Oswego Daily Palladium*, August 6, 1917, 3.

10 A King of Nowhere

1. The First Nighter, "A World of Pleasure" *The New York Dramatic Mirror*, October 23, 1915, 8.
2. "The Little Bird on the Rialto Says" *The New York Sun*, April 9, 1916, 4.
3. "Tree, As Wolsey, Gains New Fame" *The Washington Times*, March 6, 1917, 11.
4. "The first Nighter: The King of Nowhere" *The New York Dramatic Mirror*, March 25, 1916, 8.
5. "Lou-Tellegen In a Rambling Play" *The Brooklyn Daily Eagle*, March 21, 1916, 12.
6. "Madame Critic" *The New York Dramatic Mirror*, April 1, 1916, 4.
7. "Lou Tellegen" *New York Evening Post*, November 2, 1929, 7.
8. "New Attractions for the New York Theatergoers" *The New York Dramatic Mirror*, August 6, 1916, 23.
9. "Music & Drama: 'Friend Martha'" *The Evening Post, New York*, August 8, 1917, 9.
10. "Combination Crook and Orphan School" *The Syracuse Herald*, November 24, 1916, 24.
11. "On the Rialto" *The New York Dramatic Mirror*, April 15, 1916, 15.

11 Sir Herbert

1. Chaplin, Charles *My Autobiography* (London: The Bodley Head, 1964), 209-10.
2. "Sir Herbert Tree Seen as Falstaff" *The New York Press*, May 22, 1916, 4.
3. "In Manhattan: The Merry Wives of Windsor" *Brooklyn Life*, June 3, 1916, 17.
4. "Notes of the Stage" *New York Herald*, May 28, 1916, 5.
5. Nelson Cunliff, "Recreation – The St Louis Idea," *The Rotarian*, January 1923, 10.
6. "Shakespeare Pageant Will Close Tonight" *The St Louis Star & Times*, June 13, 1916, 43.
7. Cecil, David *Max: A Biography* (London: Constable & Co, Ltd., 1964)
8. "Girth Brings Fat Roles for Sydney Greenstreet: Next at Curran With Lunt-Fontanne" *Oakland Tribune*, February 2, 1941, 29.
9. Trewin, J. C. *The Edwardian Stage* (Oxford, England: Basil Blackwell, 1976), 134.
10. "Sir Herbert Tree in Shakespeare's 'Henry VIII'" *The Newark Union-Gazette*, March 17, 1917, 4.
11. "Sir Herbert Tree in Shakespeare's Henry VIII" *The Newark Union-Gazette*, March 17, 1917, 4.
12. "Beerbohm Tree and Anna Held Lead Theater Attractions" *The Washington Herald*, March 6, 1917, 13.
13. "Lyceum Theater" *Rochester Democrat & Chronicle*, March 20, 1917, 9.
14. "Reports from Mirror Correspondents: His Majesty's, Montreal" *The Dramatic Mirror*, April 7, 1917, 17.
15. "Pittsburgh, Pennsylvania" *The Dramatic Mirror*, March 24, 1917, 15.

16. "Stage Speech Not Relished by Some: Actor-Manager Makes Reference to Great War" *Rochester Democrat & Chronicle*, March 20, 1917, 17.
17. "Sir Herbert in Henry VIII Scores Triumph at Star" *Buffalo Courier*, March 23, 1917, 13.
18. Draft Registration Cards, September 1918; Family Search.org: Service Records, United Kingdom National Archives, Kew Gardens, London, 1914-21.
19. "New York Sees Sir Herbert Tree in "Colonel Newcome" *The Christian Science Monitor* (Boston), April 17, 1917, 14.
20. "New Amsterdam Theater: Colonel Newcome" *New York Theater*, April 16, 1917. 10.
21. Cecil, David *Max: A Biography* (London: Constable & Company, Ltd, 1964), 364.
22. "On Stage and Screen: Davis-Guernon Play & Cap'n Tinney's Soldiers Show Coming This Week" *Syracuse Herald*, February 9, 1919, 4.

12 The Rainbow Girl

1. "Asbury Tennis Player Now on the Stage" *Asbury Park Press*, October 15, 1919, 7.
2. "Few Tennis Players" *The Asbury Park Press*, July 25, 1919, 2.
3. "Celebrates Birthday" *Asbury Park Press*, August 11, 1911, 11.
4. "Oldest Undertaker" *The Courier-News* (Bridgewater, New Jersey), March 17, 1916, 13.
5. Gail Greenstreet, email to the author, June 6, 2017. Gail recalled seeing her grandmother's Daughters of the American Revolution membership papers.
6. "Auto for Prize in Baby Parade" *Trenton Evening Times,* August 18, 1910, 9.
7. "Three Are Injured When Autos Collide" *Asbury Park Press,* June 12, 1911, 1.
8. "Prices and Wages by Decade 1908-1910" http://libraryguides.missouri.edu/c.php?g=28284&p=174165
9. "Audience Likes Open Air Play: Queen Titania Sees Her Pageant Interpreted by Ben Greet Players" *Asbury Park Press*, August 24, 1910, 10.
10. "Queen Rides in Borden Buick" *Asbury Park Press*, August 24, 1910, 10.
11. "Threatening Weather Frowns Upon Baby Parade" *Asbury Park Press*, September 2, 1910, 1.
12. "Miss Myers Wins Auto" *Asbury Park Press*, September 6, 1910, 3.
13. "Greenstreet-Ogden" *Asbury Park Press*, May 15, 1918, 15.
14. "Sidney Greenstreet" *Asbury Park Press*, July 23, 1919, 2.
15. "Mitzi Will Be Present at the Rechristening" *The New York Times-Union*, December 28, 1920, 16.
16. Myriam Sieve, "Sydney Greenstreet Jumps from Shakespeare to Musical Comedy – Tells Why Classical Productions Don't Pay" *The Billboard*, August 20, 1921, 22.
17. "On Stage and Screen: Davis-Guernan Play & Cap'n Tinney's Soldiers Show Coming This Week" *Syracuse Herald*, February 9, 1919, 4.
18. "Shakespeare Staged a la Ziegfeld Will Make Coin, Says Sydney Greenstreet" *Syracuse Journal*, November 26, 1921, 7.

19. H. T. C., "Both Sides of the Curtain" *Evening Public Ledger* (Philadelphia), December 23, 1917, 12.
20. "The Rainbow Girl" *The Christian Science Monitor* (Boston), February 26, 1918, 8.
21. "'The Rainbow Girl' Gay and Tuneful Comedy" *The New York Clipper*, April 3, 1918, 10.
22. "National – The Rainbow Girl" *The Washington Herald*, March 3, 1919, 7.
23. "The Theaters: "The Rainbow Girl" Breaks Though the Clouds" *The Indianapolis News*, December 3, 1918, 6.
24. Burton Rascoe, "Don't Let the Plot Keep You Away From "The Rainbow Girl"" *The Chicago Daily Tribune*, August 27, 1918, 11.
25. "Repeating Plays: Forrest: Rainbow Girl" *The Philadelphia Inquirer*, March 16, 1919, 20.
26. "Friars Dine Billy Van" *The New York Clipper*, July 3, 1918, 5.
27. "Broadway Goes to Motor Show" *The Evening Telegram – New York*, January 12, 1918, 19.
28. "Miss Viola Allen Returns to Stage to Play Viola at Sleepy Hollow for Hospital" *New York Herald*, May 31, 1919, 10.
29. "The Dramatic Stage: Twelfth Night Given at Sleepy Hollow Country Club, with Viola Allen & Brilliant Cast" *Billboard*, June 7, 1919, 22.

13 Lady Billy

1. "On Stage and Screen: Davis-Guernan Play & Cap'n Tinney's Soldiers Show Coming This Week" *Syracuse Herald*, February 9, 1919, 4.
2. "Liberty – 'Lady Billy'" *Theater Magazine*, February 1921, 107.
3. "Mitzi Charms at the American in 'Lady Billy'" *The St Louis Star & Times*, January 3, 1922, 8.
4. "The New Plays on Broadway" *The Stage*, December 18, 1920, 1155.
5. "In the Brooklyn Theaters: Mitzi Delightful in Show at Montauk" *The Brooklyn Daily Eagle*, November 1, 1921, 8.
6. *Dorothy Parker Complete Broadway 1918-23* Parker, Dorothy & Fitzpatrick, Kevin C. 41.
7. "Mitzi Returns to New York" *The Daily Republican* (Rushville, Indiana), January 4, 1921, 6.
8. "Mitzi Charms at The American in Lady Billy" *The St. Louis Star & Times* (St Louis, Missouri), January 3, 1922, 8.
9. "Plays and Players" *The New York Call*, May 16, 1923, 4.
10. "From Shakespeare to Musical Comedy" *The Brooklyn Standard-Union*, October 28, 1923, 5.
11. "The Stage Door" *New York Tribune*, March 3, 1921, 8.
12. "From Shakespeare to Lady Billy's Butler" The Evening Telegram – New York, March 6, 1921, 16.

13. "Dramatic Festival Opens Three-Day Session" The New York Times, May 11, 1926, 24
14. "Behind the Scenes by the Onlooker" The Evening Telegram – New York, March 26, 1921, 22.
15. "Boston Benefit for Actor's Fund" The Morning Telegraph, April 28, 1923, 12.
16. Ward Morehouse, "Broadway After Dark: Chicago's Passing Show" The New York Sun, July 19, 1927, 23.
17. Gail Greenstreet, email to the author, June 6, 2017.
18. Ann Grosvenor Ayers to Charles Pike Sawyer "The Mirror" New York Evening Post, August 11, 1921, 7.
19. "United States Census, 1910, Harry C. Greenstreet in household of Frederick Baker, Omaha Ward 11, Douglas, Nebraska" Family Search https://familysearch.org/ark:/61903/1:1:ML44-TYP. "United States Census, 1920, Harry C. Greenstreet, Omaha Ward 9, Douglas, Nebraska" Family Search https://familysearch.org/ark:/61903/1:1:MCVB-X3D
20. "Greenstreet-Curtis Wedding" *Omaha Daily Bee,* March 23, 1913, 14.
21. "UK Incoming Passenger Lists, 1922" "U. S. Incoming Passenger Lists, 1921"

14 Comedian for Mitzi

1. Earle Dorsey, "Emma Dunn at Garrick in Paul Wilstach's Play" *The Washington Herald,* October 3, 1922, 4.
2. Harold Phillips, "Garrick Offers Paul Wilstach's 'Her Happiness'" *The Washington Times,* October 3, 1922, 13.
3. "The Whole Town's Talking a Real Laugh Provider" *The Daily Review, Freeport, New York,* November 14, 1922,1.
4. "The Whole Town's Talking" *The Wilkes-Barre Record* (Wilkes-Barre, Pennsylvania), November 21, 1922, 7.
5. Agnes Smith, "John Emerson & Anita Loos: How and What to Tell a New Idea" *The Morning Telegraph Sunday Magazine,* September 23, 1923, 1.
6. "This Week at the Theaters: The Majestic" *The Buffalo Express,* January 22, 1924, 6.
7. "Theaters: The Capitol: Mitzi in The Magic Ring" *The Albany Evening Journal,* January 15, 1924, 6.
8. "Majestic – Mitzi with "The Magic Ring"" *Buffalo Evening News,* January 22, 1924, 8.
9. "Minnie & Me" *The Christian Science Monitor* (Boston), April 17, 1923, 3.
10. "Mitzi Returns as Star of 'The Magic Ring'" *New York Morning Telegraph,* October 2, 1923, 4.
11. "Theaters: The Capitol: Mitzi in The Magic Ring" *The Albany Evening Journal,* January 15, 1924, 6.
12. "In the Theaters" *Long Island News & Owl,* October 25, 1923, 7.
13. "From Shakespeare to Musical Comedy" *The Evening Telegram – New York,* November 14, 1923, 14.

14. "20 Wealthiest Showmen" *Variety,* May 4, 1927, 1
15. "Student Prince Still Sticks to Broadway" *The Indianapolis Star,* December 27, 1925, 49.
16. John Mason Brown, "Two on the Aisle" *New York Post,* December 1, 1925, 14.
17. Gilbert W. Gabriel, "Dostoievsky to the Contrary, *The New York Sun,* October 14, 1926, 26.
18. Arthur Pollock, "Plays and Things: A Play Called "Junk," About a Hobo, a Girl and A Governor, is Presented at the Garrick Theater" *The Brooklyn Daily Eagle,* January 6, 1927, 10.
19. Arthur Pollock, "Plays and Things: A Play Called "Junk," About a Hobo, a Girl and A Governor, is Presented at the Garrick Theater" *The Brooklyn Daily Eagle,* January 6, 1927, 10.
20. Agnes Taaffe, "Mitzi to Open September 11 in 'Madcap'" *The Minneapolis Star,* August 27, 1927, 26.
21. Edward Dobson, "Mitzi the Cut-up" *The Brooklyn Standard Union,* February 1, 1928, 4.
22. George L. David, "On the Stage: Lyceum Theater" *Rochester Democratic & Chronicle,* January 24, 1928, 8.
23. "Mitzi Delights in "Madcap" Show" *Albany Evening News,* January 27, 1928, 8.
24. See Shay Delcurla, "The Passing Show: Newsletter of the Shubert Archive, Volume 25, 2006/2007." http://www.shubertarchive.org/pdf/passingshows/PS2006Final.pdf

15 Mrs. Fiske's Dream Company

1. "Fiske Players at Wedgeway" The Morning Herald Gloversville and Johnstown New York, December 15, 1928, 2.
2. "Admits Players in His Company Are All Stars" The Philadelphia Inquirer, December 23, 1928, 15.
3. "Fiske Players at Wedgeway" The Morning Herald Gloversville and Johnstown New York, December 15, 1928, 2.
4. "Mrs. Fiske in Famous Comedy" The Philadelphia Inquirer, December 26, 1928, 15.
5. "Admits Players in His Company Are All Stars" The Philadelphia Inquirer, December 23, 1928, 15.
6. "The Art of Comedy" The Theater, New York, 1916, 362.
7. "The Call Boy's Chat" The Philadelphia Inquirer, January 13, 1929, 7.
8. "Mrs. Minnie Maddern Fiske Passes Away" The Olean Times-Herald, February 16, 1932, 9.

16 The Theater Guild

1. "Plays and Players: The Madcap: Mitzi" Brooklyn Life and Activities of Long Island Society, April 30, 1927, 18.
2. "United States Census, 1930," database with images, FamilySearch (https://familysearch.org/ark:/61903/1:1:X4KP-ZBS : accessed 24 March 2017), Sydney Green-

street, Manhattan (Districts 0251-0500), New York, New York, United States; citing enumeration district (ED) ED 398, sheet 25A, line 2, family 625, NARA microfilm publication T626 (Washington D.C.: National Archives and Records Administration, 2002), roll 1553; FHL microfilm 2,341,288.
3. "The People History: 1930s" http://www.thepeoplehistory.com/1930s.html
4. "The Theater: Wilson" The Detroit Free Press, December 10, 1929, 6.
5. Walter Prichard, "Our Berkshires: Dudley Digges" The Berkshire Eagle (Pittsfield, Massachusetts), April 29, 1947, 3.
6. "Amusements: "Volpone"" The Cincinnati Enquirer, February 11, 1930, 26.
7. "Amusements: "Volpone"" The Cincinnati Enquirer, February 11, 1930, 26.
8. "'R.U. R.' Returns; Novel Guild Play Revival at Martin Beck" The Brooklyn Daily Eagle, February 18, 1930, 21.
9. "'R.U. R.' Returns; Novel Guild Play Revival at Martin Beck" The Brooklyn Daily Eagle, February 18, 1930, 21.
10. Luhrssen, David Mamoulian: A Life on Stage and Screen (Lexington, KY: University of Kentucky Press, 1989), 41.
11. "Herbert Druse Dead; English Actor On American Stage for 40 Years Succumbs to Pneumonia" The New York Times, April 7, 1931, 34.
12. George L. David, "Theater Review: Lyceum Theater" *Rochester Democrat & Chronicle,* October 14, 1931, 13.
13. Rollin Palmer, "Servant Becomes Master of Family" *Buffalo Evening News,* October 17, 1931, 4.
14. "Theater Review: Erlanger: "The Admirable Crichton" *Buffalo Courier-Express,* October 16, 1931, 4.
15. Donald Mulhern, "The Greeks Bear Gifts" June 6, 1930, 7.
16. "Westchester Theater, Mount Vernon," *The Bronxville Press,* February 26, 1932, 7.
17. "Plays & Players: Sydney Greenstreet to Have Leading Role in Lysistrata at Majestic This Week" *The Brooklyn Daily Eagle,* February 8, 1932, 19.
18. Arthur Pollock, "The Theaters: 'Berlin.' A Melodrama about Spies, Sinister Secret Police And the Days Just Before the War, Opens at the Cohan Theater." *The Brooklyn Daily Eagle,* December 31, 1931, 11.
19. Bruno Mantle, "New Primitive Drama in Gotham – Again the Watsons" *Buffalo Courier-Express,* January 10, 1932, 6.
20. John Mason Brown, "The New Plays: "Berlin" Opens at the Cohan Theater – Two New Comedies are in Town" *New York Evening Post,* December 31, 1931, 5.
21. Roy Pickard, "Sydney Greenstreet A Gifted Shakespearean Actor Who Chuckled Wickedly in Films and Made Fat Sinister" *Films in Review,* Aug-Sept 1972, 386.
22. *Catalog of Copyright Entries Part 1, Group 3: Dramatic Compositions Motion Pictures* (Library of Congress, 1932), 1055.
23. "Clever Comedy Makes Hit" *The Morning News* (Wilmington, Delaware), April 5, 1932, 8.

24. Wilella Waldorf, "Forecasts & Postscripts, *New York Evening Post*, April 7, 1932, 12.
25. "Plays Out of Town: The Good Earth" *Variety*, September 27, 1932, 53.
26. "A Shakespeare Dinner" *New York Evening Post*, April 27, 1932, 17.

17 *The Show Goes On*

1. "Letter to Seaver Buck," quoted in As Ever, Sydney: Letters from Sydney Greenstreet to Seaver Buck" *Berkshire Bulletin*, Fall 2011/Winter 2012, 45.
2. Resume from Headmaster of New York Collegiate School, quoted in "As Ever, Sydney: Letters from Sydney Greenstreet to Seaver Buck" *Berkshire Bulletin*, Fall 2011/Winter 2012, 46
3. Letter to Seaver Buck, quoted in "As Ever, Sydney: Letters from Sydney Greenstreet to Seaver Buck" *Berkshire Bulletin*, Fall 2011/Winter 2012, 45.
4. Letter to Seaver Buck quoted in "As Ever, Sydney: Letters from Sydney Greenstreet to Seaver Buck" *Berkshire Bulletin*, Fall 2011/Winter 2012. 46.
5. Letter to Seaver Buck from New York dated August 9, 1934 "As Ever, Sydney: Letters from Sydney Greenstreet to Seaver Buck" *Berkshire Bulletin*, Fall 2011/Winter 2012, 46
6. Arthur Pollock, "The Theaters: 'Roberta' a Musical Comedy by Jerome Kern and Otto Harbach, Opens Modestly at the New Amsterdam" *Brooklyn Daily Eagle*, November 20, 1933, 6.
7. Hischak, Thomas S. *The Jerome Kern Encyclopedia* (Lanham, Maryland: The Scarecrow Press, 2013), 112.
8. "Hope Recalls Original 'Roberta'" *The Knickerbocker News*, September 19, 1958, 18-A.
9. "Nice Thought" *Reno Gazette-Journal*, April 28, 1938, 4.

18 *Life with the Lunts*

1. "Letter to Seaver Buck sent from Hotel Iroquois, New York, April 10, 1935," quoted in "As Ever, Sydney: Letters from Sydney Greenstreet to Seaver Buck" *Berkshire Bulletin*, Fall 2011/Winter 2012, 48.
2. John Mason Brown, "Two on the Aisle: A Theatergoer's Guide to the Season's New Plays" *New York Post*, October 5, 1935, 10.
3. "Taming of Shrew A Sprightly Play" *Buffalo Evening News*, May 22, 1935, 26.
4. John Ferris, "Broadway: The Lunts to Have Own Versatile Company" *Buffalo Courier-Express*, June 28, 1936, 9.
5. "Donald Found Easy Does It" *The Brooklyn Daily Eagle*, May 14, 1944, 21.
6. John Mason Brown, "Two on the Aisle: Mr. Lunt and Miss Fontanne Seen in 'Idiot's Delight'" *New York Post*, March 25, 1936, 17.
7. John Mason Brown, "The Mixed Moods of Robert Sherwood's 'Idiot's Delight'" *New York Post*, March 28, 1936, 2.
8. "Theater Review: Erlanger" *Buffalo Courier-Express*, March 12, 1937, 13.
9. Willard Keefe, "Sherwood Combines Comedy with His War on War" *Buffalo Courier-Express*, March 29, 1936, 10.

10. "Entertainments: Lyric Theater: "Amphitryon 38" Theater Guild" *The Times* (London), May 18, 1938, 14.
11. "Plays Out of Town" *The Brooklyn Daily Eagle,* June 30, 1937, 56.
12. "Entertainments: Lyric Theater: "Amphitryon 38" Theater Guild" *The Times* (London), May 18, 1938, 14.
13. "Amphitryon 38: The Lunts at the Lyric" *The Bystander,* May 25, 1938, 7.
14. "Letter to Seaver Buck sent from Lyric Theater, Sussex, June 29, 1938," quoted in *Berkshire Bulletin,* Fall 2011/Winter 2012, 52.
15. "Inside Stuff – Legit" *Variety,* May 3, 1939, 48.
16. Peters, Margot *Design for Living: Alfred Lunt and Lynn Fontanne: A Biography* (New York: Alfred A. Knopf, 2003), 170.
17. Ward Morehouse. "Seeing America" *Long Island Star-Journal,* April 24, 1961, 11.
18. "Letter to Seaver Buck sent from Hotel Warren, Indianapolis, Indiana, April 17, 1939," quoted in "As Ever, Sydney: Letters from Sydney Greenstreet to Seaver Buck" *Berkshire Bulletin,* Fall 2011.Winter 2012, 53.
19. Seaver Buck Trustee about Greenstreet, quoted in "As Ever, Sydney: Letters from Sydney Greenstreet to Seaver Buck," *Berkshire Bulletin,* Fall 2011/Winter 2012, 45.
20. Gail Greenstreet, email to the author, June 6, 2017.
21. Del De Windt quoted in "As Ever, Sydney: Letters from Sydney Greenstreet to Seaver Buck" *Berkshire Bulletin,* Fall 2011/Winter 2012, 45.
22. "Letter to Seaver Buck sent from Hotel Carteret, New York City, August 3, 1938," quoted in "As Ever, Sydney: Letters from Sydney Greenstreet to Seaver Buck" *Berkshire Bulletin,* Fall 2011/Winter 2012, 52.
23. "Letter to Seaver Buck sent from Hotel Severin, Indiana, Indianapolis, March 5, 1935," quoted in "As Ever, Sydney" *Berkshire Bulletin,* Fall 2011/Winter 2012, 52.
24. "Letter to Seaver Buck sent from Hotel St Paul, St Paul, Minnesota, May 16, 1937," quoted in "As Ever, Sydney: Letters from Sydney Greenstreet to Seaver Buck" *Berkshire Bulletin,* Fall 2011/Winter 2012, 52.
25. "Letter to Seaver Buck sent from Lyric Theater, Sussex, June 29, 1938," quoted in "As Ever, Sydney: Letters from Sydney Greenstreet to Seaver Buck" *Berkshire Bulletin,* Fall 2011/Winter 2012, 52. Greenstreet's role in *Idiot's Delight* (1939) was played by Charles Coburn.

19 *There Shall Be No Night*

1. "Entertainments: The Lunts in a Tchekhov Play" *The Times,* April 13, 1938, 12.
2. "Lunts' Revival of 'Sea Gull' is Lively Drama" *Chicago Daily Tribune,* April 10, 1938, 62.
3. Arthur Pollock, "Stage, Screen, Music: The Theater: Theater Guild Presents the Lunts in 'The Sea Gull' – Shubert" *The Brooklyn Daily Eagle,* March 29, 1938, 9.
4. Arthur Pollock, "Spotlight on Chekhov" *Drama Trend, The Brooklyn Daily Eagle,* April 3, 1938, 8.
5. "Two on the Aisle: Chekhov's "The Seagull" Revived with the Lunts" *New York Post,* March 29, 1938, 14.

6. Barringer, Millie *Margaret Webster: A Life in the Theater* (Ann Arbor, Michigan: The University of Michigan Press, 2007), 83.

7. Webster, Margaret *Don't Put Your Daughter on the Stage* (New York: Alfred A. Knopf, Inc., 1972), 21.

8. Don O'Malley "New York Inside Out" *The Citizen Advertiser, Auburn, New York*, April 8, 1938, 12.

9. Robert G. Tucker, "Plays and Players" *The Indianapolis Sunday Star*, April 30, 1939, 69.

10. Michael Buckley, "Stages to Screens: A Chat with Theresa Rebeck: Remembering Uta Hagen" *Playbill*, January 18, 2004.

11. Arthur Pollack, "The Theaters: Alfred Lunt & Lynn Fontanne Come Back" *The Brooklyn Daily Eagle*, February 6, 1940, 7.

12. Blanche Shoemaker Wagstaff, "There Shall Be No Night" *Wilton Bulletin*, (Wilton, Connecticut), July 11, 1940, 2.

13. "Apes His God in Musical Heavens" *The New York Sun*, August 5, 1940, 19.

14. Blanche Shoemaker Wagstaff, "There Shall Be No Night" *Wilton Bulletin*, (Wilton, Connecticut), July 11, 1940, 2.

15. Bosworth, Patricia *Montgomery Clift: A Biography* (New York: Harcourt Brace Jovanovic, 1978), 79.

16. Bosworth, Patricia *Montgomery Clift: A Biography* (New York: Harcourt Brace Jovanovic, 1978), 115.

17. Witham, Barry B. "There Shall Be No Night and the Politics of Isolationism" in *Theater Symposium Volume 9: Theater & Politics in the Twentieth Century* (University of Alabama Press, 2001), 123.

18. Kaspar Monahan, "Show Shops: Lunts and Sherwood Triumph in Tragedy" *The Pittsburgh Press*, November 12, 1940, 10.

19. "Legit Follow Up: 'There Shall Be No Night'" *Variety*, September 1, 1940, 44.

20 *The Black Bird*

1. Luhr, William [Ed.] *The Maltese Falcon, John Huston, director* (New Brunswick, New Jersey: Rutgers University Press, 1996), 116.

2. Young, Jordan R., *Reel Characters* (Beverly Hills, CA: Moonstone Press, 1986), 19.

3. Young, Jordan R., *Reel Characters* (Beverly Hills, CA: Moonstone Press, 1986), 19.

4. Gobel, Laurence *The Hustons: The Life and Times of a Hollywood Dynasty* (New York: Scribner, 1989), 220.

5. Long, Robert Emmet [Ed] *John Huston Interviews* (University Press of Mississippi, 2001), 93.

6. Steven H. Scheuer, "TV Keynotes: Peter Lorre Returns Tonight" *Citizen Register, Ossining, New York*, February 24, 1960, 14.

7. Shipman, David *Humphrey Bogart: Great Stars* (London: Penguin Books, 2009), 78.

8. Long, Robert Emmet [Ed] *John Huston Interviews* (University Press of Mississippi, 2001), 163.

9. Luhr, William [Ed.] *The Maltese Falcon, John Huston, director* (New Brunswick, New Jersey: Rutgers University Press, 1996), 116.

10. Astor, Mary *A Life on Film* (London: W. H. Allen, 1973), 160.

11. Long, Robert Emmet [Ed] *John Huston Interviews* (University Press of Mississippi, 2001), 23.

12. Huston, John *An Open Book* (New York: Knopf, 1980), 78-9.

13. "The Maltese Falcon" *Variety*, October 1, 1941, 9.

14. Sara Hamilton, "Who's News? Devil with a Cherub's Face" *Photoplay*, June 1943, 35.

15. Erskine Johnson, "In Hollywood" *Ogdensburg Journal*, April 4, 1946, 13.

16. "New Films in London: A Respite from War: Regal: The Maltese Falcon" *The Times* (London), June 22, 1942, 8.

17. Mosher, Jerry "Hard-Boiled and Soft-Bellied" in Gabbard, Krin & Luhr, William [Eds.] *Screening Genders* (New Brunswick, New Jersey: Rutgers University Press, 2008), 142.

18. "Warner Bros. To Make "Maltese Falcon" Sequel" *Showmen's Trade Review*, December 6, 1941, 36.

19. Gabbard, Krin & Luhr, William [Eds.] *Screening Genders* (New Brunswick, New Jersey: Rutgers University Press, 2008), Note 3, 154.

21 The Blue Parrot

1. "Errol Flynn in Stirring Role in Proctor Show" *The Bronxville Press*, January 15, 1942, 4. General Scott's long military career began with the War of 1812. When the Civil War began in April 1861 he was 74 and after his 'Anaconda plan' of attacking and encircling the South was vetoed he resigned in November 1861.

2. Hillel Italie, "You Must Remember This; 'Casablanca' at 50, *The Recorder*, Greenfield, Massachusetts, April 9, 1992, 18.

3. Lebo, Harlan *Casablanca: Behind the Scenes* (New York: Simon & Schuster, 1992), 145.

4. Lebo, Harlan *Casablanca: Behind the Scenes* (New York: Simon & Schuster, 1992), 137.

5. Pontuso, James F. [Ed.] *Political Philosophy Comes to Rick's: Casablanca and American Civic Culture* (Lanham, MD: Lexington Books, 2005), 10.

6. Hillel Italie, "You Must Remember This; 'Casablanca' at 50, *The Recorder*, Greenfield, Massachusetts, April 9, 1992, 18.

7. Harmetz, Aljean *Round Up the Usual Suspects: The Making of Casablanca: Bogart, Bergman & World War II* (New York: Hyperion, 1992). 286.

8. Eco, Umberto *Travels in Hyper-Reality* (London: Picador, 1986), 462.

9. Leonard Maltin, "Casablanca to be shown on the big screen in Oklahoma City" *NewsOK*, March 9, 2012, 69.

10. Hillel Italie, "You Must Remember This; 'Casablanca' at 50, *The Recorder*, Greenfield, Massachusetts, April 9, 1992, 18.

11. "WB's War Front Sequel" *Variety*, January 20, 1943, 48.

12. Harold V. Cohen, "The Drama Desk: Hollywood Notes" *The Pittsburgh Press*, July 29, 1942, 21.
13. "Warner Bros. To Glorify U. S. Merchant Marine" *Showmen's Trade Review*, May 2, 1942, 25.
14. Hedda Hopper "In Hollywood" *The Los Angeles Times*, March 3, 1943, 32.
15. "Screen News Here and In Hollywood" *The New York Times*, October 1, 1943, 32.

22 Bogie and Sydney

1. "Greenstreet Role One to His Liking" *The Jackson Sun*, June 7, 1942, 23.
2. "Cushion Helps Ease Actor's Death" *The Pittsburgh Press*, July 6, 1942, 14.
3. Harold Heffernan, "Hollywood Today" *The Long Island Star Journal*, August 3, 1942, 12.
4. "Reviews of the New Films: Across the Pacific" *The Film Daily*, August 18, 1942, 6.
5. Bosley Crowther, "The Screen; 'Across the Pacific' Featuring Humphrey Bogart and Sydney Greenstreet in a Tingling Thriller, Arrives at Strand" *The New York Times*, September 5, 1942, 43.
6. Astor, Mary *A Life on Film* (London: W. H. Allen, 1973), 169.
7. "Greenstreet Again Villain in Drama Due at Paramount" *Syracuse Journal*, July 28, 1943, 15.
8. "New Films in London: Murder and Conscience: Warner – Conflict" *The Times* (London), October 1, 1945, 6.
9. Bob Porfirio, "Conflict (1945)" Silver, Alain & Ward, Elizabeth *Film Noir* (London: Secker & Warburg, 1980), 63.
10. Bernhardt, Curtis & Kiersch, Mary *Curtis Bernhardt: A Director's Guild of America Oral History* (Berkeley, CA: University of California Press/Director's Guild of America, 1986), 99.
11. "TCM Notes: Conflict (1945)" http://www.tcm.com/tcmdb/title/95/Conflict/notes.html
12. "Psychiatrist Advises on Film" *The Los Angeles Times*, June 27, 1945, 13.
13. Patricia Clary, "Hollywood" *The Daily News* Huntingdon, Pennsylvania, August 29, 1945, 2.
14. "South West Pictures" *The Blackwood Times, Bunbury, Western Australia*, May 9, 1947, 10.

23 Background to Danger

1. McGilligan, Patrick [Ed.] *Backstory: Interviews with Screenwriters of Hollywood's Golden Age* (Berkeley, CA: University of California Press, 1986), 70.
2. "Ex-Comic Now Villain" *The Los Angeles Times*, March 13, 1944, 10.
3. Gene Handsaker, "Hollywood: Mongrel Dog Becomes Star" *Daily Sentinel, Rome, New York*, December 17, 1947, 4.
4. Halliwell, Leslie *Halliwell's Film Guide: Fourth Edition* (London: Guild Publishing, 1983), 53.

5. "Greenstreet Again Villain in Drama Due at Paramount" *Syracuse Journal*, July 28, 1943, 8.
6. Phillips, Gene D. *Fiction, Film & Faulkner: The Art of Adaptation* (Knoxville, Tennessee: University of Tennessee Press, 1988), 32-33.
7. Youngkin, Stephen D., *The Lost One: A Life of Peter Lorre* (Lexington, KY: The University Press of Kentucky, 2005), 217.
8. Sperber, A. M. & Lax, Eric *Bogart: The Biography* (New York: Harper Collins, 1996), 174.
9. Hirschhorn, Clive *The Warner Bros. Story* (London: Octopus Books, 1979), 247.
10. Richard Mallett in *Punch*, quoted in Halliwell, Leslie *Halliwell's Film Guide: Fourth Edition* (London: Guild Publishing, 1983), 629.
11. Bosley Crowther, "The Screen: 'Passage to Marseille,' a Heavy Action Drama in Which Free Frenchmen Figure, with Bogart, at the Hollywood" *The New York Times*, February 17, 1944, 31.

24 A Star of Tomorrow at 64

1. "Stars of Tomorrow" *Motion Picture Herald*, August 26, 1944, 14.
2. "Pix Paid Most of Biggest Salaries During 1943-44; Report 75G or More" *Variety*, June 27, 1945, 25.
3. Harrison Carroll, "Hollywood" *The Wilkes-Barre Record* (Pennsylvania), August 27, 1943, 15.
4. Gail Greenstreet, email to the author, June 5, 2017.
5. Bob Thomas, "Greenstreet Meets Ford; Fails to Get New Auto" *The Knickerbocker News, Albany, New York*, February 22, 1946, B-3.
6. "A Town Called Hollywood" *Chicago Daily Tribune*, January 17, 1943, 50.
7. "Pix Paid Most of Biggest Salaries During 1943-44; Report 75G or More" *Variety*, June 27, 1945, 25.
8. Edwin Schallert, "Horror Star Karloff Here" *The Los Angeles Times*, June 16, 1942, 16.
9. Ward Morehouse: "London After Dark: The Lunts: Reunion on Thames" *The New York Sun*, June 5, 1945, 14.
10. Hal Eaton, "Going to Town: Rialto Ramblings" *Long Island Star-Journal*, September 24, 1943, 14.
11. Inger Arvad, "Sydney Greenstreet, Film Menace, Is Charming Host" *The Indianapolis Star*, May 21, 1944, 71.
12. Hedda Hopper "Looking at Hollywood" *Buffalo Courier-Express*, July 19, 1943, 15.
13. Wood Soames, "Curtain Calls: Welles Plans 'King Lear' Tour: Orson, Sydney Greenstreet Both Want to Assume Great Shakespeare Role" *Oakland Tribune*, August 9, 1943, 7.
14. Edwin Schallert, "Greenstreet Plans London Repertoire" *The Los Angeles Times*, October 13, 1944, 10.

15. "Greenstreet Clings to Footlights Habit" *Daily World* (Opelousis, Louisiana), June 19, 1942, 5.
16. "Letter to Seaver Buck sent from Hotel Carteret, New York City, September 21, 1939, quoted in "As Ever, Sydney: Letters from Sydney Greenstreet to Seaver Buck" *Berkshire Bulletin*, Fall 2011/Winter 2012. 53.
17. "Actor's Housekeeper is His Severest Critic" *The Brooklyn Daily Eagle*, May 26, 1946, 28.
18. Virginia Macpherson, "Sydney Greenstreet is a Practical Joker at Home" *The Schenectady Gazette*, August 1, 1945, 23.
19. Hedda Hopper "In Hollywood" *The Daily Clintonian* (Clinton, Indiana), October 13, 1944, 4.
20. "Sydney Greenstreet Will Star in a Two-Reel Dramatic Subject" *Showmen's Trade Review*, September 5, 1942, 39.
21. Louella O. Parsons "Private Holle, Marine Boy Hero, Signed by Warner Brothers Studio" *Albany Times-Union*, December 28, 1942, 13.
22. "Coast Flashes" *Motion Picture Daily*, April 6, 1944, 4.
23. "The Hollywood Scene: Frank Lloyd a Major in Army Air Force" *Motion Picture Herald*, January 16, 1943, 42.
24. "Warners Have 79 Properties in Material Pool: Ann Sheridan to Star in Calamity Jane" *Motion Picture Herald*, August 19, 1944, 30.

25 *The Mask of Dimitrios*

1. Halliwell, Leslie *Halliwell's Film Guide: Fourth Edition* (London: Guild Publishing, 1983), 301.
2. Negulesco, Jean *Things I Did and Things I Think I Did: A Hollywood Memoir* (New York: Linden Press/Simon & Schuster, 1984), 118.
3. "Crime Does Pay If Fat Enough" *The Brooklyn Daily Eagle*, July 2, 1944, 18.
4. "Zachary Scott Fills Idea of Handsome Guy" *Daily Press Newport News* (Virginia), December 31, 1944, 4.
5. Sidney Skolsky, "Hollywood is My Beat: Watching Them Make Movies" *New York Post*, January 23, 1945, 35.
6. Youngkin, Stephen D., *The Lost One: A Life of Peter Lorre* (Lexington, KY: The University Press of Kentucky, 2005), 217-18.
7. "TV Keynotes: Screen Villain is Getting Roles" *Tarrytown, New York, Daily News*, March 20, 1963, 35.
8. "Don't Pad the Part – Just the Place Where Syd Falls" *Buffalo Evening News*, February 12, 1944, 4.
9. "The Selling Approach on New Products" *Motion Picture Herald*, July 29, 1944, 76.
10. Negulesco, Jean *Things I Did and Things I Think I Did: A Hollywood Memoir* (New York: Linden Press/Simon & Schuster, 1984), 122.
11. Rudy Behlmer *Shoot the Rehearsal! Behind the Scenes with Assistant Director Reggie Callow* (Scarecrow Press, Inc., 2010), 53.

12. Negulesco, Jean *Things I Did and Things I Think I Did: A Hollywood Memoir* (New York: Linden Press/Simon & Schuster, 1984), 122.
13. "Other Recommended Pictures: The Conspirators" *National Board of Review Magazine,* November 1944, 4.
14. Youngkin, Stephen D., *The Lost One: A Life of Peter Lorre* (Lexington, KY: The University Press of Kentucky, 2005), 221-2.

26 Between Two Worlds

1. Roy Pickard "Sydney Greenstreet: A Gifted Shakespearean Actor Who Chuckled Wickedly in Films and Made Fat Sinister" *Films in Review,* August – September 1972, 391.
2. Thomas F. Brady, "Hollywood Collides with the Wage Cutting" *The New York Times,* November 6, 1942, 12.
3. Donati, William, *Ida Lupino: A Biography* (Lexington, Kentucky: The University of Kentucky Press, 1996), 101-2.
4. "Green Fruit Lasts Well in Film Sets" *The Brooklyn Daily Eagle,* May 21, 1944, 26.

27 Comedy at last – almost

1. Sherman, Vincent *Studio Affairs: My Life as a Film Director* (Lexington, Kentucky: University Press of Kentucky, 2015), 152.
2. Hirschhorn, Clive *The Warner Bros. Story* (London: Octopus Books, 1979), 254.
3. Sherman, Vincent *Studio Affairs: My Life as a Film Director* (Lexington, Kentucky: University Press of Kentucky, 2015), 152.
4. Donati, William, *Ida Lupino: A Biography* (The University of Kentucky Press, 1996), 117.
5. "Greenstreet is Shady Again" *The Brooklyn Daily Eagle,* March 31, 1946, 28.
6. Hirschhorn, Clive *The Warner Bros. Story* (London: Octopus Books, 1979), 256.
7. Madsen, Axel *Barbara Stanwyck: A Biography* (New York: Open Road Media), 171.
8. "Christmas In Connecticut" *The Film Daily,* August 8, 1945, 6.
9. Hedda Hopper, "Looking at Hollywood" *Harrisburg Telegraph,* February 20, 1946, 6.
10. "Flashes from the Studios" *Examiner, Launceston, Tasmania,* May 10, 1947, 6.
11. Sheilah Graham, "Hollywood Today" *Asbury Park Press,* April 15, 1946, 4.
12. Halliwell, Leslie *Halliwell's Film Guide: Fourth Edition* (London: Guild Publishing, 1983), 811.
13. Why Should We Consider? 'That Way with Women' *Freeport New York Daily Review,* February 18, 1947, 9.
14. "For Clark, Greenstreet" *Showmen's Trade Review,* April 26, 1947, 47.
15. Sam Zolotow, "Elliott Presents New Farce Tonight" *The New York Times,* May 2, 1945, 45.
16. Hedda Hopper, "On the Sunny Side of the Greenstreet" *Chicago Sunday Tribune,* September 10, 1944, 2.

28 Still Learning

1. Hedda Hopper, "On the Sunny Side of the Greenstreet" *Chicago Sunday Tribune*, September 10, 1944, 2.
2. Erskine Johnson, "In Hollywood" *The Daily Tribune* (Wisconsin Rapids, Wisconsin), February 23, 1946, 6.
3. "On Parade" *The Akron Beacon Journal* (Ohio), May 2, 1948, 97.
4. "Greenstreet in New Assignment" *The Berkshire Eagle*, December 21, 1945, 14.
5. "Greenstreet Best Friends Form 'Local Angle'" *The Berkshire Eagle* (Pittsfield, Massachusetts), May 29, 1946, 8.
6. "Berkshire Festivities" *The Brooklyn Daily Eagle*, August 6, 1933, 2 B-C.
7. Robbin Coons, "Hollywood Sights & Sounds" *Niagara Falls Gazette*, December 21, 1945, 19.
8. "Sydney Greenstreet Has Useless Hobby" *The Pittsburgh Press*, November 24, 1946, 48.
9. Bob Thomas, "Joan Crawford No. 1 Setter of Hairstyles" *The Ottawa Journal*, April 29, 1946, 14.
10. Sheilah Graham, "In Hollywood Today" *The Indianapolis Star*, February 23, 1946, 11.
11. John Todd, "Fat Man to Cut 75 Pounds" *Salt Lake Telegram*, August 6, 1945, 8.
12. Bessie M. Gant, "Bess' Secrets 'Bout Good Things to Eat" *The Pittsburgh Courier*, September 15, 1945, 8.
13. Ida Jean Kain, "Keeping in Trim" *Albany New York Times-Union*, June 9, 1949, 20.
14. Harold Heffernan, "Shirley Temple Aids Husband in Debut" *The Winnipeg Tribune*, (Canada), June 26, 1947, 8. 15. "Hefty Actor Refutes Claim Food is Romance Substitute" *The Greenville News*, April 19, 1946, 25.
16. "Disabled Veterans to Extend Motion Picture Public Service into Post War Era" *The Medina Journal-Register*, September 25, 1947, 5.
17. Sheilah Graham, "Hollywood Today" *The Indianapolis Star*, December 23, 1944, 8.
18. Erskine Johnson, "In Hollywood" *Ogdensburg New York Journal*, July 16, 1948, 2.
19. "Sydney Greenstreet" *The Cincinnati Enquirer*, December 9, 1945, 75.
20. "UK Incoming Passenger Lists, 1932, 1935, 1938."
21. "Movie Stars Providing for Rainy Day" *The Ottawa Journal*, June 19, 1948, 2.
22. Hedda Hopper "In Hollywood" *Harrisburg Telegraph*, October 1, 1942, 25.
23. Gail Greenstreet, Email to the author, June 6, 2017. As far as I have been able to ascertain, Arthur and Guy didn't have children. Frank had at least three children, Peter (b.1916), Pamela (b.1918) and Mary W. (b.1920).
24. "Chinese Get Aid" *Buffalo Evening News*, July 3, 1943, 5.
25. Gail Greenstreet, Email to the author, June 6, 2017.
26. Erskine Johnson, "Hollywood Victory Gardens Sprouting Behind Movie Mansions" *The Ithaca Journal*, April 14, 1943, 12.

27. "Greenstreet Joins Class in Dancing" *The Pittsburgh Press*, March 10, 1943, 26.
28. Hugh Dixon, "Hollywood" *Pittsburgh Post-Gazette*, February 6, 1947, 11.
29. Hedda Hopper, "In Hollywood" *The Akron Beacon Journal*, August 22, 1943, 32.
30. Gail Greenstreet, email to the author, June 5, 2017.
31. "Laughton on Stage in 'Galileo'" *Binghampton Press*, July 31, 1947, 18.
32. Hyatt Downing, "She Knows What She Wants and She'll Get It! Phyllis Thaxter" *Screenland*, September 1945, 85.

29 The Laurel and Hardy of Crime

1. "'Three Strangers' Starts Tuesday at The." *The Sheboygan Press*, June 3, 1946, 56.
2. "Enshrined" *The Amarillo Globe-Times*, December 26, 1945, 15.
3. Bogdanovich, Peter *Who the Devil Made It? Conversations with Legendary Film Directors* (New York: Ballantine Books, 1997), 98.
4. "Greenstreet Ill; Film Work Halts" *The Los Angeles Times*, November 20, 1945, 15.
5. Eileen Creelman, "Picture Plays and Players: Rosalind Ivan Discusses Her Latest Films, 'Three Strangers' and 'The Suspect'" *The New York Sun*, December 4, 1945, 25.
6. "New Films in London: Murder & Mystery: Warner – The Verdict" *The Times* (London), November 18, 1946, 8.
7. Edwin Schallert, "Musical 'Shrew' Looms, Brent in 'Bella Donna'" *The Los Angeles Times*, March 7, 1946, 15.
8. Bob Thomas, "Hollywood Comment: Broadway Shows Short on Talent, Full of Propaganda, Says Catlett" *Harrisburg Telegraph*, May 18, 1946, 21.
9. Sheilah Graham, "In Hollywood: Maria 'Learns' Twins on Way" *The Des Moines Register*, September 12, 1945, 12.
10. Steven H. Scheuer, "TV Keynotes: Peter Lorre Returns Tonight" *Citizen Register, Ossining, New York*, February 24, 1960, 14.
11. Edwin Schallert, "McLaglen, Morris Will Play 'Men of the Deep'" *The Los Angeles Times*, November 2, 1944, 11.

30 Prelude to Night

1. Davis, Ronald L. *Zachary Scott: Hollywood's Sophisticated Cad* (University of Mississippi Press, 2009), 85.
2. Williams, Tony in Chapter Beyond *Citizen Kane: Ruthless* as Radical Psychobiography," in Rhodes, Gary *Edgar G. Ulmer: Detour on Poverty Row* (Lanham, MD: Rowman & Littlefield, 2009), 197.
3. Erskine Johnson, "In Hollywood" *Ogdensburg Journal*, April 4, 1946, 13.
4. "'Ruthless' Player Takes Pains with Make Believe" *The Brooklyn Daily Eagle*, September 5, 1948, 21.
5. Glenn Erickson, "DVD Savant Review: Ruthless" April 23, 2013. http://www.dvdtalk.com/dvdsavant/s4137ruth.html
6. Hedda Hopper, "Looking at Hollywood" *The Los Angeles Times*, November 6, 1947, 19.

7. Erskine Johnson, "In Hollywood" *Ogdensburg Journal,* August 9, 1948, 7.

31 *"Most Unfortunate!"*

1. Ralph Wilk "Hollywood Speaking" *The Film Daily,* April 2, 1945, 12.
2. "Warner-Cinema: The Woman in White" *The Times* (London), July 17, 1948, 2.
3. Sheilah Graham, "In Hollywood: Chaplin's Newest Film a Secret" *The Des Moines Register,* December 31, 1946, 6.
4. Anne McIlhenny, "41 Years on Stage; Then Movies" *Buffalo Courier-Express,* March 2, 1947, 13-A.
5. "Regent Theatre" *The Ottawa Journal,* October 30, 1948, 15.
6. Harold Heffernan, "Screen Death of a Fat Man" *St Louis Post-Dispatch,* March 16, 1947, 80.
7. Hedda Hopper "Looking at Hollywood: Greenstreet Rattigan" *The Los Angeles Times,* November 8, 1946, 7.
8. Leonard Wallace, "The Film Fat Man: Sydney Greenstreet" *Picturegoer,* January 21, 1950, 39.
9. Bubbeo, Daniel *The Women of Warner Brothers: The Lives & Careers of 15 Leading Ladies* (Jefferson, NC: McFarland & Co, Inc., 2002) 220.
10. Hedda Hopper, "Six More Short Movies Being Made By Smith" *Buffalo Courier-Express,* February 1, 1947, 6.

32 *The Velvet Touch*

1. Capua, Michelangelo *Deborah Kerr: A Biography* (Jefferson, NC: McFarland & Co, Inc., 2010), 41.
2. Bob Thomas, "From Filmland: Sidney Will Get a Lot of Moola in 'Hucksters'" *The Knickerbocker News* (Albany, New York), December 27, 1946, 10-A.
3. Herbert Cohn, "Screen; 'The Hucksters' Caustic Drama at Capitol" *The Brooklyn Daily Eagle,* July 18, 1947, 4.
4. "Greenstreet Plays the Great Huckster" *Life,* March 31, 1947, 51-54.
5. Capua, Michelangelo *Deborah Kerr: A Biography* (Jefferson, NC: McFarland & Co, Inc., 2010), 43.
6. Bosley Crowther, "The Screen: The Hucksters" *The New York Times,* July 18, 1947, 35.
7. "The Hucksters" *Variety,* December 31, 1946, 45.
8. Stephens, Michael *Art Directors in Cinema: A Worldwide Biographical Dictionary* (Jefferson, NC: McFarland & Co, Inc., 2008), 109.
9. "Star Gets Ibsen Role: Rosalind Russell Will Play Title Role in 'Hedda Gabbler' On Screen" *Lansing State Journal,* June 27, 1948, 27.
10. Harold Heffernan, "Rosalind Russell Hailed as Smart Film Producer" *Long Island Star-Journal,* November 5, 1947, 17.
11. William R. Weaver, "The Hollywood Scene: Independent Arts Adopt "Damn Torpedoes" Policy" *Motion Picture Herald,* January 31, 1948, 23.
12. "Studio Sign-Ups: Warner Bros. 75 Grand for Greenstreet" *Film Bulletin,* 1947.

13. Sheilah Graham, "Hollywood Today" *The Indianapolis Star,* June 7, 1947, 17.
14. "Los Angeles Briefs: Actor's Son to Wed," *The Los Angeles Times,* February 15, 1948, 13.
15. "Head All-Star Cast" *Showmen's Trade Review,* December 20, 1947, 30.
16. Ralph Wick, "Hollywood Vine-Yard" *The Film Daily,* July 21, 1948, 65.
17. Sam Zolotow, "Revival of 'Sally' Closed Saturday" *The New York Times,* June 7, 1948, 56.

33 Flamingo Road

1. Skal, David J. & Rains, Jessica, *Claude Rains: An Actor's Voice* (The University Press of Kentucky, 2008), 125.
2. "Mr. Greenstreet Has Awful Ordeal" *The Pittsburgh Press,* April 24, 1949, 66.
3. "He Always Dies Gently" *The Mail* (Adelaide, South Australia), September 2, 1950, 6.
4. Quirk, Lawrence J. & Schoell, William *Joan Crawford: The Essential Biography* (Lexington, KY: University Press of Kentucky, 2002), 148.
5. "Telephone-Throwing Made into Art" *Elmira Star-Gazette,* April 14, 1949, 41.
6. "Focus; Film Review: Our Panel of Priests: Flamingo Road" *A Film Review,* 1948-9, 205.
7. "Box Office Slant: Flamingo Road" *Showmen's Trade Review,* April 9, 1949, 13.
8. Hedda Hopper, "MGM Gets Fitzgerald Story and Jennifer" *The Los Angeles Times,* November 18, 1948, 44.
9. "Hokum About Malaya" *The Singapore Free Press,* December 24, 1949, 2.
10. "Sunday Cineview: Malaya" *The Straits Times,* January 15, 1950, 10.
11. "Advert for *East of the Rising Sun*" *Picturegoer,* January 21, 1950, 42.
12. Dewey, Donald *James Stewart: A Biography* (Atlanta, GA: Turner Publishing, Inc., 1996), 307.

34 Radio Swansong

1. "Inside Stuff – Radio" *Variety,* September 5, 1945, 32.
2. Sleeve notes from *The Cask of Amontillado,* Brunswick OE9171 (October 1955)
3. "ABC Preps Flock of Radio Shows for Testing" *The Billboard,* April 29, 1950, 11.
4. McBride, O. E. *Stout Fellow: A Guide Through Nero Wolfe's World* (Lincoln, NE: IUniverse, 2003), 153.
5. McBride, O. E. *Stout Fellow: A Guide Through Nero Wolfe's World* (Lincoln, NE: IUniverse, 2003), 138-9.

35 Finis

1. "Capitol: Sydney Greenstreet One of Supporting Stars Seen in Current Screen Drama" *Shamokin News-Dispatch,* July 8, 1949, 9.
2. "Screen's Noted 'Fat Man' Follows Serene Policy" *The Pittsburgh Press,* August 5, 1945, 30.

3. "Actor Gives Hopeful Tips to Tired Old Businessmen" *The Pittsburgh Press,* July 22, 1945, 26.

4. Erskine Johnson, "In Hollywood" *Ogdensburg Journal,* May 12, 1947, 7.

5. Edith Gwynn, "Hollywood" *Pottsdown Mercury* (Pennsylvania), March 16, 1949, 4.

6. Louella O. Parsons, "Greenstreet May Do 'Fat Man' Roles" *The Philadelphia Inquirer,* July 22, 1949, 25.

7. Sheilah Graham, "Hollywood Today: Dana Andrews, Gene Tierney, Will Co-Star in New Film" *Asheville Citizen-Times* (North Carolina), December 18, 1949, 29.

8. Sheilah Graham, "In Hollywood" *Honolulu Star-Bulletin,* June 8, 1948, 18.

9. Louella Parsons, "Hollywood" *Albany, New York, Times-Union,* February 20, 1948, 13.

10. Edith Gwynn, "Hollywood" *The Cincinnati Enquirer,* March 20, 1951, 16.

11. Sheilah Graham, "Hollywood Today: Liz Taylor Nixes Bids for Story of Her Life" *The Indianapolis Star,* February 5, 1951, 9.

12. Morley, Sheridan *Robert, My Father* (London: Weidenfeld & Nicholson, 1993), 145.

13. Williams, Tennessee *27 Wagons Full of Cotton & Other One-Act Plays* (Ann Arbor, Michigan: New Directions, University of Michigan, 1946), 73.

14. "English Actor Dies" *The Winnipeg Tribune* (Manitoba, Canada), March 8, 1948, 2.

15. "Church Filled at Last Rites for S. B. Buck" *The Berkshire Eagle,* May 19, 1950, 46.

16. Sheilah Graham, "In Hollywood: Filmland Sights and Sounds" *Honolulu Star-Bulletin,* November 17, 1952.

17. Gene Handsaker "What's Become of the Old Stars? Sydney Greenstreet Told By Doctor to Take Rest" *The Courier-Journal* (Louisville, Kentucky), April 22, 1952, 21.

18. Herb Klein *The Philadelphia Inquirer,* December 29, 1952, 17.

19. "Sydney Greenstreet, Great Mausoleum, Utility Columbarium, Niche 523330; Record Added January 1, 2001, Find a Grave Memorial No. 420." https://www.findagrave.com/cgi-bin/fg.cgi?page=gr&GRid=420

20. "Actor Greenstreet Leaves $150,000" *The Los Angeles Times,* February 2, 1954, 4.

21. "Dorothy N. Greenstreet d. April 23, 1972, Ocla, Wisconsin, 78: Certificate No. 017487." Wisconsin Death Index, 1959-1997, Ocla, Wisconsin, Wisconsin Dept. of Health, Madison, Wisconsin.

22. Mike Connolly, "Star Gazing" *Asbury Park Press,* September 15, 1954, 6.

23. "John Ogden Greenstreet '43" Hamilton Alumni Necrology. https://www.hamilton.edu/magazine/fall05/necrology/1940s "Greenstreet, John Ogden" Funeral Notices, *Tucson Citizen,* March 8, 2005. http://tucsoncitizen.com/morgue2/2005/03/08/144366-funeral-notices/

24. See *Some details of Sydney's family.* Imdb claims that Mark Greenstreet is a great nephew of Sydney, which is not true. The connection between them is more distant

and goes back further than Sydney's great grandfather William Greenstreet who was born in 1786 and Mark's 3 x great grandfather John (b. 1820). Mark was an actor on British television in the 1980s. A blond, handsome light leading man he was once tested for the role of James Bond but lost out to Timothy Dalton.

Epilogue

1. Harold Heffernan, "Movieland" *The Baltimore Sun*, November 22, 1942, 116.
2. Erskine Johnson, "Not Fat, Says Sidney; Stylish Stout at 260" *The Saratogian*, April 2, 1946, 4.
3. Cowsill, Alan *Spider-Man Chronicle: A Year By Year Visual History* (London: DK Publishing, 2012), 8.
4. Mosher, Jerry Dean *Weighty Ambitions: Fat Actors & Figurations in American Cinema 1910-1960* (ProQuest, 2007), 271.
5. "The Fat Man Dies" *Life*, February 1, 1954, 20.

Theater

1. "Auditorium (Harry G. Sommers) My Cinderella Girl" *The New York Dramatic Mirror*, September 28, 1910, 21.

Radio

1. "Sydney Greenstreet" *The Morning Call* (Allentown, Pennsylvania), November 3, 1926, 33.
2. "Radio: From the Production Centers: In New York City" *Variety*, June 4, 1941, 28.
3. "P & G Ganders 'Below'" *Variety*, April 2, 1947, 31.
4. "Main Street: California Commentary: Hollywood" *Radio Daily*, November 22, 1949, 3.
5. "ABC Preps Flock of Radio Shows for Testing" *The Billboard*, April 29, 1950, 11.

Some details of Sydney's family

His father John Jarvis Greenstreet (1847-1913) Died Strand, London aged 65.

His mother Anne Greenstreet (nee Baker) (1852-1931). Died May 18, 1931 in Birmingham, England, aged 79.

John Jarvis Greenstreet was the son of William (circa 1820-58) and Eliza Cooper (circa 1818-55).

William Greenstreet (1786-1869) was born in Frinsted, Kent, married Martha Mantle (c1788-1859). They lived in Eastchurch, Kent.

William Cooper (1788-1871), tanner, born Steyning, Sussex, married Susannah (circa 1793-1870). Lived on Chalkwell Road, Milton. Many children including Venn Cooper (circa 1829-1872)

Anne Baker's parents Henry Baker (c1813-1867) and Ann nee Pollard (c1814-91?) m. January 17, 1839, Sandwich. Booksellers & Stationers, Market Street, Sandwich, Kent. Business carried on by Charles Baker (1843-1908)

Children of John and Ann Baker:

Harry Cooper Greenstreet (1875-?) emigrated to the United States in 1907. He went to stay with his uncle Frederick Baker, his mother's brother, who was working as a clerk in a packing firm in Douglas, Omaha, Nebraska. Frederick Baker had lived in America since 1894. Harry Greenstreet also worked as a clerk and later became a land examiner. He stayed in Douglas and married Lucille Curtis Race; their son was named after his brother Sydney (b. 1917). Harry became a naturalized U. S. citizen in 1919. Sydney was best man at his wedding in 1913.

Frank Baker Greenstreet (1877-1926) was a fine art dealer who lived in London. He died July 12, 1926 aged 49 at 306 Goldhawk Road, Middlesex. Children: Peter, Pamela and Mary W. Greenstreet.

Arthur Venn Greenstreet (1878-1959) stayed in the brewing business and worked as a Hop Merchant. He moved to Birmingham and married twice; his second wife, Gwendolyn, was 35 years younger than him but pre-deceased him in 1957.

Olive Julia Greenstreet b. March 23, 1881, Sandwich, Kent. d. May 14, 1981, Brighton, East Sussex aged 100.

Guy Seaman Greenstreet (1882- Sept 1943) was a manager and lived in Camberwell, South London, where he died aged 61 in 1943.

Hilda Greenstreet (b. April 19, 1883) married Arthur Hayward in Kensington, September 1913. died Hove, Sussex, March 1972 aged 89.

Margery Greenstreet (b. May 1, 1886-1972) married Frederick W. Davis September 1912 in Kensington; d. June 1972, Merton, Surrey aged 86.

Index

Abbott & Costello 206, 234
Abbott, John 215
Academy Awards 132, 170
Across the Pacific 142-5, 146, 148, 234, 244
Actor's Equity Union 81
Actor's Fund of America 39, 81
The Admirable Crichton 100-1
The African Queen 239
Agee, James 152
Alfonso XIII, King of Spain 23
Allen, Viola 76
Allgood, Sara 176
Aloha Means Goodbye 142
The Amazing Dr. Clitterhouse 154
Ambler, Eric 150, 152, 164
American Dramatic Guild 36
American Theatrical Association 80
American Women's Association 104
Amphitryon 38 115, 118, 122
Anderson, Bobby 211
Andrews, Pattie 172
Anglin, Margaret viii, 46, 49-53, 55, *63*
Antony & Cleopatra 49, 51, 52
Arbutny, Jerome K. 200
Are You a Mason? 32
Aristophanes 100, 101
Arling, Joyce 212
Arliss, George 184, 186
Armstrong, Louis 181
Army Relief Society 46
Arnold, Albert 213
Arnold, Edward 131
Arthur, Jean 101
Asbury Park Journal 70
Astaire, Fred 132, 170
"As Time Goes By" 138
Astor, Mary *129*, 130, *131*, 132, 142, 144, *146*, 234
As You Like It 12, 18, 19, 20, 22, 26, 31, 32, 49, 50, 56, 63-4
Atwill, Lionel 200
Audrey 30

Background to Danger 148, 150-4
Bainter, Fay 101, 185

Baker, Charles 3
Baker, Frank 3
Baker, Frederick 82
Baker, Henry 3, 8
Ball, Lucille 234
Barrett, Edith 212
Barrie, J. M. 100
Barrymore, Lionel 232
The Beast with Five Fingers 206
Beat the Devil 240
Beerbohm, Max 67
Behrman, S. N. 160
Belch, Sir Toby *13*, 49, 51, 56, 76
The Beloved Blackguard 163
Benchley, Robert 121
Bendix, William 165
Ben Greet School of Acting 8-9, 10, 236
Bergen, Edgar 234
Bergman, Bernard 206
Bergman, Ingrid 137, 138, *139*
Berlin 101-2
Bernhardt, Curtis 146-7, 148, 173-4
Bernhardt, Sarah 60
Between Two Worlds 173, 176-8
The Big Country 225
Biggers, Earl Derr 184
Big Town 233
Bijou Theater, London 9, 11
The Billboard 76
The Black Cat 210
Blanke, Henry 166
Blatt, Edward A. 177
Blind, Eric 31, 53-3
Bogart, Humphrey viii, 115, 128, 129, 130, 131, 133, 137, 141, 142-9, 152, 154, 155, 158, 160, 166, 195, 197, 198-9, 206, 234, 240, 243
Bolton, Guy 42
Bomberg, J. Edward 137
Boocock. Cornelius B. 105-6
Boston University 80
Bottomley. Roland 102
Bradbury, Jim 83
Brautigan, Richard 245
Brazzaville 140

Bremer, Lucille *209, 211,* 212
Brent, George 234
Bressart, Felix *162*
Brian, David 225, 227
Bring on the Girls 42
Brisson, Frederick 222
Broad Street Theater, Philadelphia 94
Bronte, Anne 173-4
Bronte, Branwell 173
Bronte, Charlotte 173-5
Brooklyn, U. S. A. 162
Brown, John Mason 102. 112, 115
Bruce, Nigel 213
"Brush Up Your Shakespeare" 113
Bryn Mawr College 26
Buck, Pearl S. 103
Buck, Dr. Seaver 108, 116, 118, 189-90, 240
Budge, Don 81
Bugs Bunny 195
Buka, Donald 114
Burnett, W. R. 152
Burr, Raymond 212
Byron, Lord George 192

Caliban *24,* 25, 190
The Call 28
Callow, Reggie 171
Canterbury Tales 1
Capek, Karel 99
Capra, Frank 142
Carlos & Inez 84
Carmen 33
Carr, John Dickson 235
Carson, Frances 52-3
Carson, Jack 230
Carter, Ann 211
Casablanca 135-41, 160, 169, 202, 244
The Cask of Amontillado 234
Castle School for Girls, Tarrytown, NY 80
Chaplin, Charles 62
Chaucer, Geoffrey 1
Chautauqua Circuit 29, 56
Chekhov, Anton 120
Chicago Tribune 55, 120
The Christian 33

Christmas in Connecticut 181-4, 187, 215
The City 38
Clark, Dane 184, 186
Clark, Fred 227
Claudius (*Hamlet*) 20
Clift, Montgomery viii, 123
Close-Ups vii
Cobb, Lee J. 131
Coburn, Charles 165
Cochran, Mary 241
A Coffin for Dimitrios 164
Cohn, Herbert 220
Collegiate School, NY 105
Collier, Constance 36
Collier, John 213
Collier's Comedy Theater, NY 41
Collins, Wilkie 208, 213
Colman, Ronald 244
Columbia Pictures 238
Columbia University 25, 31, 38
A Confederate General from Big Sur 245
Conflict 142, 146-8, 149, 173, 244
The Conspirators 169-72
Conte, Richard 237
Continental Memorial Hall, NY 23
Conway, Jack 220
Cook, Jr., Elisha 103, 128, 129, *131*
Cooper, William 2
Cooper, Susannah 2
Cooper, Venn (great-uncle) 2-3
Corbett, James L. 74
Cormas, Carroll 81
Cornell, Katherine 159
The Corn is Green 204
Cortese, Valentina 231, 232
Cort Theater, Chicago 56
Coulouris, George 177, 202, *203*
Coward, Noel 116, 117, 146
Crawford, Joan 162, 226-7, *228,* 229, 230,
Crawley, John Sayre 11, 21, 104, 190, 240
Crime and Punishment 87
Crisp, Donald 132, 200
Criterion Theater, NY 36
Crowther, Bosley 144, 157, 220
Crystal Palace 14

Curse of the Cat People 212
Curtiz, Michael 140, 154, 156, 225, 227, 228-9

The Dairy Farm 32
Dallas Little Theater 80
Daly's Theater, NY 31
Danbury, Captain 218, 220-2
Dandridge, Dorothy 181
Dane Hill House Prep. School, Margate 4
Dangerous Female 127
Davis, George L. 90
Davis Cup 4
Davis, Donald 103
Davis, Frederick W. 44, 118, 194
Davis, Harry 31-3
Davis, Owen 103
Davis, Ralph W. 37, 39
Day, Doris 230
de Balzac, Honore 160, 187
Decca Records 234
de Cordoba, Fred 184, 185
de Cordoba, Pedro 94
de Courville, Albert 217
de Havilland, Olivia 135, 173, *174*
Dekker, Albert 99
del Ruth, Roy 128
de Malherbe, Francois 105
De Mille, Cecil B. 38, 41
de Mille, William C. 38
The Desert Song 55
Design for Living 116
Detour 210
Deutsch, Adolph 130, 168
Devotion 173-5, 187
Dickens, Charles 1, 2, 175
Dickens, Homer vii
Digges, Dudley 31, 97, 127-8
Disabled American Veterans National Service Fund 193
Doctor Faustus 21
Dodd, Lee Wilson 41
Dogberry, Constable *93*, 94
Donnelly, Ruth 181
Dostoievsky, Feodor 87
A Double Life 222
Downing College, Cambridge 12
The Dragon Seed 149

Drake, Oliver *140*
"Drink, Drink, Drink" 86
Dr. Jekyll and Mr. Hyde 99
Druse, Albert 99
The Duchess of Suds 36
Duff, Howard 237
Dugas, John-Don 15
Dunn, Emma 83
Dunne, Irene 110
Duquesne Theater, Pittsburgh 31-3
Duse, Eleanora 60

E & G High School, Washington, DC 27
East Lynn 32
East of the Rising Sun 230
Eaton, Walter Prichard 51
Eco, Umberto 139
Eddy, Nelson 85
Edeson, Arthur 130, 143
Edward VII, King of England 23
Elsom, Isobel 177
Emerson, John 83, 84
Enobarbus 51, *52*
The Era 20
Erwin, Stuart 181
The Eternal City 11, 12
Evans, Evan Llewellyn 218, 222
The Evening Telegram 83
Everson, William K. 245
Everybody Comes to Rick's 137
Everyman 12, 15, 16, 17, 21, 23, 36
Excuse Me 40, 42-4, 45

The Fabulous Mr. Manchester 235
Falstaff, Sir John 14, 46, 63, 190
Fanny and the Servant Problem 73
Farrar, Geraldine 59
The Fat Man 163, 235, 237
Faulkner, William 154
Ferrari, Senor 135, 231
Fields, W. C. 17
The Film Daily 143
Films in Review vii
Finnish War Relief Fund 123
Fisher, King 45
Fiske, Harrison Grey 91
Fiske, Mrs. Minnie Maddern viii, 91-5, *92*

Fitzgerald, Barry 222
Fitzgerald, Geraldine 140, *199*,
Flamingo Road 225-30, 244
Flannery, William 222
Fletcher, John 65
Flynn, Errol 135, *136*, 152
Fontanne, Lynn viii, 64, 112-7, 119, 120-5, *124*, 132, 135, 159, 160, 240, 243
Forbes-Robertson, Sir Johnston 73
Ford, Jr., Henry 185
Fortinbras 20
Fosco, Count 208, 213-5, 217
Fragments from Shakespeare 80
France, Anatole 36
Francen, Victor *156*, 165, 170
Franklin, Benjamin 160
Friend, Budd 177
Friend Martha 59, 60
"The Friends of Mr. Cairo" 245
Further Adventures of the Maltese Falcon 134

Gabin, Jean 153
Gable, Clark 218, *219*, 220
Gaiety Theater, NY 54
Galileo 195
Gant, Bessie 191
Gardiner, Reginald *182*
Gardner, Ava 218, *219*
Garfield, John 163, 176, *177*
"Garry Owen" 136
Garson, Greer *162*
George, Gladys 130, 227
George V, King of England 23
Gilbert, Billy 131
Gilbert, W. S. 31, 85
Giradout, Jean 115
Give and Take 61
Gobbo, Lancelot 33
The Goddess of Reason 30, 31
Godfrey, Peter 215, 216
Gogol, Nikolai 224
Goldsmith, Oliver 21
Gomez, S. Thomas 113
Gone With the Wind 32
The Good Earth 103-4
Good Morning Boys 215
Goulding, Edmund 171-2

Graham, Sheilah 241
Gratiano 41
Gray, Tommy 54
Greeley, Horace 15
Greenstreet, Ann (nee Baker) 1-4, *5*, 6, 8, *9*, 44, 82
Greenstreet, Arthur Venn 2, 7, 44, 66, 194, 238, 242
Greenstreet, Eliza (Aunt) 2
Greenstreet, Eliza (nee Cooper) 2
Greenstreet, Frank 2, 44, 194
Greenstreet, Gail 194
Greenstreet, Gail H. ix, 7, 82-3, 106, 158, 194, 238, 241
Greenstreet, James O. 241
Greenstreet, John Jarvis 1-4, 5-6, 8, 44
Greenstreet, John Ogden (Son) Birth of, 72, *73*, *78*, *79*, *80*, *86*, *89*, 99, 105, 108-9, 110, *117*, 118, 185, 189, *202*, *223*, Marriage of, *224*, *239*, 241-2
Greenstreet, Guy Seaman 2, 44, 66, 194
Greenstreet, Harry Cooper 2, 44, 66, 82, 194
Greenstreet, Hilda 2, *5*, 44, 82, 118, 194, 241, 242
Greenstreet, Margery 2, 44, 194, 241, 242
Greenstreet, Martha 2
Greenstreet, Olive Julia 2, *5*, 44, 82, 194, 241, 242
Greenstreet, Sarah (Great-aunt) 3
Greenstreet, Sydney (Nephew) 82
Greenstreet, William (Grandfather) 2
Greenstreet, William (Great-grandfather) 2, 4
Greenstreet, William (Uncle) 2
Greet, Sir Philip Ben 8-12, 15-18, 20-1, 22-9, 30, 31, 32, 40, 46, 52, 56, 70, 104, 127, 171, 245
"Gunga Din" 40
Gutman, Kaspar vii, 126, 127-9, 130, 133-4, 151
Gwenn, Edmund 176

"Hail to the Chief" 28
Haines, Mrs. 39

Haines, Robert T. 35, 37-9, 40
Hajos, Mitzi 72, 77-8, 82, 83, 84-5, 88, 90, 94
Hale, Alan 184-5
Hamilton College, NY 162
Hamlet 17, 19, 20, 27, 31, 35-6
Hammett, Dashiell 126, 130, 133, 134, 163, 234, 235
"The Hangman Won't Wait" 234
The Happy Times 224
Harding, Lyn 66
Harding, Warren G. 23
Harvard College 20, 24, 42
Harworth, Joseph 35-6
Hawthorne, Nathaniel 25, 27, 234
Hay, Will 215
Hayes, Helen 159
Hays, Will H. 128
Hayward, Arthur D. 44
Hayward, Louis 208
Head Over Heels 78
Hedda Gabler 221
Hepburn, Katherine 239
Heflin, Van 163
Henreid, Paul 137, 138, 169, 176, 177
Henry V 80
Henry VII 1
Henry VIII 58, 190
Henry VIII 57, 64, 65-6
Henry VIII and His Court 66
Her Happiness 83
Heroes Without Uniform 141
Hill, George Washington 220
His Majesty's Theater, Montreal 49
Hitchcock, Alfred 53, 152
Hitler, Adolf 154
Hitler Lives 202
H. M. S. Pinafore 31
Hobart, Rose 146, *149*
Hodiak, John 232
Hoey, Dennis 212
Holbein, Hans 59
Hollaender, Friedrich 148
Hollis Theater, Boston 95
Hollywood Canteen 172
Holmes, Helen 38
Hope, Bob 105, 109, 110, 205, 234
Hopkins, Miriam 101
Hopper, Hedda 158

Hotel Berlin 206
Howe & Hummel 224
Howe, William 224
How Green Was My Valley 132
The Hucksters 217, 218-20
Hudson Theater, NY 46, 47, 48, 51
Hughes, Rupert 42, 45
The Humble 87
The Hunchback of Notre Dame 215
Huston, John 124, 125, 126, 128, 129-30, 131-2, 142-6, *146*, 152, 200, 239, 240
Huston, Walter 145, 181, 202

Ibsen, Henrik 91
Idiot's Delight 114, 115, 122
Idiot's Delight (1939) 119
"I Dreamt I Dwelt in Marble Halls" 200
"If I Could Be With You One Hour Tonight" 229
The Importance of Being Earnest 21
The Inspector General 224
In This Our Life 145
Ironside 115
It's A Great Feeling 230
It's A Wonderful Life 211
Ivanhoe 238
Ivan, Rosalind 200, 204

Jackson, Barry 10
James, Henry 213
Jane Eyre 174
Jerome, Jerome K. 73
Johnston, Mary 30
Jon & Vangelis 245
Jonson, Ben 21, 97
Joseph and His Brethren 65
Julius Caesar 8, 18, 80
Junk 87

Kape, Curtis 102
Kaye, Charlotte 120
Kaye, Danny 224
Keighley, William 56
Kemble, Lillian 32
Kennedy, Arthur 173
Kentucky 12
Kern, Jerome 105, 110

Kerr, Deborah 218, *219*
"The Key" 235
Key Largo 113
Khan, Kublai 96-7
King, Cecil 63
King, Dennis 176
King Lear 160
King Midas & the Golden Touch 27
A King of Nowhere 57, 58-60
Kipling, Rudyard 40
Kiss Me Kate 113
Klaw & Erlinger 72
Korngold, Erich Maria 178
Kurnitz, Harry 223

Lady Billy 77-8, 80, 82, 83
Lady Windermere's Fan 48, 49
Lamarr, Hedy 169, 170, *171*
Lamour, Dorothy 191
Lancaster, Burt 225, 237
Lang, Fritz 99
Larimore, Earle *98*, 99
"The Lass with the Delicate Air" 47
The Last of My Solid Gold Watches 240
La Torre, Charles 156
Laughton, Charles 141, 195
Laurel & Hardy 131
Leigh, Vivien 117
Leland Stanford, CA 24
Le Vay, John 46
Lewis, Ada 54
Lewton, Val 212
The Liars 38
Liberty Magazine 163
Life 220, 246
The Lion and the Mouse 38
Lockhart, Gene 224
Look Magazine 194
Loos, Anita 83
Lorenz, Dr. H. F. G. 143-4, 145
Lorre, Peter vii, viii, *129*, 130, 138, 142, 144, 150, 152, 153, 154, 158, 159, 164-5, 166, *167*, 169-72, 197-207, 233, 234, 240, 243, 245
Lorring, Joan 204, *205*
Lowther Lodge, Kensington 11
Lucky Penny 223
Lucky Strike 220
Lugosi, Bela 245

Lukas, Paul 163
Lunt, Alfred viii, 64, 112-7, 119, 120-5, *124*, 132, 135, 159, 160, 240, 243
Lupino, Ida 163, 173, 179, *180*, 181
Lyceum Theater, New York 65
Lydy, Beth 73
Lyons, Arthur 239
Lyons & Wakefield 84
Lyric Theater, London 14
Lysistrata 100, 101

Macauley, Richard 143
Macbeth 19
MacDonald, Jeanette 85
MacMurray, Fred 110
Macpherson, Virginia 96
The Madcap 88, 90
The Magic Ring 84-5, 161
Majestic Theater, Boston 30-1
Malaya 225, 230, 231-2, 244
Mallett, Richard 157
The Maltese Falcon vii, 126-34, 142, 143, 145, 148, 150, 153, 233, 234, 237, 243
Maltin, Leonard 139
Mamoulian, Rouben 99
The Man from Planet X 210
Mankind 36
The Man Who Played God 163
Marco Millions 96-7
Marlowe, Christopher 21
Marlowe, Julia 30-1, 77
The Mask of Dimitrios 164-9, 234, 243-4
Masques & Faces 25
Massanet, Jules 36
Ma Tante d'Honfleur 54
Maxine Elliot Theater, NY 57
Mayer, Louis B. 194
McEntee, Frank 31
McGill College, Montreal 20
McGuffey the Great 186
McLaren, James 47
Meet Me in St Louis 212
Menjou, Adolphe 218, *219*
The Merchant of Venice 33, 41, 234
The Merry Wives of Windsor 14, 26, 63
Metro Goldwyn Mayer 224, 238
Metropolis 99

Middleton, George 160
Middleton, Robert 110
A Midsummer Night's Dream 10, 14, 19, 31, 65, 70, 104, 204
Mills, Grace Halsey 56
Minnie & Me 84
Mission to Moscow 140
Moliere 21
Montesole, Max 63
The Moonstone 213
Moorehead, Agnes 214
Morgan, Beatrice 37-8
Morgan, Dennis 142, 183
Morgan, Michele 155
Morley, Robert 240
Morris Bros. 193
Mosher, Jerry 133
Mosley, Leonard vii
Motion Picture Herald 169
Mr. Skeffington 181
Mrs. Dow's School for Girls, Briarcliff, NY 80
Mrs. Temple's Telegram 33
Much Ado About Nothing 19, 94
Murdock, Janet "Scotty" 84, *159*, 160-2, 185, *193*, 241
My Aunt 54
My Cinderella Girl 35
My Favorite Brunette 205

Napier, Alan *201*
Nazimova, Alla 103
NBC Kraft Theater 240
NBC Radio 234
Negulesco, Jean 164-6, *167*, 168, 170, 171, 200
Nero, Emperor 141
The Nest Egg 35
Neumann, Alfred 147
The New Adventures of Nero Wolfe 233, 235-6, 238
New Amsterdam Theater, NY 63
The Newcomes 67
New Model 223
The New York Dramatic Mirror 37, 60
New York Press 36
The New Yorker 62
The New York Sun 57
Nordstrom, Marie 37

Notman, Mrs. 47
Now, Voyager 178

O'Brien, Pat 140
O'Connor, Una 183
Office of War Information 138
Ogden, Dorothy Marie 69-72, *71*, *73*, *78*, *80*, *81*, *86*, *89*, 105-9, *106*, *107*, 110-1, 117, 119, 158, 241
Ogden, Frank 70
Ogden, Harold 70
Ogden, James Crawford 69-70, 72
Ogden, Jennie (nee Whitehead) 69-70, 72
Ogden, John 69
Old Acquaintance 181
Old Vic Theater, London 30, 104
"O Little Town of Bethlehem" 183
Olivia Bows to Mrs. Grundy 102-3
Olivier, Laurence 117
One Man's Secret 163
Ossining Hospital, NY 76
Our Boarding House 233
Outward Bound 127, 176

Pacific Bomber Command 162
A Pair of Queens 55-6
Pallette, Eugene 131
Pandora – The Box of Mischief 255, 27
Paramount Studios 205, 222
Parker, Dorothy 78
Parker, Eleanor 176, 213
Passage to Marseille 145, 148, 154-7
Patrick, Lee 194
Pearls of Everyday Wisdom 167
Peple, Edward 60
"Perfidia" 168
The Petrified Forest 115
Philemon & Baucis 25
Phillips, Harold 83
The Pickwick Papers 1
Picturegoer 217
Pillow to Post 148, 179-81
Plews, Herbert 228
The Pirate 160
Please Murder Me 215
Poe, Edgar Allan 234
Poel, Frederick 17
Pollock, Arthur 88, 120

Polo, Marco 96
Polonius 20, 27
Pomander Walk 47
Pom Pom 78
Porfirio, Robert 147
Porter, Cole 113
Possessed 163
Power, Sr., Tyrone 36
Pratt, Hannah (nee Greenstreet) 3
Prelude to Night 208
Preminger, Otto 160
"Pretty Red Wing" 211
Price, Vincent 224
Princeton 20, 23
The Prison Chaplain 162
Prisoner's Aid & City Missionary Society 23
Private Eye 205
Production Code Administration 128
Public School 64, NY 40
Pulitzer Prize 113, 115, 124
Punch 157
Pyke, Dr. Ralph W. 148

Quixote, Don 46
Quo Vadis? 141

Race, Lucille Curtis 82
Racquet Club, Palm Springs 189
Raft, George 141, 150, 152-3
The Rainbow Girl 73-4, 185
Rains, Claude 103, 138, 154, 159, 200, 225, 227, 244
Ralph, Jessie *103*
Ranson's Folly 32
Rappacini's Daughter 234
Rapport, Helena *102*
Raquello, Edward 114
Ratcliff, Edward J. 35
Rathbone, Basil 206, 244
Rattigan, Terence 216
Reade, Charles 25
Reed, Carol 62
Reed, Oliver 62
Reeves, Dr. George H. 191-2
Richie, Lady Anne 67
Ringling, John 85
The Rivals 21

The Road to Rome 115
The Road to Yesterday 32
Roberta 109-10, 112
Robert, Lyda 110
Robinson, Colonel 150-4
Robinson, Edward G. 141
Robinson, William A. 69
Rodin, Auguste 60
Rogers, Ginger 110
The Romancers 46
Romberg, Sigmund 55, 86
Roosevelt, Edith 27
Roosevelt, Franklin D. 23
Roosevelt, Theodore 22, 27-8
Rosenberg, Walter 39
Rosenberg, W. J. 237
Rose of the Rancho 32
Rovere, Richard 224
Royal Academy of Dramatic Art (RADA) 62
Royal Naval School 12
Royal St George's Golf Club 5
R. U. R. 99
Russell, Rosalind 220-3
Ruthless 208-12, 244

St Albin, Raymond 156
Sakall, S. K. "Cuddles" 183
San Francisco Dramatic Review 48
Sari 78
Satan Met a Lady 128
Saturday Evening Post 141
Savage, Col. Henry W. viii, 40, 42-3, 77, 85
Savoy Theater, Asbury Park, NJ 38
School for Scandal 21
Scott, Lt. Gen. Wingfield 135-6
Scott, Zachary viii, 165, 166, *167*, 208, 209, 229
Screen Guild Theater 234
Screening Genders 133
The Seagull 120-2, 240
Sears, Zelda 35, 85
The Second Shepherd's Play 36
Secret Service 38
Self, Edwin B. 87
Semple, Sheriff Titus 225-7, 229-30
Shadow of a Doubt 53
Shakespeare for Everyman 15-16

Shakespeare, William viii, 10, 15, 16, 18, 19, 21, 25, 29, 30, 40, 51, 58, 62, 65, 85, 91-2, 93-4, 97, 112, 122, 142, 160, 186, 235, 243, 246
"Shakespearian Clowns" 80
Sheridan, Ann 142, 225
Sheridan, Richard Brinsley 21
Sherlock Holmes 11, 190
Sherman, Vincent 145, *145*, 181
Sherwood, Robert 114, 115, 123
She's In Again 54
She Stoops to Conquer 21
Shipman, David 131
Shock Treatment 114-5
Short, Frank Lea 46
The Showmen's Trade Review 229
Shylock 186, 234
Sibelius, Jean 123
Siegel, Don 202, 204
Sieve, Myriam 77
The Sign of the Cross 33
Siodmak, Robert 147
Skipworth, Alison 128
Sleepy Hollow Country Club, NY 76
Slick Hare 195
The Smiling Corpse 205-6
Smith, Alexis 146, *149*, 214, 216
Smith College, Northampton, MA 20
Soldiers of Fortune 37
Sorin, Peter 120-2
Sorma, Agnes 60
Sothern, E. H. 30, 31, 77
South London Harrier's Club 4
Speed 41
Stanwyck, Barbara *182*, 183
The Star of Bethlehem 20
"Stars of Tomorrow" 158
Steiner, Max 136, 138, 169
"Step to Paris Blues" 90
Stevens, Craig 217
Stewart, James *230*, 231-2
Stoddart, Dayton 208
Stout, Rex 235-6
Straforel 46-7
Strickling, Howard 194
Stromberg, Hunt 238
Strongheart 38
Studebaker Theater, Chicago 19, 43

The Student Prince 55, 86-7
Suffragettes 47
Suspense 235
Sweatnam, William P. 43
Sydney, Basil 87
The Sydney Greenstreet Blues 245

Tales of Wonder 25, 27
The Taming of the Shrew 31, 48, 112, 114, 122
Tamiroff, Akim 141
"Tango of Love" 147
Taylor, Matt 163
Tellegen, Lou viii, 57, 59-60
A Temperance Town 33
The Tempest 20, 24-6, 31
Tennyson, Alfred Lord 21
Thackeray, William Makepeace 67, Greenstreet as, 173-5, *174*, 187, 190
Thais 36-7
That Hagen Girl 215
That Was Balzac 160
That Way with Women 162, 184-7
Thaxter, Phyllis 196
Theater Guild 96-9, 103-4, 127, 179
Theatrical Syndicate 91
There Shall Be No Night 120, 123-4, 196
They Died With Their Boots On 135-6
They Knew What They Wanted 116
Thompson, Barry 113
Thorndike, Russell 15
Thorndike, Sybil 15, 18-19, 27
The Three Musketeers 224
Three on a Match 239
Three Strangers 198-201, 244
The Times (London) 116, 133, 214-5
Tobias, George 176
To Have and To Hold 30
Toler, Sidney 206
Too Hot for Maneuvers 286
Touchstone 49, *50*, 56, 63
Tracy, Spencer *230*, 231-2
Travers, Henry 99
Treacher, Arthur 90
Tree, Sir Herbert Beerbohm viii, 8, 49, 55, 62-8, *64*
Trevor, Claire 221
Trewin, J. C. 10

Trilling, Steve 154
Tucker, Robert G. 122
Tuppy (Lord Augustus Lorton character) *48*, 49
Twelfth Night 13, 21, 25, 49, 51, 56, 76, 80
Twentieth Century Fox 160
Two Gentlemen of Verona 20
The Two Mrs. Carrolls 215

Ulmer, Edgar G. 208, 209-10
Uncommon Danger 150
Union Station 222
U. S. War Department 194
University of California, Berkeley 17, 24

Van, Billy B. 74-5, *75*
Van Curler Theater, New York 93
Vane, Sutton 176
Variety 37, 45, 55, 103, 132, 220
Vassar College 20
Veidt, Conrad 138
The Velvet Touch 218, 220-3
The Verdict 162, 198, 201-5, 206
Vickers, Martha *184*, 185
Vinson, Helen *102*
Volpone 97-9, 127

Wakeman, Frederick 218, 220
Wald, Jerry 154, 163
Waldemar, Uncle 123-6
Waldrup, Oza *59*
Wallace, Leonard 243
Wallis, Hal 137, 170
Warner Bros. 133-5, 154, 157-60, 162, 163, 165, 166, 169, 178, 181, 194, 205, 206, 218, 223, 230, 235,
Warner, Jack L. 134, 137, 166, 202, 204
The Washington Herald 74
The Washington Times 27
Watney, Coombe & Reid Brewery 7
Wayburn, Ted 54
Wayne, John 234
Webster, Margaret 9, 122
Weiman, Rita 163
Welford, Dallas 94
Welles, Orson 160

West End Theater, 125th Street, NY 37-9
West Point 46
What Ails You? 45
What Happened to Jones? 33
When Knighthood Was in Flower 32
When We Were Twenty-One 33
Which is Which? 234
White House Lawn 22, 23, 27-8, 29
Whitney Opera House, Chicago 35
Whitty, Dame May 9
The Whole Town's Talking 83-4
Whorf, Richard 112, 113, 116
"Who Threw the Overalls in Mrs. Murphy's Chowder" 186
Wilde, Oscar 21, 48, 49, 62, 186
Wilder, Robert 225, 229
William Smith College, Geneva, NY 23
Williams, Tennessee 240
Williams, Tony 209
Wilson, Dooley 138
Wilson, Thomas Woodrow 22-3
Wilstach, Paul 83
Winter Garden Theater, NY 55
Wodehouse, P. G. 42
Wolf, Rennold 74
Wolfe, Nero 186, 233, 235
The Woman in White 208, 213-7, 227, 244
A Woman of No Importance 49
Woodland Players 22, 30, 104, 245
Worcester College, Oxford 12
A World of Pleasure 55
"The Worm's Revenge" 78, 80
Wyantenuck Country Club, MA 190
Wylie, Philip 206

Yale University 20
Yardley, Alexander 183
Young, Collier 223
Young, Gig 214
Young, Sen 143

Zangwill, Israel 202, 204
Zeus 25
Ziegfeld Follies 212

About the Author

Derek Sculthorpe is an archivist and researcher from England with a background in the visual arts. He has had a lifelong love of golden age cinema and has written several biographies, including those of Van Heflin and Claire Trevor.

CPSIA information can be obtained
at www.ICGtesting.com
Printed in the USA
BVHW032315020822
643591BV00006B/81